The Best Informational
Diagrams 2

A collection of graphics that communicate information visually

PIE
BOOKS

The Best Informational
Diagrams 2

PIE BOOKS
2-32-4, Minami-Otsuka, Toshima-ku, Tokyo 170-0005 Japan
Phone: +81-3-5395-4811 Fax: +81-3-5395-4812

e-mail: editor@piebooks.com
e-mail: sales@piebooks.com
http://www.piebooks.com

ISBN4-89444-392-9 C3070
Printed in Japan

CONTENTS

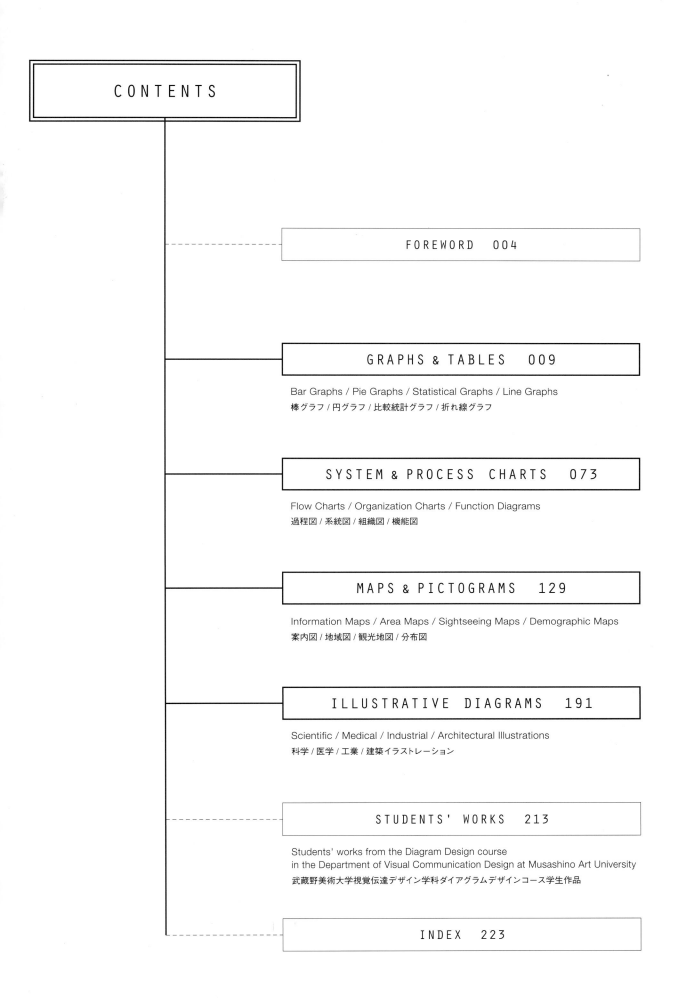

"Now and Future Diagrams"

By Katha Dalton
Project Manager; Hornall Anderson Design Works, Inc.

Today we share a world where visual information is simultaneous and omnipresent in staggering amounts. Growth of online, electronic and interactive media ensures that in the future still more of it will come alive, not only in two and three dimensions, but in a potent fourth: motion. This is good news, not only for the public, but also for designers whose palette for expressing visual information is enriched. Why? Because the old cliché is, and will remain, true: "A picture is worth 1,000 words."

How does this work? It is in part because through design, visually presented facts and statistics are able to simultaneously communicate data and trigger emotional responses to that information based on its appearance.

In the past, designers typically used diagrams for a more aesthetic purpose—as visual filler on the page—than to relay information. However, in today's world, we are continuously barraged with an onslaught of information, and diagrams are more important than ever. They are a critical form of communication that helps us assimilate complex information and respond to it in appropriate ways.

One such example of using diagrams in this manner can be found in the 2002 annual report for an aircraft-operating lessor client. In an effort to illustrate fiscal results in a more reader-friendly manner, the client distills a complex global business into digestible bits using simple, illustrative diagrammatic metaphors, such as "don't put all your eggs in one basket," the Wall Street bulls and bears, and the team success of bees in a hive.

With the ongoing challenge of filtering the myriad details we receive on a daily basis, informational diagrams will continue to play a key role in softening, simplifying and supporting clients' messages now and in years ahead.

Profile

At Hornall Anderson Design Works, we have always had two main goals: first, to give our clients design solutions in tune with their marketing objectives; and second, to do the best work in the business, striving to elevate every job above the ordinary. The plan has succeeded. Started in 1982, Hornall Anderson has become one of the largest, most respected design firms on the West Coast.

ダイアグラムの現在と未来

キャサ・ダルトン
ホーナル・アンダーソン・デザイン・ワークス　プロジェクト・マネージャー

現在、世界には驚くほど多くの視覚情報が同時に遍在している。インターネットや電子媒体、そしてインタラクティブなメディアは、平面や立体だけではなくモーションという面でも今後さらに発達していくに違いない。これは一般人だけでなく、視覚情報を表現する手法が豊かなデザイナーにとっても朗報だ。なぜなら、昔から良く言われている「一枚の絵は千の言葉に値する」という言葉が、今も、そしてこれから先もまさに真実だからだ。

これらは実際にはどう作用しているのだろうか。ひとつとして、事実と統計をデザインによって視覚的に提示することで、データを理解したり、見たままの情報に対して感情的な反応を引き起こしたりが同時に行えるという点が挙げられる。

昔、デザイナーは情報を伝えるというよりもページを視覚的に埋めるといった、デザインを美しく見せる目的でダイアグラムを使うのが一般的だった。しかし、現在の私たちは絶え間なく情報の集中砲火を浴びており、ダイアグラムはかつてないほど重要性を帯びている。複雑な情報を理解し、適切な方法で情報に反応する手助けをしてくれるダイアグラムは、コミュニケーションに欠かせないひとつの形態だ。

こうした意味でダイアグラムを使ったひとつの例に、航空機リース業者であるクライアントのために作成した2002年度アニュアル・レポートがある。決算報告を読者に分かりやすく表現するため、クライアントの複雑なグローバル・ビジネスを、「ひとつのカゴからすべての卵を取り出してはいけない」、「ウォールストリートの雄牛と熊」、「蜂の巣の蜜蜂チームの成功」といった、シンプルで一目瞭然なダイアグラムのメタファーを使用した具体例へと落とし込んだ。

日々受け取る大量の情報を常に選別していくという挑戦のために、インフォメーショナル・ダイアグラムは、現在も、そしてこれから先も、クライアントのメッセージを分かりやすく明快にし、支援するのに中心的な役割を果し続けるだろう。

プロフィール
ホーナル・アンダーソン・デザイン・ワークスでは、常にふたつのゴールを目指している。ひとつは、クライアントのマーケティング目標に合ったデザイン・ソリューションを提供することで、もうひとつは、すべての仕事で水準以上の結果を目指し、ベストを尽くすことだ。このプランは非常に成功している。1982年の設立以来、ホーナル・アンダーソンはアメリカ西海岸で最も大きく評判の高いデザイン会社の地位を保っている。

"No change"

By Gilmar Wendt, Creative Director; SAS

My favourite diagram is the London Underground Map, perhaps not a surprising choice. But living in London makes things slightly different. When I mention it to my English friends they either say 'you are such a tourist', or start to moan about the dirt and the delays they experience every day. Londoners love to hate the tube. To them, the diagram is just part of it, a commodity, helping you find the quickest way from A to B.

I don't mind that. After all, helping you understand something better is what diagrams are about. The tube map has simply become so much part of my friends' daily routine that they're unable to see what it really is. Which is, a perfect piece of information design. Designed by an engineer, Harry Beck, in 1931, with the single aim to make it as easy to understand as possible, it has revolutionised the way we design tube maps around the world. And even though it has been altered over the years, to me it has lost none of its graphic qualities. I love the colour coding, the clarity, simplicity, and, of course, the beautiful Johnston typeface.

These are interesting times for designers. New media has brought new dimensions to information design-and new challenges too. I'm fascinated as to how animation and interactivity can be used to explain a complex structure, or make a process clear. But as we expand our tool box and explore ever-changing fashion styles, there's one thing that remains. Information design is for the user. Helping him understand how to get from A to B is what its all about.

Profile
Gilmar Wendt is the creative director of SAS, the London based corporate design company. SAS has been running for 15 years, helping their various blue-chip clients communicate more effectively with their investors, business customers and employees.
www.sasdesign.co.uk

ノー・チェンジ：今も昔も変わりなく。

ギルマー・ベント
SAS　クリエイティブ・ディレクター

私の大好きなダイアグラムはロンドンの地下鉄マップだ。おそらく、この答えはあまり意外ではないだろう。しかし、ロンドンに住んでいると多少事情が異なってくる。私がこのことをイギリス人の友人に話すと、「君は旅行者みたいだな」と言われるか、日々経験している地下鉄の遅れやら汚さに不満を言い始めるかのどちらかだ。ロンドンっ子は地下鉄の悪口を言うのが好きなのだ。彼らにとって、そのダイアグラムは愛すべき嫌われものの一部でしかなく、A地点からB地点へ最も早く行ける方法を探すための必需品なのだ。

私にしてみればそんな事はどうでもいい。結局、ある物事を良く理解するための助けになることがダイアグラムの目的だ。地下鉄マップは単に、私の友人たちの日常にあまりにも深く関わっているため、彼らには本当はそれが何なのか、ということが見えなくなってしまったのだ。つまり、本当は地下鉄マップは完璧なるインフォメーション・デザインのひとつなのだ。1931年、できる限り分かりやすいものを作るというたったひとつの目標のもと、エンジニアであるハリー・ベックがデザインした地下鉄マップは、世界中の地下鉄マップのデザイン方法に革命を起した。さらに何年もの時を経て部分的な修正はされてきたものの、私からみればそのグラフィックの質は少しも失われていない。色分けの仕方や明快でシンプルなところがたまらなく好きだ。そしてもちろん、美しいジョンソンのタイプフェイスも。

今はデザイナーにとって興味深く、面白い時代だ。ニューメディアはインフォメーション・デザインに新しい面だけでなく、新たな挑戦をももたらした。複雑な構造を説明したり、プロセスを明確にするのに、アニメーションやインタラクティビティがどう使われているのかに私は魅了されている。しかし、私たちがどんどん新しい手法を取り入れ、絶えまなく変化するファッション・スタイルを探究している最中にも、ひとつだけ変わらないことがある。インフォメーション・デザインはユーザのためにあるということだ。A地点からB地点までどう行けばいいのかを教えてくれるのに役立つ。それがすべてなのだ。

プロフィール
ギルマー・ベントは、ロンドンを拠点にするコーポレイト・デザイン・カンパニー、SASのクリエイティブ・ディレクター。SASは15年間にわたり、様々な一流企業のクライアントが、出資者や取引先、従業員などとより効果的なコミュニケーションが取れるように支援している。
www.sasdesign.co.uk

CREDIT FORMAT　クレジットフォーマット

■Caption　作品説明文

■Country from which submitted / Year of completion　制作国／制作年

■Creative staff　制作スタッフ

CD: Creative Director（クリエイティブディレクター）

AD: Art Director（アートディレクター）

D: Designer（デザイナー）

P: Photographer（カメラマン）

I: Illustrator（イラストレーター）

CW: Copywriter（コピーライター）

DF: Design Firm（デザイン事務所）

CL: Client（クライアント）

S: Submittor（作品提供者）

* Full names of all others involved in the creation / production of the work.
　上記以外の制作スタッフの呼称は略さずに記載しています。

* Please note that some credit data has been omitted at the request of the submittor.
　作品提供者の意向によりクレジット・データの一部を記載していないものがあります。

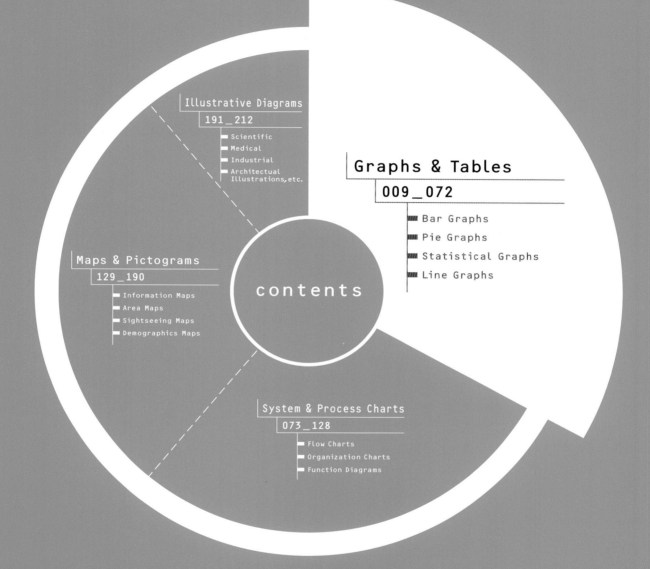

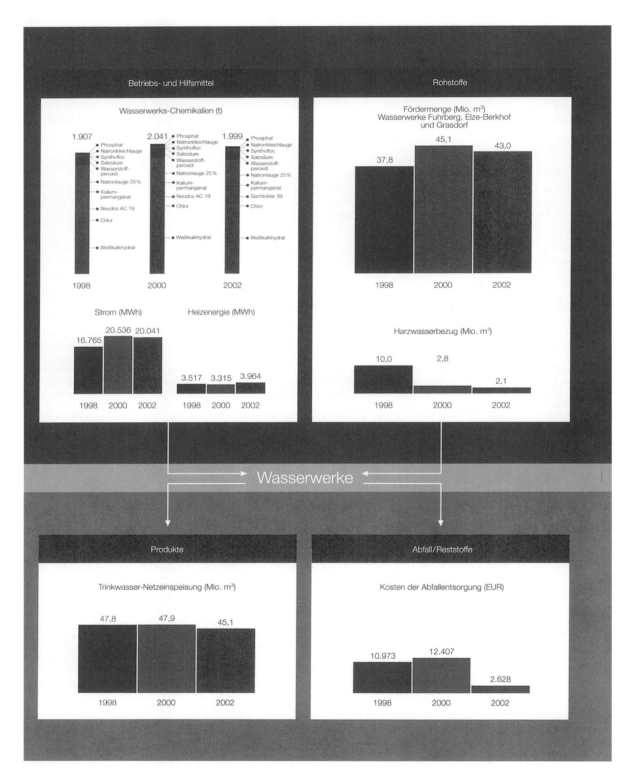

Graphs providing the information on environmental facts and figures of power stations and water companies.

発電所や水道会社の環境に関する情報を示すグラフ。

Germany   2003
CL, S: Stadtwerke Hannover AG

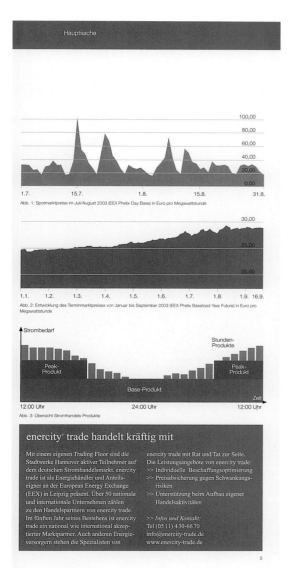

Abb. 1: Spotmarktpreise im Juli/August 2003 (EEX Phelix Day Base) in Euro pro Megawattstunde

Abb. 2: Entwicklung des Terminmarktpreises von Januar bis September 2003 (EEX Phelix Baseload Year Future) in Euro pro Megawattstunde

Abb. 3: Übersicht Stromhandels-Produkte

enercity® trade handelt kräftig mit

Mit einem eigenen Trading Floor sind die Stadtwerke Hannover aktiver Teilnehmer auf dem deutschen Stromhandelsmarkt. enercity trade ist als Energiehändler und Anteilseigner an der European Energy Exchange (EEX) in Leipzig präsent. Über 50 nationale und internationale Unternehmen zählen zu den Handelspartnern von enercity trade. Im fünften Jahr seines Bestehens ist enercity trade ein national wie international akzeptierter Marktpartner. Auch anderen Energieversorgern stehen die Spezialisten von

enercity trade mit Rat und Tat zur Seite. Die Leistungsangebote von enercity trade:
>> Individuelle Beschaffungsoptimierung
>> Preisabsicherung gegen Schwankungsrisiken
>> Unterstützung beim Aufbau eigener Handelsaktivitäten

>> *Infos und Kontakt:*
Tel (05 11) 4 30-66 70
info@enercity-trade.de
www.enercity-trade.de

5

Klimafreundlichkeit wird belohnt

Der Strom kommt aus der Steckdose, das weiß jeder. Was sich aber genau hinter der Abkürzung KWK oder den KWK-Gesetzen verbirgt und warum ökologisches Handeln belohnt wird, kann man hier nachlesen.

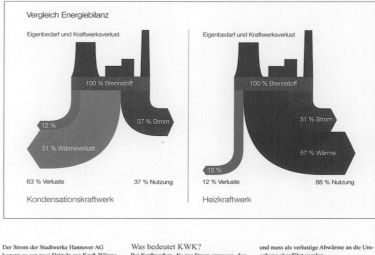

Der Strom der Stadtwerke Hannover AG kommt zu gut zwei Dritteln aus Kraft-Wärme-Kopplungs-Anlagen. Diese Anlagen zeichnen sich durch eine umweltfreundliche Stromerzeugungstechnik aus und werden seit März 2000 durch die KWK-Gesetzgebung gefördert.

Was bedeutet KWK?
Bei Kraftwerken, die nur Strom erzeugen, den Kondensationskraftwerken, wird die Energie des eingesetzten Brennstoffes wie Kohle oder Erdgas in einem thermischen Prozess nur in mechanische Energie sprich Kraft umgewandelt. Mit dieser Kraft, dem Wasserdampf, wird ein Generator angetrieben, der dann das eigentliche Produkt, den Strom erzeugt. Ein großer Teil der durch die Verbrennung frei werdenden Wärme kann nicht genutzt werden

und muss als verlustige Abwärme an die Umgebung abgeführt werden.
Die Abkürzung KWK steht für Kraft-Wärme-Kopplung. In einem Heizkraftwerk werden eben diese beiden Produkte erzeugt. Gegenüber dem Kondensationskraftwerk verzichtet ein Heizkraftwerk auf einen kleinen Teil der Stromerzeugung und kann dafür den Teil der

14

a

b

Each graph showing the current of market price in July/August 2003, the option market price in September 2003, and the trade in a day. (a)
Graphs comparing the energy balance between the condensation power station and the combined heat and power station. (b)

それぞれ、2003年7〜8月の市場価格、9月のオプション市場価格および1日あたりの取引の推移を示すグラフ。 (a)
蒸気凝縮方式の発電所と熱併給発電所のエネルギーのバランスを比較するグラフ。 (b)

Aantal gerechtigden AOW/Anw en AKW per vestiging

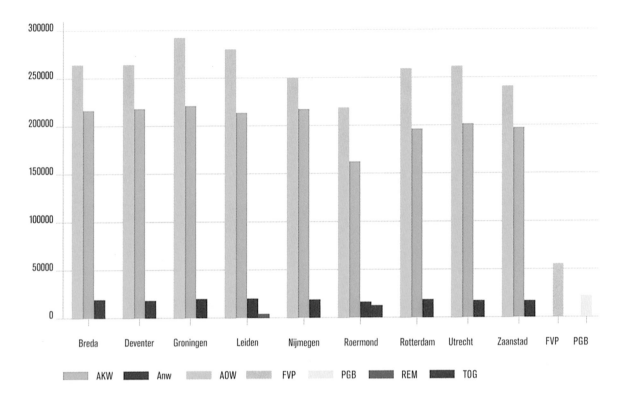

AKW	Anw	AOW	FVP	PGB	REM	TOG

Aantal AOW-gerechtigden per leeftijdsklasse

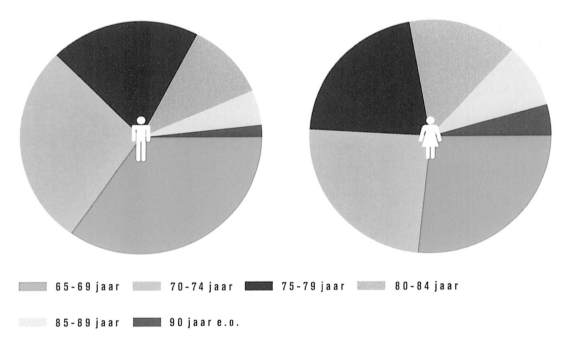

65-69 jaar	70-74 jaar
75-79 jaar	80-84 jaar
85-89 jaar	90 jaar e.o.

Charts from a social annual report which introduces the activities of the empoyees working in the bank. Showing not the financial status but the social aspects of the bank.

銀行の従業員の活動を紹介するソーシャルアニュアル・レポートより。銀行の財政状況ではなく、社会的な面を明らかにしている。

Netherlands 2001
CD, AD, D: Wout De Vringer   AD, I: Bob Van Dijk   CW: Corporate Communication SVB   DF, S: Faydherbe / De Vringer   CL: SVB (Sociale Verzekerings Bank)

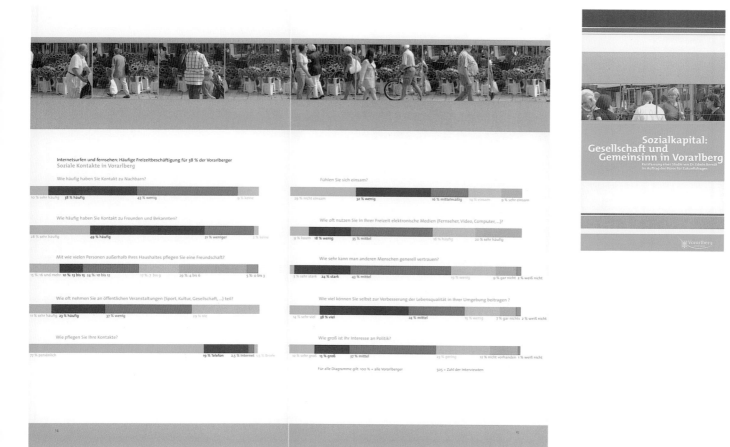

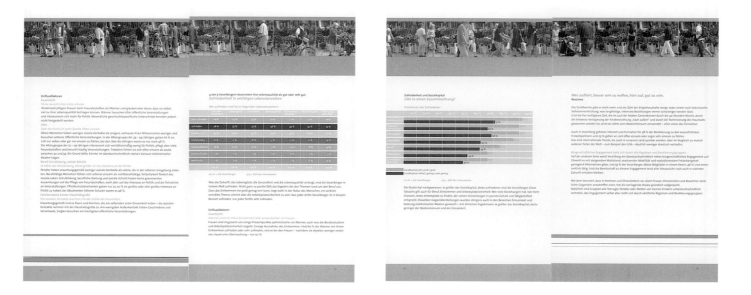

Graphs indicate social capital and life satisfaction in Austria.

オーストリアにおける社会資本や人生に対する満足度を表すグラフ。

Austria 2002
CD, AD: Sigi Ramoser   D, P, I: Sabine Sowieja   CW: Petra Zudrell   DF, S: Sägenvier   CL: Land Vorarlberg

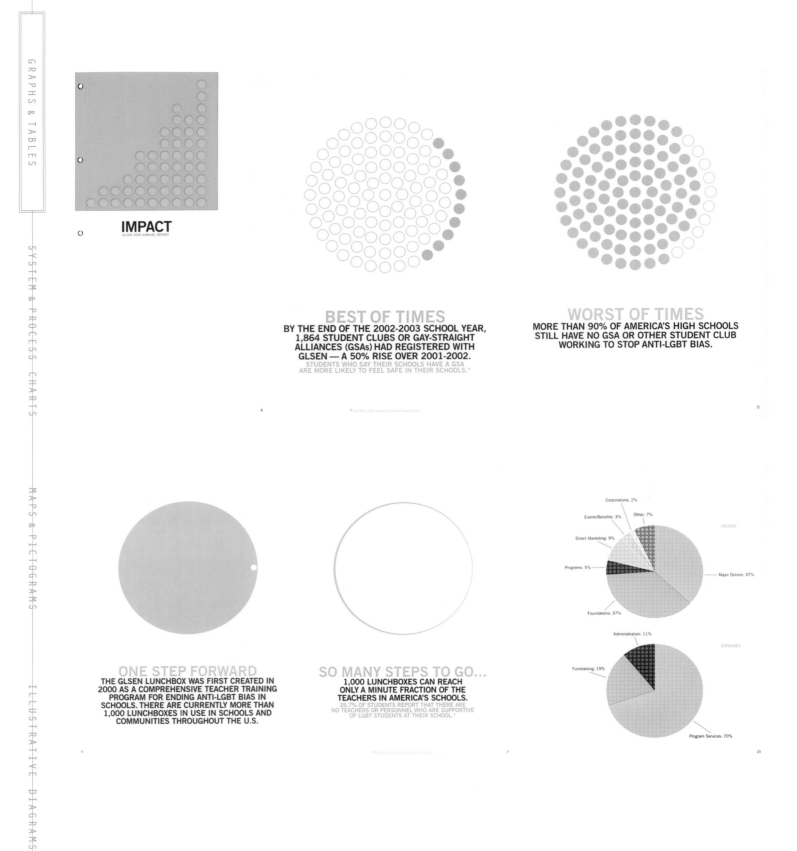

IMPACT
GLSEN 2003 ANNUAL REPORT

BEST OF TIMES
BY THE END OF THE 2002-2003 SCHOOL YEAR,
1,864 STUDENT CLUBS OR GAY-STRAIGHT
ALLIANCES (GSAs) HAD REGISTERED WITH
GLSEN — A 50% RISE OVER 2001-2002.
STUDENTS WHO SAY THEIR SCHOOLS HAVE A GSA
ARE MORE LIKELY TO FEEL SAFE IN THEIR SCHOOLS.*

WORST OF TIMES
MORE THAN 90% OF AMERICA'S HIGH SCHOOLS
STILL HAVE NO GSA OR OTHER STUDENT CLUB
WORKING TO STOP ANTI-LGBT BIAS.

ONE STEP FORWARD
THE GLSEN LUNCHBOX WAS FIRST CREATED IN
2000 AS A COMPREHENSIVE TEACHER TRAINING
PROGRAM FOR ENDING ANTI-LGBT BIAS IN
SCHOOLS. THERE ARE CURRENTLY MORE THAN
1,000 LUNCHBOXES IN USE IN SCHOOLS AND
COMMUNITIES THROUGHOUT THE U.S.

SO MANY STEPS TO GO...
1,000 LUNCHBOXES CAN REACH
ONLY A MINUTE FRACTION OF THE
TEACHERS IN AMERICA'S SCHOOLS.
39.7% OF STUDENTS REPORT THAT THERE ARE
NO TEACHERS OR PERSONNEL WHO ARE SUPPORTIVE
OF LGBT STUDENTS AT THEIR SCHOOL.*

INCOME

Corporations: 2%
Other: 7%
Events/Benefits: 3%
Direct Marketing: 9%
Programs: 5%
Major Donors: 37%
Foundations: 37%

EXPENSES

Administration: 11%
Fundraising: 19%
Program Services: 70%

GLSEN is an organization devoted to building tolerance and acceptance for gay and transgender high school students. Charts represent the financial statements in 2003.

GLSENはゲイや性同一性障害の高校生に対する理解を深めるために活動している団体。2003年の決算報告を表すグラフ。

USA 2003
CD, AD, D, I: Brian Wong　DF, S: Suka Design　CL: GLSEN (Gay, Lesbian and Straight Education Network)

2

Recoletos
en Cifras

Total ingresos **EBITDA** **EBIT** **Resultado consolidado**

Número medio de empleados

Cuenta de explotación consolidada

Estado de flujo de caja consolidado

Balance

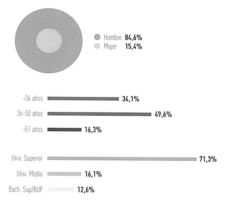

R
RECOLETOS

Sectores anunciantes de Expansión
(en % de páginas de publicidad)

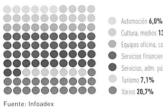

- Automoción **6,0%**
- Cultura, medios **13,6%**
- Equipos oficina, comercio **10,2%**
- Servicios financieros **24,6%**
- Servicios, adm. públicas **17,8%**
- Turismo **7,1%**
- Varios **20,7%**

Fuente: Infoadex

Cuota de mercado
Difusión OJD 2002 preliminares a Junio

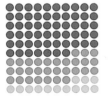

- Expansión **57,0%**
- Cinco Días **29,8%**
- Gaceta de los negocios **13,2%**

Sectores anunciantes de Marca
(en % de páginas de publicidad)

- Automoción **26,7%**
- Bebidas **5,2%**
- Cultura, medios **17,3%**
- Distribución, restauración **13,8%**
- Servicios financieros **4,5%**
- Servicios, adm. públicas **2,8%**
- Telecomunicciones e intern **11,7%**
- Varios **18%**

Fuente: Infoadex

Cuota de mercado
Difusión OJD 2002 datos preliminares a junio 2002

- Marca **49,5%**
- AS **22,4%**
- Sport **14,3%**
- Mundo Deportivo **13,8%**

Expansión Perfil del lector

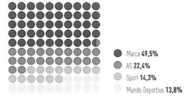

- Hombre **84,6%**
- Mujer **15,4%**

- ‹36 años **34,1%**
- 36-50 años **49,6%**
- ›51 años **16,3%**

- Univ. Superior **71,3%**
- Univ. Medio **16,1%**
- Bach. Sup/BUP **12,6%**

Various graphs and charts for an annual report of a media company providing market information.

市場に関する情報を提供する、メディア企業のアニュアル・レポートのためのグラフやチャート。

Spain   2002
CD: Emilio Gil   D: Ingrid Forbord   DF, S: Tau Diseño   CL: Recoetos Group

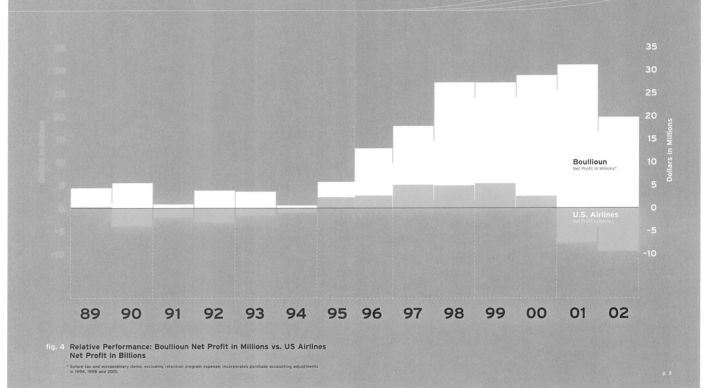

In 2002, Boullioun performed well ahead of the curve.

強いフラットな色調を使用した隠喩的なイラストとグラフは、リースにおけるリスクを最小限にする方法、グローバルな企業が直面するリスク、最高の専門性を誇る航空機のリース企業がどのように経営されているかなどを示している。

fig. 4 **Relative Performance: Boullioun Net Profit in Millions vs. US Airlines Net Profit in Billions**

* Before tax and extraordinary items; excluding retention program expense; incorporates purchase accounting adjustments in 1994, 1998 and 2001.

p. 3

Boullioun
Net Profit in Millions*

U.S. Airlines
Net Profit in Billions

Dollars in Millions

89 90 91 92 93 94 95 96 97 98 99 00 01 02

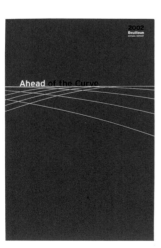

Metaphoric illustrations and charts are used in strong flat colors to show how risk is minimized in leasing, how global presence helps spread risk, and how the Boullioun team operates at the highest professional level.

強いフラットな色調を使用した隠喩的なイラストとグラフは、リースにおけるリスクを最小限にする方法、グローバルな企業が直面するリスク、最高の専門性を誇る航空機のリース企業がどのように経営されているかなどを示している。

USA 2003
AD: Jack Anderson   AD, D: Katha Dalton   D, I: Belinda Bowling   D: Michael Brugman   CW: John Koval   DF, S: Hornall Anderson Design Works, Inc.   CL: Boullioun Aviation Services

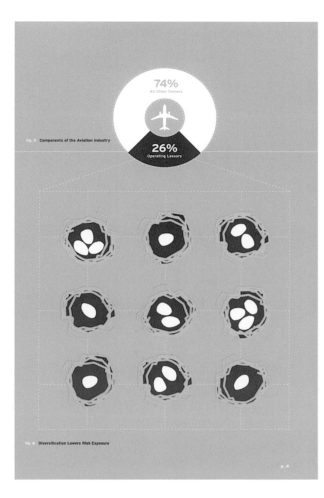

fig. 5 Components of the Aviation Industry

74%
All Other Owners

26%
Operating Lessors

fig. 6 Diversification Lowers Risk Exposure

p. 4

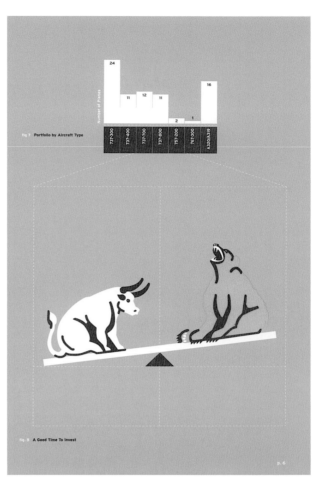

fig. 7 Portfolio by Aircraft Type

fig. 8 A Good Time To Invest

p. 6

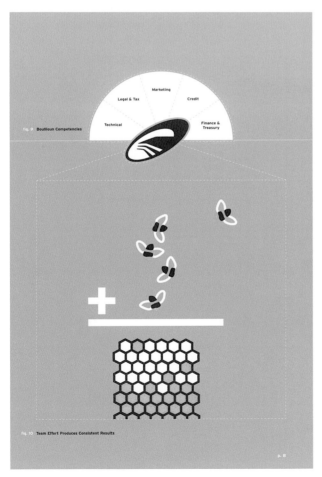

fig. 9 Boullioun Competencies

Marketing
Legal & Tax
Credit
Technical
Finance & Treasury

fig. 10 Team Effort Produces Consistent Results

p. 8

President's Message

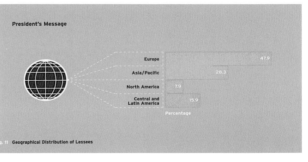

Europe 47.9
Asia/Pacific 28.3
North America 7.9
Central and Latin America 15.9

Percentage

fig. 11 Geographical Distribution of Lessees

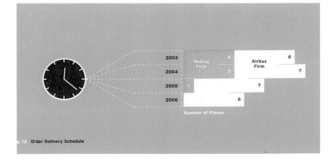

Boeing Firm
Airbus Firm

2003   5   6
2004   5   7
2005   1   7
2006   6

Number of Planes

fig. 12 Order Delivery Schedule

Graphs in simple but various forms indicating the market shares, increase of sales turnover, and business perspectives of a electronic devices distributor.

シンプルだが様々な形態で表したグラフは、電子機器販売会社のマーケット・シェア、販売額の増加、ビジネスの展望などを示している。

Germany 2002
CD: Jochen Rädeker   AD, D: Kirsten Dietz   D: Stephanie Zehender   CW: Eberhard Kaiser   DF, S: Strichpunkt GmbH   CL: 4MBO International Electronic AG

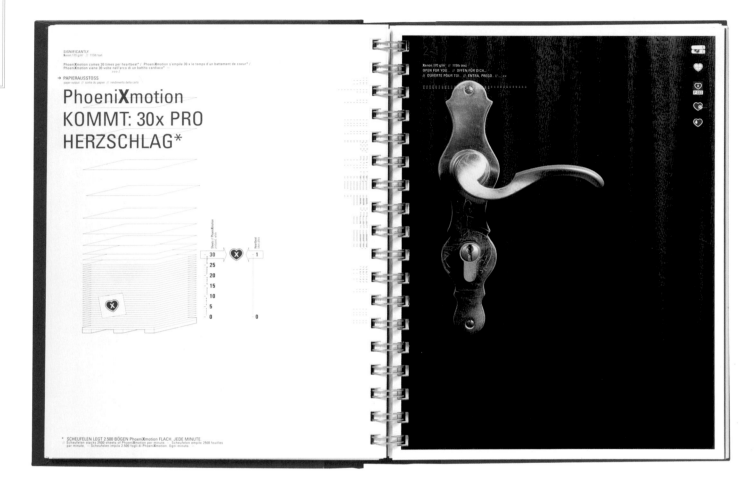

SIGNIFICANTLY
Xenon 170 g/m² // 115lb text

PhoeniXmotion comes 30 times per heartbeat* / PhoeniXmotion s'empile 30 x le temps d'un battement de coeur* /
PhoeniXmotion viene 30 volte nell'arco di un battito cardiaco* —
>>> /

→ PAPIERAUSSTOSS
paper output // sortie du papier // rendimento della carta

PhoeniXmotion
KOMMT: 30x PRO
HERZSCHLAG*

* SCHEUFELEN LEGT 2.500 BÖGEN PhoeniXmotion FLACH, JEDE MINUTE.
// Scheufelen stacks 2500 sheets of PhoeniXmotion per minute. // Scheufelen empile 2500 feuilles
par minute. // Scheufelen impila 2.500 fogli di PhoeniXmotion. Ogni minuto.

From a diary for a papermill using diagrams comparing the characteristics of the paper brand "Phoenixmotion:paper with heart" with the features of human heart.

製紙会社のために作成されたダイアリーから抜粋。「Phoenixmotion：ハートのこもった紙」という紙のブランドの特徴を、人間のハートの特徴と比較したダイアグラムを使用している。

Germany   2003
CD, AD, D: Kirsten Dietz   CD, CW: Jochen Rädeker   D: Tanja Günther / Felix Widmaier   P: Jan Steinhilber   DF, S: Strichpunkt GmbH   CL: Papierfabrik Scheufelen GmbH+Co. KG

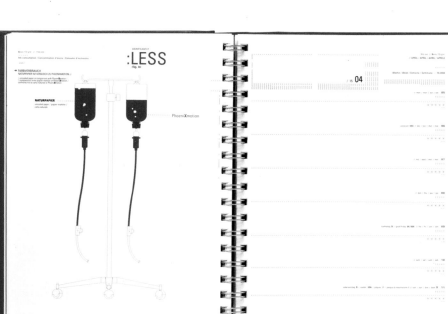

:LESS (fig. to)

NATURPAPIER

PhoenXmotion

09

#10 ≙ HEARTFACT, NR 10
heartbeat
MOMENT

HERZPROBLEME? — DAS HILFT —

H E L P

| 1 stk. /TAG | 70 g /TAG | 2,5 stk. /TAG | 2 EL /TAG |
| KNOBLAUCH | SCHOKOLADE | CITRUSFRÜCHTE | LEBERTRAN |

07-08

#08 ≙ HEARTFACT, NR 9
heartbeat
MOMENT

80 % ALLER SEEMÄNNER SIND TÄTOWIERT.
84 % DAVON HABEN EIN HERZ AUF DER HAUT.
und zwar für

5%
AKTUELLER
FREUND

10%
AKTUELLE
FREUNDIN

N.N.

40%

45%
EX FREUNDIN

LAGEBERICHT DES 4MBO-KONZERNS

// GESCHÄFTSJAHR 2002

GESAMTWIRTSCHAFTLICHE ENTWICKLUNG

Entgegen vielen zu Beginn des Jahres 2002 abgegebenen Prognosen kam die weltweite Konjunktur auch 2002 nicht in Fahrt. So wuchs das Bruttoinlandsprodukt in den Industrieländern nach Angaben des Hamburgischen Weltwirtschaftsarchivs (HWWA) lediglich um 1,5% und in der Euro-Zone sogar nur um 0,8%. In diesem schwierigen Umfeld ist das Wachstum in Deutschland im Jahr 2002 nahezu zum Stillstand gekommen. Real stieg das Bruttoinlandsprodukt um magere 0,2% – der schlechteste Wert seit 1993.

Ein Abrutschen in die Rezession verhinderte lediglich der starke Export, der einen Wachstumsbeitrag von 1,5% lieferte. Enttäuschend entwickelte sich hingegen der private Konsum – er war 2002 erstmals seit der Wiedervereinigung schwächer als im Jahr zuvor. Dies schlägt sich in Zahlen nieder: Nach Erhebungen des Statistischen Bundesamtes hat der Einzelhandel in Deutschland im Jahr 2002 nominal (in jeweiligen Preisen) 2,0% und real (in konstanten Preisen) 2,3% weniger umgesetzt als im Vorjahr. Einen Umsatzrückgang im Einzelhandel im Jahresvergleich gab es zuletzt 1997.

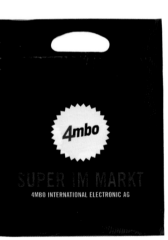

From an annual report of a hardware distributor. Using various graphics for visualization of the turnover and business development.
Annual report is placed inside a bag "SUPER IM MARKT."

ハードウェアの販売会社のアニュアル・レポートより。売上高やビジネスの成長度を視覚化するために様々なグラフィックを使用している。
このアニュアル・レポートは「SUPER IM MARKT」という袋に入れられている。

Germany 2003
CD, AD, D: Kirsten Dietz   CD, AD, CW: Jochen Rädeker   CW: Eberhard Kaiser   DF, S: Strichpunkt GmbH   CL: 4MBO International Electronic AG

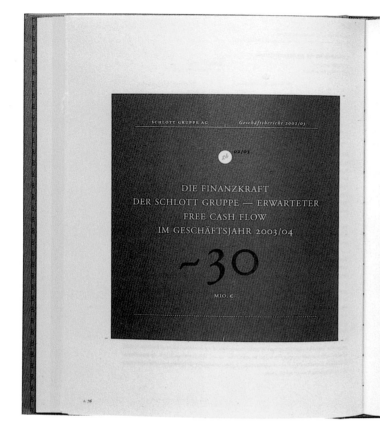

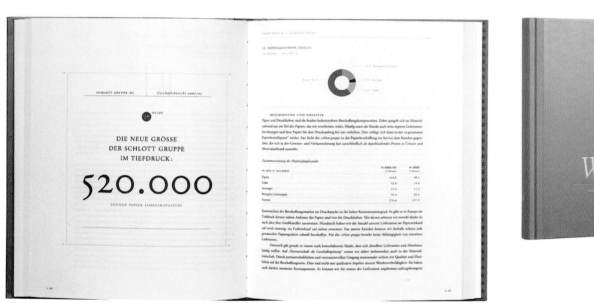

From an annual report of a printing company. Showing facts and figures of the fiscal year.

印刷会社のアニュアル・レポートより。本年度の売上などの情報を示している。

Germany   2003
CD, AD: Kirsten Dietz   CD: Jochen Rädeker   D: Stephanie Zehender / Gernot Walter   P: Andreas Langen / Kai Loges   CW: Pr + Co.
DF, S: Strichpunkt GmbH   CL: Schlott Gruppe AG

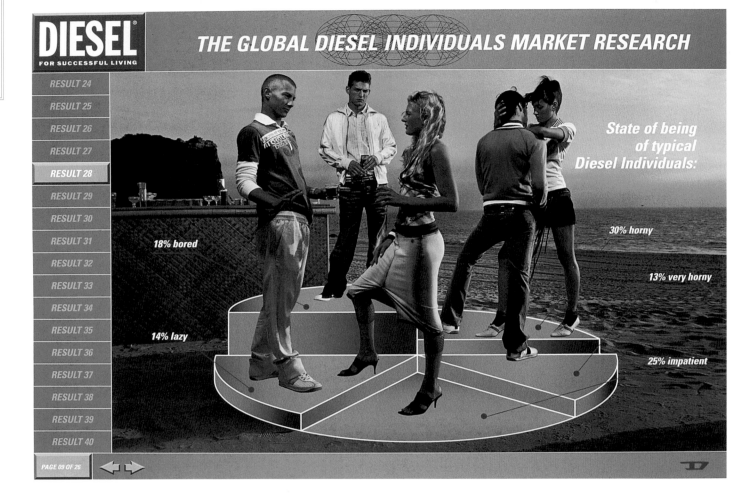

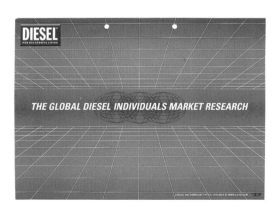

A pie chart showing the state of being of typical Diesel individuals.

典型的なディーゼル愛好者の性格を示す円グラフ。

Netherlands   2003
AD: Pim Van Nunen   P: Luiz Sanchez   CW: Lorenzo De Rita   DF, S: Kesselskramer   CL: Diesel

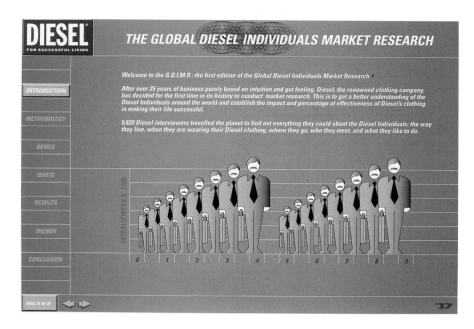

Graphs showing the result of market research
to provide a better understanding of the Diesel individuals
around the world and establish the impact
and percentage of effectiveness of Diesel's clothing
in making their life successful.

世界中のディーゼル愛好者を良く理解し、彼らの人生を成功に導いた同社の
洋服の効果や、影響の度合いを立証するマーケット・リサーチの結果を
示すグラフ。

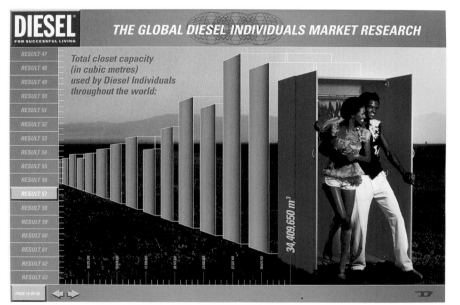

A graph illustrating total closet capacity (in cubic meters)
used by Diesel individuals throughout the world.

世界中のディーゼル愛好者が使用しているクローゼットの広さの
合計（立方平方メートル）を表すグラフ。

A graph showing a number of sand castles accidentally
destroyed by Diesel swimsuit wearers during the summer.

夏の間、ディーゼルの水着を着た人に偶然壊されてしまった砂の城の数
を示すグラフ。

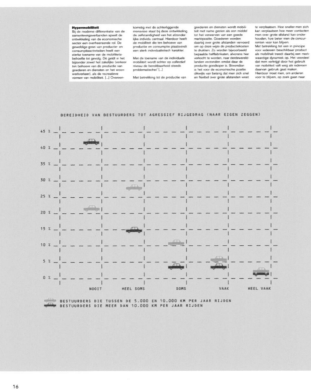

a

b

Diagram showing the aggressive behavior in traffic:drivers who drive between 5,000 and 10,000km versus those who drive more than 10,000km per year. (a)
Diagram showing average income per person versus travelling time per person per day in Africa, USA, and the Netherlands. (b)

渋滞における攻撃的な行動を示すダイアグラム。年間5,000〜10,000キロを運転するドライバーと年間10,000キロ以上運転するドライバーの比較。 (a)
アフリカ、アメリカおよびオランダの個人の平均収入と1日の移動時間を比較したダイアグラム。 (b)

Netherlands 2003
CD, AD: André Toet   CD: Jan Sevenster   D: Bas Meulendijks   CW: Paul Van Koningsbruggen   DF, S: Samenwerkende Ontwerpers   CL: Grafische Cultuurstichting

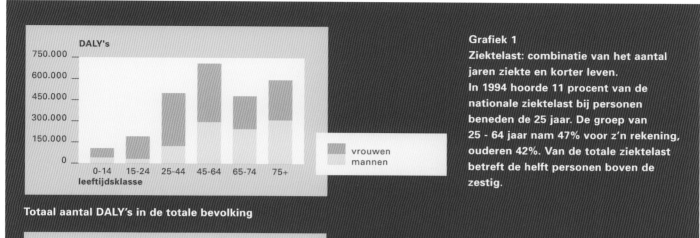

Grafiek 1
Ziektelast: combinatie van het aantal jaren ziekte en korter leven.
In 1994 hoorde 11 procent van de nationale ziektelast bij personen beneden de 25 jaar. De groep van 25 - 64 jaar nam 47% voor z'n rekening, ouderen 42%. Van de totale ziektelast betreft de helft personen boven de zestig.

Totaal aantal DALY's in de totale bevolking

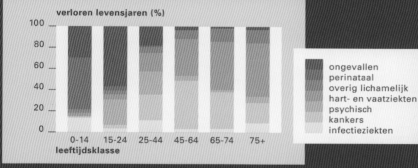

Grafiek 2
Verloren levensjaren zijn mede bepalend voor de ziektelast.
Ze komen bij de meest jeugdigen voor rekening van ongevallen en problemen tijdens zwangerschap en geboorte.
De belangrijkste oorzaken, naar leeftijd, in beeld.

Aantal verloren levensjaren

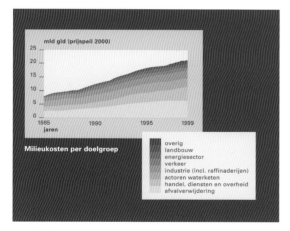

Milieukosten per doelgroep

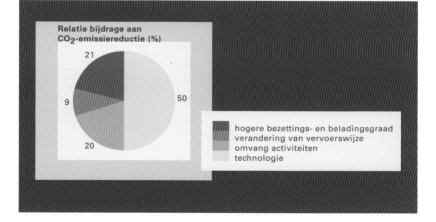

Various diagrams showing studies and statistics on environmental issues : population, CO2 emission, temparature, and etc.

人口、二酸化炭素排出量、気温など、環境問題に関する研究と統計を示す様々なグラフ。

Netherlands   2001
CD: Annemieke Later   D: Edwin Van Praet   DF, S: TelDesign   CL: RIVM

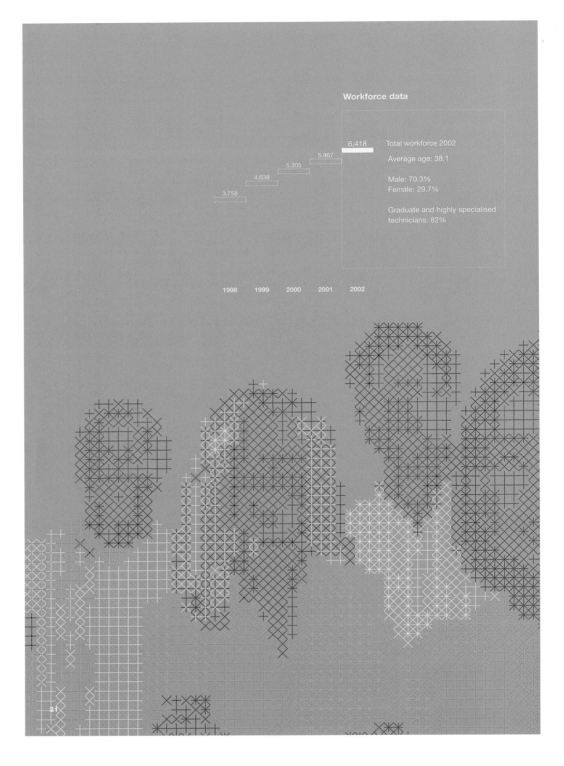

Workforce data

6,418

Total workforce 2002

Average age: 38.1

Male: 70.3%
Female: 29.7%

Graduate and highly specialised
technicians: 82%

5,967

5,305

4,638

3,758

1998　1999　2000　2001　2002

From an annual report of a telecommunication company. Graphs showing average daily trading volume per month, workforce data, average share value, and profit and revenues.

テレコミュニケーション会社のアニュアル・レポートより。1ヶ月あたりの平均的な日常の取引高、従業員数のデータ、平均的な株価、利益と収入を示すグラフ。

Spain　2003
CD: Emilio Gil　AD: Jorge García　CW: Angel Alloza　DF, S: Tau Diseño　CL: Indra

General Evolution

A weak economy that performed below initial expectations and the slowdown in growth had an adverse impact on overall confidence in 2002. The information technologies industry, in which the majority of Indra's operations take place, has not been immune to these circumstances, growth rates having declined with respect to 2001 in all markets, including Spain.

Despite this scenario, Indra has again fulfilled its permanent medium-term goal of rapid growth in turnover and profitability, significantly above the Spanish and European markets, in a year of negative results for many industry companies.

All objectives set for 2002 have been met, even though the general economic outlook at the end of 2001, when the company's aims were defined, was not as adverse as the situation that unfolded during the year:

	Initial objectives	Year end
Growth in IT revenues (ex balloting projects)	12%-15%	15%
Growing in SIM/ATS + DEE revenues	15%	17%
Operating profitability (EBIT margin as % of sales)	10.8%	11%
Net profit growth	**15%**	**20%**

Total revenues for 2002 reached €873.6m, entailing a rise of 13% on 2001 (15% ex balloting projects).

Order intake amounted to €927.3m, a figure 6% higher than total revenues for the year and similar to the total for 2001, when order intake grew 29%.

At the year end the order backlog totalled €1,177m or 1.35 times revenues for the year, ensuring a good coverage level for coming years.

The IT business performed well despite the industry scenario previously referred to. Total revenues of €669.4m represent 12% year-on-year growth (15% ex balloting projects). The following issues should be noted:

• 15% growth (20% ex balloting projects) was achieved in the three institutional markets (accounting for 62% of revenues), the two most significant in terms of revenues and visibility being Defence & Security Forces and Transport & Traffic. Balloting projects declined in 2002 as no elections were held in Indra's habitual markets, although business was secured in new regions;

• as regards the remaining vertical markets, significant progress was made in Industry & Commerce (18%) and Finance & Insurance (10%). In spite of the general weak performance in this market in 2002, Indra's Telecommunications & Utilities business grew 3% on 2001, when it rose 50% compared with the previous year.

(*) Normalised data for 1998

IT Revenues by market	2002 (€M)	2001 (€M)	Variation
Transport & Traffic	189.0	156.9	20%
Defence & Security Forces	177.2	142.7	24%
Telecommunications & Utilities	157.9	153.2	3%
Public Administration & Healthcare	47.5	44.5	7%
Public Administration Balloting Projects	3.6	19.9	-82%
Finance & Insurance	52.0	47.1	10%
Industry & Commerce	42.2	35.7	18%
Total IT Revenues	**669.4**	**600.1**	**12%**

The following should be noted in relation to the Simulation and Automatic Test Systems (SIM/ATS) and Defence Electronics Equipment (DEE) businesses, where turnover totalled €204.2m:

• 17% overall rise in revenues, SIM/ATS having grown 30%;
• continued high visibility and a large order backlog equal to 2.6 times 2002's turnover;
• major projects have been identified that should generate new contracts as from 2004.

Significant developments relating to total revenues by geographical areas are as follows:

• 19% growth in the Spanish market, which accounts for 70% of total revenues;
• 20% growth in international markets, not including Latin America, which has offset the decline in revenues in this area caused by a decrease in balloting projects and the depreciation of the main currencies.

In general, Indra's international business has again helped to support the company's development, representing 30% of total revenues.

2002 has been a positive year from a commercial viewpoint, in terms of revenues and order intake; profitability has also improved, despite price pressures accompanied by slow growth in demand and stricter customer requirements, factors that have caused a reduction in profits recorded by the industry's leading European companies, whose operating margins have declined by an average of 37%.

EBITDA has risen 18% to reach €113.6m, totalling 13% of revenues in 2002 compared with 12.4% in 2002.

EBIT has increased to €96.0m, amounting to 11% of revenues in 2002 versus 10.8% in 2001 and exceeding the initial target for the year. This growth in profitability is explained by a rise in the contribution from added value products, a flexible funding structure and ongoing measures to control costs and optimise production.

Net profit totals €57.4m, entailing a rise of 20% on the figure for 2001.

Indra also continues to generate a substantial cash flow, which amounted to €86m in 2002, 22% up on 2001. This factor, coupled with a considerable rise in working capital, has resulted in a net cash position of €36.5m at the year end after investing €100m, of which €73m relates to acquisitions (a 49% stake in Indra EWS and 60% of the Portuguese company CPC).

ROCE (return on capital employed) and ROE (return on equity) stand at 51% and 29%, respectively (excluding financial coverage for option plans in both cases).

Indra's stock has performed above average in 2002 thanks in part to sound economic and financial figures, as described above, and the company's sustained growth since the IPO, all yearly targets having been fulfilled and even exceeded.

During the year, stock markets have been highly volatile due to the loss of confidence in an economic recovery. The major indices have registered substantial losses, particularly IT industry indices.

2002 was a poor year from an economic viewpoint and this is also true in the financial markets, the world's stock exchanges having suffered for the third year running as a result of the recession in the real economy.

In this adverse context, Indra's performance was clearly above average, even though the stock fell 32% over the year. The European IT services sector lost 67%, the main Spanish index (IBEX-35) closed at a loss for the third consecutive year (28%) and the technological indices have shown no signs of recovering: the Nasdaq fell 33% and Spain's New Market lost 47%.

The following graph shows the evolution of Indra's share price, the IBEX 35 and the average share prices for the main European IT services companies in 2002 (base 100):

This above-average market performance becomes even clearer based on Indra's performance since the IPO in March 1999. While Indra's stock has risen in value by 45%, the average share value for the principal European IT companies has fallen 80% and the IBEX 35 has lost 39%, as shown in the following graph (base 100):

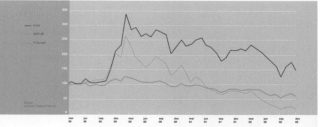

We may therefore conclude that Indra's position has improved both in absolute terms and, more importantly, in comparison with the rest of the industry, following three years of unfavourable and even crisis conditions (2000-2002). This has been possible thanks to a number of specific features that may be identified in the company's business model, including:

• selective growth policy as regards retaining customers, securing new business and providing services.
• strong commitment to project execution and delivery.
• focus on cost control and production optimisation.
• major emphasis on cash generation by projects and working capital management.
• all the above is supported by a selective acquisitions policy, alliances forged to access wider markets and a proven capacity to generate projects in emerging markets.

Meggitt PLC Report and Accounts 2003

Around 3,700 employees.
Four integrated divisions.
One Meggitt.

Meggitt is more than the responsible custodian of first-class, operationally independent businesses.

Within or across the four divisions through which we manage them, you'll find Meggitt's operating units increasingly marching in step; sharing research, engineering, operational and marketing expertise; and orchestrating technical solutions of increasingly high value to customers—in ways they want them delivered.

Aerospace Systems

90% of the world's aircraft carry the engine vibration monitoring systems we have developed over half a century. Today, we enjoy a wider diagnostic capability, evidenced by our recent launch of the world's first, comprehensive, on-engine condition monitoring unit for the A380 Airbus. With our electronics, this unit adds parameters of temperature, pressure and speed from digital engine control systems to our oil debris and vibration analysis tools, sharpening maintenance scheduling and enhancing the readiness of mission critical aerospace applications.

The division's electronic cockpit displays are compact, information-rich yet optically-clear, and function in extreme conditions. With 2002's acquisition of best-in-class air data computers, specialised avionics sensors and data acquisition units, discrete flight instrumentation is now being integrated into comprehensive, higher value systems for military aircraft.

£124.1m
Turnover 2003
31%
Percentage of group turnover

2003	124.1
2002	100.7
2001	107.7
2000	86.7
1999	77.5

Defence Systems

43 countries favour our aerial targets, electronic scoring systems and unmanned air vehicles, which are used to train personnel and develop and evaluate anti-aircraft weapon systems. Turnkey systems and services add value to these products. Our aero-mechanical launch and recovery systems—deploying targets or towed decoys to foil missile threats—are installed on numerous military aircraft the world over. These innovative proprietary technologies are protected and developed through total systems control, guaranteeing a high degree of customisation for each client.

Two acquisitions in 2003 widened the scope of the division's offer. Caswell International extended our targetry expertise to ground-based stationary and mobile target equipment for small arms and armour training. Meggitt Western Design enhanced our weapons systems development capability with its world class, automated ammunition handling technology and environmental control systems.

£52.0m
Turnover 2003
13%
Percentage of group turnover

2003	52.0
2002	36.9
2001	37.1
2000	29.7
1999	26.6

Aerospace Equipment

The flight time of our fire detection systems, which have never missed a true fire warning, exceeds one billion hours. Our high speed fuel control and shut-off valves operate in less than 50 milliseconds at extreme temperatures. Our unique Bleed Air Leak Detection system is now on the CS jet and Aermacchi M346 jet trainer and our tank pressurisation ducts on the Space Shuttle. Our quick disconnect products, used on interconnecting lines involving corrosive and other exotic fluids found on military aircraft and space vehicles, are made to the highest specifications, ready to be uncoupled at speed with zero leakage and air inclusion.

When you consider that our products transmit signals, help control engine clearance, regulate de-icing, cool avionics, select landing gear, manage fuel and control cabin pressure and temperature, you can see why our products and systems—also repaired and replaced by us over the average 30-year life of an aircraft—are on virtually every aircraft flying today. We work on the ground, too: on transfer cooling solutions involving proprietary printed circuit heat exchange technology, and fire and gas detection systems for industrial applications.

The newly acquired, high performance products of Meggitt Airdynamics will increase the military-grade content of the division's environmental control systems. In turn, with access to complementary products across the division, Meggitt Airdynamics will advance its systems offer.

£151.4m
Turnover 2003
38%
Percentage of group turnover

2003	151.4
2002	169.3
2001	173.6
2000	155.4
1999	95.2

Electronics

We design and manufacture high-value, active sensors for mission critical applications. Our markets are characterised by the need for absolute measurement from high performance products that function in demanding environments.

Our customers, who operate in regulated business sectors of the medical, flight, military and transportation safety markets, demand the highest standards of product reliability. After all, life can depend on the integrity of systems that include Meggitt technology. At one end of the spectrum, our sensor technology developments support new ideas in human condition monitoring like in vitro drug delivery systems and blood pressure monitoring and, at the other, networked intelligent sensors that guide orbiting satellites.

The division also produces high volume, position sensors, potentiometers and encoders for a diverse range of automotive and domestic applications including audio volume and tuning controls, climate management and airflow distribution, and equipment positioning and mode switching.

£71.2m
Turnover 2003
18%
Percentage of group turnover

2003	71.2
2002	68.6
2000	67.4
2001	66.5
1999	42.0

...leading to record profits—
the highest in Meggitt's history.

In 2003, we delivered another set of outstanding results.

We did this by maintaining investment in new products—even in depressed markets there are always customers for innovation.

We continued to take a balanced approach to market diversification within our chosen niches with a portfolio designed to offset demand changes in our primary aerospace and defence markets.

We realised intrinsic value from current operations and, through another year of

And we supported customers in other sectors hungry for the aerospace quality which characterises Meggitt's engineering-rich, information-oriented products.

We continued to integrate our divisions so that we can, as a group, manage the select core of customers that drive many of our businesses.

astute acquisitions, positioned ourselves to refresh core technologies, deliver new products and exploit new markets.

And that's how we will continue to deliver value to our customers—and the kind of returns to which Meggitt shareholders have become accustomed.

£75.5m
Profit before tax, exceptional items and goodwill amortisation

2003	75.5
2002	70.3
2001	72.4
2000	66.1
1999	49.1

£81.7m
Cash flow from operating activities

2003	81.7
2002	81.6
2001	88.3
2000	81.6
1999	49.8

18.3p
Earnings per share (EPS basis)

2003	18.3
2002	17.1
2001	17.4
2000	16.2
1999	13.2

7.5p
Dividends per share

2003	7.5
2002	7.0
2001	6.8
2000	6.4
1999	5.7

Cash generation [£m]

2003	
2002	78.4
2002	81.6
2001	84.5
2001	88.3
2000	80.6
2000	81.6
1999	56.0
1999	49.8

■ Operating profit before goodwill amortisation   ■ Cash flow from operations

Turnover by geographical destination [%]

■ UK: 15% (2002: 16%)
■ Continental Europe: 23% (2002: 21%)
■ North America: 52% (2002: 52%)
■ Rest of World: 10% (2002: 11%)

Exchange rates effective for 2003

	Balance Sheet Year end rate		Profit & Loss Account Weighted average	
	2003	2002	2003	2002
US dollar	1.79	1.61	1.63	1.46
Euro	1.42	1.53	1.45	1.57
Swiss franc	2.21	2.23	2.21	2.34

Currency profile of net debt [£m]

	2003	2002
Sterling	(22.8)	(29.4)
US dollar	141.2	144.8
Euro	(3.2)	(6.3)
Swiss franc	25.7	31.3
Other	(0.4)	(0.7)
Total net debt	140.5	139.7

Gearing [%]

118.6	
83.1	
60.7	
54.2	

1999 2000 2001 2002 2003

Graphs indicating data on employees and analysis of turnover for 2001-2003.

2001年から2003年の売上高の分析や従業員に関するデータを表すグラフ。

UK 2004
CD: David Stocks / Gilmar Wendt   AD, D, I: Rachael Godfrey   DF, S: SAS   CL: Meggitt PLC

Principali dati economici e finanziari consolidati

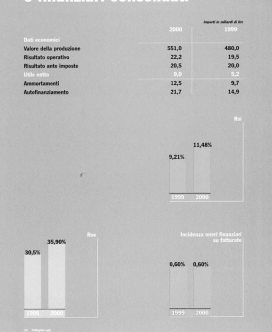

Importi in miliardi di lire

Dati economici	2000	1999
Valore della produzione	551,0	480,0
Risultato operativo	22,2	19,5
Risultato ante imposte	20,5	20,0
Utile netto	9,0	5,2
Ammortamenti	12,5	9,7
Autofinanziamento	21,7	14,9

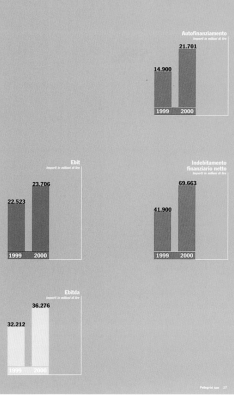

Autofinanziamento *Importi in milioni di lire*
- 1999: 14.900
- 2000: 21.701

Roi
- 1999: 9,21%
- 2000: 11,48%

Ebit *Importi in milioni di lire*
- 1999: 22.523
- 2000: 23.706

Indebitamento finanziario netto *Importi in milioni di lire*
- 1999: 41.900
- 2000: 69.663

Roe
- 1999: 30,5%
- 2000: 35,90%

Incidenza oneri finanziari su fatturato
- 1999: 0,60%
- 2000: 0,60%

Ebitda *Importi in milioni di lire*
- 1999: 32.212
- 2000: 36.276

16 Pellegrini spa — Pellegrini spa 17

Ristorazione in Italia
- 249.569 2000
- 224.217 1999

Dati in milioni lire

orienterà verso queste soluzioni, la Pellegrini si è adeguatamente strutturata per rispondere a tali esigenze.

Il numero dei pasti erogati nel corso del 2000 è stato di 29,2 milioni con un incremento rispetto all'anno precedente pari al 9,8%.

La ristorazione commerciale

È stato inaugurato a novembre il primo ristorante commerciale a marchio Valentina presso il centro commerciale Bennet di San Martino Siccomario, in provincia di Pavia. I primi risultati confermano la validità dell'investimento e la bontà della formula adottata tanto che è stato recentemente aperto il secondo ristorante presso il Museo della Scienza e della Tecnica di Milano.

Quello che era l'obiettivo di inserirsi nel settore della ristorazione commerciale è stato raggiunto e sarà ulteriormente rinnovato con la costante apertura di nuovi punti vendita.

Distribuzione automatica

Il settore ha prodotto un fatturato di oltre un miliardo raddoppiando le vendite rispetto all'esercizio precedente. Il numero dei clienti serviti è passato da 2 a 7.

Distribuzione automatica
- 1.129 2000
- 597 1999

Dati in milioni di lire

Notevoli sono le prospettive di sviluppo con tassi di crescita certamente non usuali in quanto il mercato, sempre di più, apprezza questo servizio svolto da società di ristorazione affermate che sono

in grado di integrare le attività di ristorazione con quelle di ristoro.

Nel corso dell'anno è stata avviata la sperimentazione di una macchina per la distribuzione di pasti caldi che può trovare impiego sia nel segmento tradizionale della ristorazione, turni notturni e servizi non presidiati, oltre a risolvere le necessità di ristoro in aree pubbliche.

Tecnologie per l'ambiente

Prosegue con grande soddisfazione il trend di sviluppo di questa divisione. L'incremento di circa 6 miliardi, pari al 61% rispetto all'anno precedente, è la testimonianza di una organizzazione che eroga un servizio apprezzato e di alto livello.

Tecnologie per l'ambiente
- 14.310 2000
- 8.882 1999

Dati in milioni di lire

Sino ad oggi lo sviluppo si è concentrato prevalentemente nel Nord Italia (Lombardia, Piemonte, Liguria) e nella città di Roma. Gli obiettivi futuri prevedono una espansione su tutto il territorio nazionale replicando il percorso storico avvenuto per le altre divisioni.

Derrate alimentari

Il totale dei ricavi è stato di 74 miliardi registrando un incremento rispetto all'anno precedente del 89%. Questo risultato ampiamente positivo è stato raggiunto a seguito dell'acquisizione delle attività F.A.C. (vendita di derrate alimentari a Comunità Religiose e a ristoranti), all'importante appalto per la fornitura al servizio di refezione scolastica del Comune di Milano, oltre al consolidamento delle vendite di carni bovine a marchio Grantaglio.

Derrate alimentari
- 74.210 2000
- 39.363 1999

Dati in milioni di lire

Negli ultimi mesi dell'anno il fenomeno "mucca pazza" ha pesantemente influenzato il mercato delle carni bovine, costringendo gli operatori a strutturarsi con sistemi di controllo che garantissero l'origine dell'animale. La divisione Central-Food grazie agli investimenti costantemente effettuati era già pronta a garantire il consumatore finale e di conseguenza, pur subendo la flessione delle vendite si è trovata avvantaggiata al momento della ripresa avvenuta da Aprile del 2001.

Buoni pasto

Pur perdurando lo stato di forte competizione già verificatosi lo scorso esercizio, il fatturato si è mantenuto in linea con l'anno precedente. Molta attenzione è stata rivolta al mantenimento della clientela esistente che ci ha costretto ad una politica di aumento degli sconti praticati ai clienti, compensati da una politica maggiormente aggressiva nei confronti dei fornitori ed alla ottimizzazione dei costi di gestione.

Buoni pasto
- 184.614 2000
- 185.843 1999

Dati in milioni di lire

In questo scenario economico il volume di buoni pasto emessi ha di poco superato i 23 milioni mantenendo inalterato il valore medio facciale.

Risorse umane e relazioni industriali

Al 31 dicembre 2000 i dipendenti del Gruppo Pellegrini risultano pari a 3857 unità, con un incremento rispetto all'anno precedente di 530 unità. I dipendenti facenti capo a società estere al 31 dicembre 2000 sono pari al 12,6% del totale.

Nel corso dell'esercizio si è puntato molto sulla formazione dei dipendenti, ad ampio spettro, in particolare modo per quanto attiene i temi relativi alla sicurezza sul lavoro, che ha già portato al risultato positivo di una flessione delle giornate perdute per infortunio.

Ai sensi dell'articolo 2428 del codice civile viene data informazione che la Pellegrini spa non detiene e non ha detenuto nel corso dell'esercizio, azioni proprie o quote di società controllanti, anche per tramite di società fiduciarie o per interposta persona. Inoltre non sono state realizzate attività di

ricerca e di sviluppo.

Infine con riferimento ai rapporti con imprese controllate, collegate, controllanti ed imprese sottoposte al controllo di quest'ultima si rinvia a quanto illustrato nella nota integrativa.

Andamento Economico Finanziario del Gruppo

A livello di bilancio consolidato il Gruppo Pellegrini ha prodotto ricavi per vendite e prestazioni di 544 miliardi che si confrontano con i 476 dell'esercizio precedente ed evidenzia un patrimonio netto di 25,9 miliardi dopo aver stanziato 12,5 miliardi per ammortamenti, 1,1 miliardi per fondo rischi su crediti e 11,4 miliardi per carico fiscale di competenza dell'esercizio. L'utile netto ammonta a 9,1 miliardi.

Ristorazione all'estero

Le attività di ristorazione all'Estero vengono svolte dalla nostra partecipata Pellegrini Catering Overseas sa che ha realizzato nel corso dell'esercizio un fatturato consolidato di 19,7 miliardi ed un utile netto di 0,8 miliardi. Il patrimonio netto ammonta a 3,46 miliardi.

Pellegrini Catering Overseas opera nei seguenti paesi:

Congo

È stato rinnovato per tre anni il contratto con il nostro principale cliente: Agip. Inoltre si è deciso di sviluppare il business in un nuovo settore gestendo il centro sportivo, Plage-sportive, per la durata di tre anni.

Libia

Si rileva una flessione dei ricavi a seguito della riduzione dei grandi lavori appaltati al nostro cliente di riferimento. Poiché il paese viene ritenuto importante si sta analizzando la possibilità di costituire una branch per poter partecipare alle gare di appalto indette dalle aziende governative operanti nel settore petrolifero.

Nigeria

Nel corso dell'anno si è concluso il contratto più importante con il nostro cliente Techint. Fatto estremamente importante è che con lo stesso cliente è stato stipulato un nuovo contratto, con decorrenza da novembre 2000 e con interessanti prospettive non solo per il 2001 ma anche per il biennio successivo.

Asia ed Est Europa

Le strategie di sviluppo dei prossimi anni passano attraverso l'insediamento nei paesi dell'Est Europa, a cominciare dalla Romania dove è già stata costituita una branch, ed in Asia, in Kazakhstan, dove sono in corso contatti di notevole importanza.

20 Pellegrini Spa — Pellegrini Spa 21

From an annual report of a catering company. Graphs detail various costs in the catering industry in Italy.

外食企業のアニュアル・レポートより。イタリアの外食産業における様々なコストを表すグラフ。

Italy 2001
CD, I: Guido Grognola   AD, D: Andrea Fanji   P: Industrial & Corporate Profiles Srl-Fiorenza Cicogna
CW: Andrea Di Gregorio   DF, S: Industrial & Corporate Profiles Srl   CL: Pellegrini Spa

REVENUE

A. Education	$4,853,016	59.6%
B. Health Systems	$2,487,765	30.5%
C. Clinical Research	$635,170	7.8%
D. Administrative, Marketing and Business Development	$166,583	2.0%
E. Health Policy Consulting	$5,868	0.1%
TOTAL REVENUE	$8,148,402	100.0%

EXPENSES

A. HMS Faculty Salaries, Honoraria & Travel, Program Fees, Harvard University Overhead and HMS Contribution	$3,588,691	44.1%
B. Operational Services and Expenses	$2,088,002	25.6%
C. Staff	$1,321,174	16.2%
D. Travel	$879,919	10.8%
E. Communications, Meetings, & Conferences	$270,616	3.3%
TOTAL EXPENSES	$8,148,402	100.0%
NET INCOME		0

Pie charts itemizing the revenus and expenses.
From an annual report for a non-profit unit of
Harvard Medical School.

収益と費用の内訳を示す円グラフ。
ハーバード大学医学部内の非営利部門のアニュアル・レポートより。

USA 2002
CD, AD, D: Natalie Pangaro / Shannon Beer
DF, S: Pangaro Beer   CL: Harvard Medical International

Industry Classification

Summary of the Funds' investment portfolio by industry and by type of ownership as of December 31, 2003.

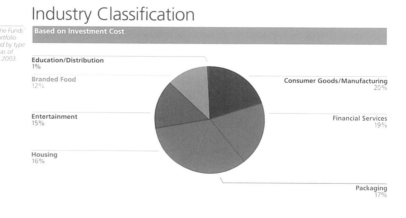

Based on Investment Cost

- Education/Distribution 1%
- Branded Food 12%
- Entertainment 15%
- Housing 16%
- Consumer Goods/Manufacturing 20%
- Financial Services 19%
- Packaging 17%

Type of Ownership

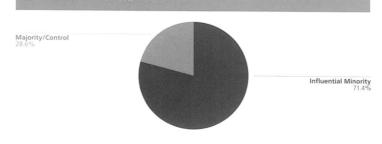

Based on Number of Investments

- Majority/Control 28.6%
- Influential Minority 71.4%

Graphs to communicate financial results for ZN Mexico Funds,
an investment fund focusing on Mexico. From an annual report.

メキシコに焦点をあてた投資ファンド、ZN Mexico Fundsの決算報告を伝えるグラフ。
アニュアル・レポートより。

USA 2004
CD, D: Graham Hanson   D: Pilar Freire   CW: Mariel Creo
DF, S: Graham Hanson Design   CL: Zephyr Management

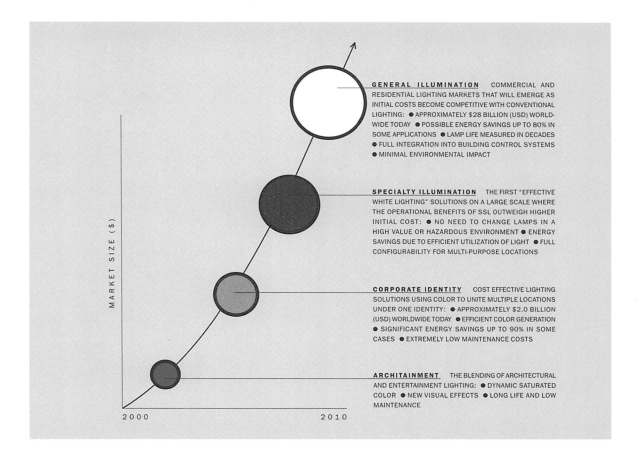

GENERAL ILLUMINATION COMMERCIAL AND RESIDENTIAL LIGHTING MARKETS THAT WILL EMERGE AS INITIAL COSTS BECOME COMPETITIVE WITH CONVENTIONAL LIGHTING: ● APPROXIMATELY $28 BILLION (USD) WORLD-WIDE TODAY ● POSSIBLE ENERGY SAVINGS UP TO 80% IN SOME APPLICATIONS ● LAMP LIFE MEASURED IN DECADES ● FULL INTEGRATION INTO BUILDING CONTROL SYSTEMS ● MINIMAL ENVIRONMENTAL IMPACT

SPECIALTY ILLUMINATION THE FIRST "EFFECTIVE WHITE LIGHTING" SOLUTIONS ON A LARGE SCALE WHERE THE OPERATIONAL BENEFITS OF SSL OUTWEIGH HIGHER INITIAL COST: ● NO NEED TO CHANGE LAMPS IN A HIGH VALUE OR HAZARDOUS ENVIRONMENT ● ENERGY SAVINGS DUE TO EFFICIENT UTILIZATION OF LIGHT ● FULL CONFIGURABILITY FOR MULTI-PURPOSE LOCATIONS

CORPORATE IDENTITY COST EFFECTIVE LIGHTING SOLUTIONS USING COLOR TO UNITE MULTIPLE LOCATIONS UNDER ONE IDENTITY: ● APPROXIMATELY $2.0 BILLION (USD) WORLDWIDE TODAY ● EFFICIENT COLOR GENERATION ● SIGNIFICANT ENERGY SAVINGS UP TO 90% IN SOME CASES ● EXTREMELY LOW MAINTENANCE COSTS

ARCHITAINMENT THE BLENDING OF ARCHITECTURAL AND ENTERTAINMENT LIGHTING: ● DYNAMIC SATURATED COLOR ● NEW VISUAL EFFECTS ● LONG LIFE AND LOW MAINTENANCE

A graph showing the market growth of solid state lighting.

半導体照明のマーケットの成長を示すグラフ。

USA   2001
CD, AD, D: Dave Mason   AD, D: Pamela Lee   D: Nancy Willett   P: Victor John Penner   DF, S: Samata Mason   CL: TIR Systems Ltd.

(2) Market share and position
We hold the leading position in the key fixed and mobile systems markets

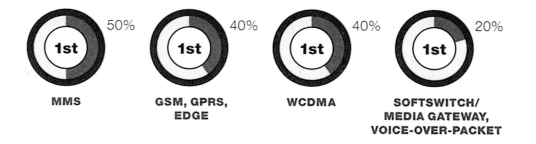

Pie charts showing market share and position.

マーケットシェアと市場を示す円グラフ。

UK   2004
CD, AD: Gilmar Wendt   CD: David Stocks   D, I: John-Paul Sykes   P: Peter Hoelstad   CW: Tim Rich / Mats Thoren   DF, S: SAS   CL: Ericsson

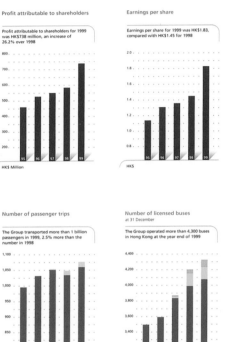

Profit attributable to shareholders

Profit attributable to shareholders for 1999 was HK$738 million, an increase of 26.2% over 1998

HK$ Million

Earnings per share

Earnings per share for 1999 was HK$1.83, compared with HK$1.45 for 1998

HK$

Number of passenger trips

The Group transported more than 1 billion passengers in 1999, 2.5% more than the number in 1998

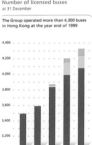
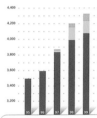

Million passenger trips

Franchised Public Bus Operations
■ KMB
▨ LWB

Number of licensed buses
at 31 December

The Group operated more than 4,300 buses in Hong Kong at the year end of 1999

Number of buses

■ KMB
▨ LWB
▨ Non-franchised bus services

3

Shareholders' funds
at 31 December

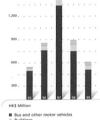
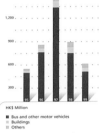

HK$ Million

Capital expenditure

HK$ Million

■ Bus and other motor vehicles
▨ Buildings
▨ Others

Debt maturity profile
at 31 December

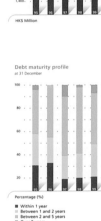

Percentage (%)

■ Within 1 year
▨ Between 1 and 2 years
▨ Between 2 and 5 years
▨ Over 5 years

Staff cost and staff per bus

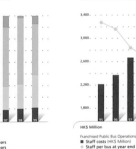

HK$ Million   Number of staff

Franchised Public Bus Operations
■ Staff costs (HK$ Million)
• Staff per bus at year end

Financial Review

A series of graphs showing corporate profitability, number of passengers and buses. From an annual report.

企業の収益性、乗客やバスの数を示す一連のグラフ。アニュアル・レポートより。

Hong Kong   2000

CD, AD, D: Freeman Lau Siu Hong   AD, D: Eddy Yu   DF, S: Kan & Lau Design Consultants   CL: The Kowloon Motor Bus Holdings Ltd.

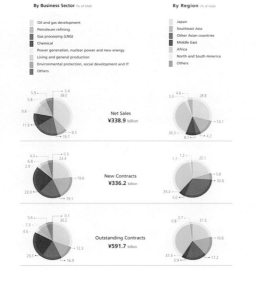

Performance Highlights—Non-Consolidated (Fiscal 2002)

By Business Sector (% of total)
- Oil and gas development
- Petroleum refining
- Gas processing (LNG)
- Chemical
- Power generation, nuclear power and new energy
- Living and general production
- Environmental protection, social development and IT
- Others

By Region (% of total)
- Japan
- Southeast Asia
- Other Asian countries
- Middle East
- Africa
- North and South America
- Others

Net Sales ¥338.9 billion
New Contracts ¥336.2 billion
Outstanding Contracts ¥591.7 billion

a

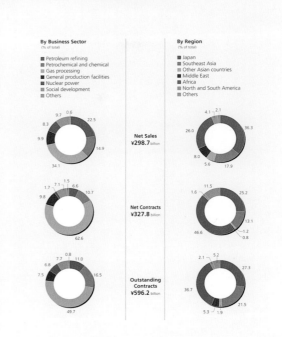

By Business Sector (% of total)
- Petroleum refining
- Petrochemical and chemical
- Gas processing
- General production facilities
- Nuclear power
- Social development
- Others

By Region (% of total)
- Japan
- Southeast Asia
- Other Asian countries
- Middle East
- Africa
- North and South America
- Others

Net Sales ¥298.7 billion
Net Contracts ¥327.8 billion
Outstanding Contracts ¥596.2 billion

b

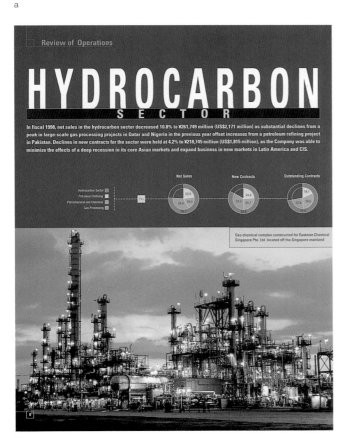

Review of Operations

HYDROCARBON
SECTOR

In fiscal 1998, net sales in the hydrocarbon sector decreased 10.8% to ¥261,749 million (US$2,171 million) as substantial declines from a peak in large-scale gas processing projects in Qatar and Nigeria in the previous year offset increases from a petroleum refining project in Pakistan. Declines in new contracts for the sector were held at 4.2% to ¥218,745 million (US$1,815 million), as the Company was able to minimize the effects of a deep recession in its core Asian markets and expand business in new markets in Latin America and CIS.

- Hydrocarbon Sector
- Petroleum Refining
- Petrochemical and Chemical
- Gas Processing

Net Sales   New Contracts   Outstanding Contracts

Oxo chemical complex constructed for Eastman Chemical Singapore Pte. Ltd. located off the Singapore mainland

c

Review of Operations

GENERAL INDUSTRIES
SECTOR

In fiscal 1998, net sales for the general industries sector increased 20.4% to ¥79,729 million (US$661 million) led by strong activity in general production facilities, nuclear energy and social development projects. New contracts for the sector declined to ¥43,728 million (US$363 million) due to contraction in the Japanese economy. However, the Company continued to win orders in a variety of new fields including large-scale shopping centers, soft drink manufacturing plants and syringe production facilities.

- General Industries Sector
- General Production Facility
- Nuclear Energy
- Social Development
- Other

Net Sales   New Contracts   Outstanding Contracts

Research and education technology center in Miyazaki, Japan

d

Pie charts showing sales, orders and backlog by region and business type. (a, b)
Pie charts showing sales, orders and backlog by sector and business type. (c, d)

事業分野別・地域別の売上高、受注高、受注残高を表す円グラフ。 (a, b)
セクターごとの事業分野別売上高、受注高、受注残高を表す円グラフ。 (c, d)

Japan   2003 (a) / 2002 (b) / 1999 (c, d)
D: Ayano Sasaki (a) / Shinji Suzuki (b) / Mayumi Noguchi (c, d)   CL: JGC Corporation   S: The IR Corporation

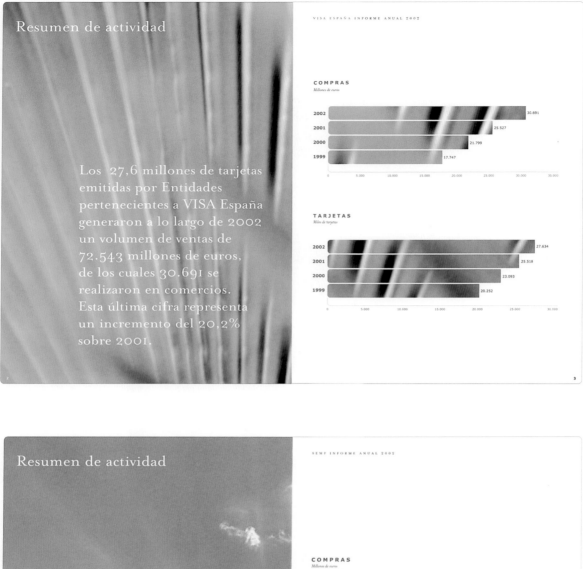

Resumen de actividad

Los 27,6 millones de tarjetas emitidas por Entidades pertenecientes a VISA España generaron a lo largo de 2002 un volumen de ventas de 72.543 millones de euros, de los cuales 30.691 se realizaron en comercios. Esta última cifra representa un incremento del 20,2% sobre 2001.

COMPRAS
Millones de euros

2002	30.691
2001	25.527
2000	21.799
1999	17.747

TARJETAS
Miles de tarjetas

2002	27.634
2001	25.518
2000	23.093
1999	20.252

Resumen de actividad

SEMP INFORME ANUAL 2002

Los 1,5 millones de tarjetas emitidas por Entidades pertenecientes a SEMP generaron a lo largo de 2002 un volumen de ventas de 1.638 millones de euros, de los cuales 823 fueron compras.

COMPRAS
Millones de euros

2002	823.182
2001	928.710
2000	385.949
1999	192.042

A series of financial chart for annual reports of the VISA Group.
VISAグループ各社のアニュアル・レポートから抜粋した、財務関連のチャートのシリーズ。

Spain   2003
CD: Emilio Gil   D: Ingrid Forbord   DF, S: Tau Diseño   CL: Sermepa

COMPRAS Y ANTICIPOS
Importes en miles de euros

OPERACIONES	Compras	Incr.	% s/ total	Anticipos	Incr.	% s/ total	Volumen de Ventas	Incr.	% s/ total
Tarjetas on/off-line	259.827.665	13,5%	39,9%	87.643.143	5,6%	19,3%	347.470.808	11,4%	31,4%
Tarjetas on-line	391.755.972	20,0%	60,1%	367.408.785	5,0%	80,7%	759.164.757	12,2%	68,6%
Total tarjetas	**651.583.637**	**17,3%**	**100,0%**	**455.051.928**	**5,2%**	**100,0%**	**1.106.635.565**	**12,0%**	**100,0%**

IMPORTES	Compras	Incr.	% s/ total	Anticipos	Incr.	% s/ total	Volumen de Ventas	Incr.	% s/ total
Tarjetas on/off-line	14.151.322	16,5%	48,1%	10.273.509	16,5%	24,9%	24.424.832	16,5%	34,5%
Tarjetas on-line	15.274.238	22,7%	51,9%	31.048.288	16,2%	75,1%	46.322.525	18,3%	65,5%
Total tarjetas	**29.425.560**	**19,6%**	**100,0%**	**41.321.797**	**16,3%**	**100,0%**	**70.747.357**	**17,7%**	**100,0%**

PORCENTAJE DE COMPRAS SOBRE VOLUMEN DE VENTAS

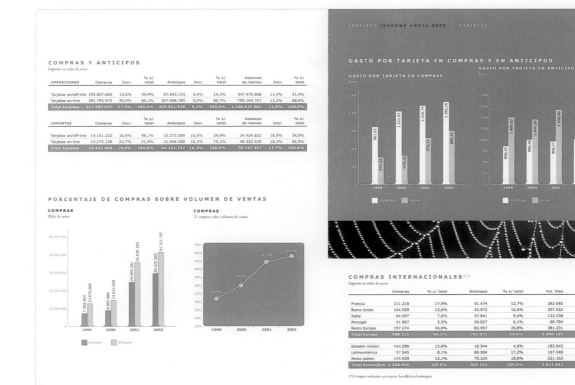

GASTO POR TARJETA EN COMPRAS Y EN ANTICIPOS

COMPRAS INTERNACIONALES(*)
Importes en miles de euros

	Compras	% s/ total	Anticipos	% s/ total	Vol. Vtas	% s/ total
Francia	211.218	17,5%	51.474	12,7%	262.692	16,3%
Reino Unido	164.059	13,6%	42.972	10,6%	207.032	12,9%
Italia	84.597	7,0%	37.841	9,4%	122.438	7,6%
Portugal	41.967	3,5%	24.827	6,1%	66.794	4,1%
Resto Europa	297.274	24,6%	83.957	20,8%	381.231	23,7%
Total Europa	**799.115**	**66,2%**	**241.071**	**59,6%**	**1.040.186**	**64,6%**
Estados Unidos	164.099	13,6%	18.544	4,6%	182.643	11,3%
Latinoamérica	97.545	8,1%	69.504	17,2%	167.049	10,4%
Resto países	145.939	12,1%	75.224	18,6%	221.163	13,7%
Total Extranjero	**1.206.698**	**100,0%**	**404.343**	**100,0%**	**1.611.042**	**100,0%**

(*) *Compras realizadas con tarjetas ServiRed en el extranjero*

VOLUMEN DE VENTAS
Miles de operaciones. Importes en miles de euros

OPERACIONES	Compras	% s/ total	Anticipos	% s/ total	Volumen de Ventas	% s/ total
ServiRed/MasterCard	18.216	67,6%	3.042	32,1%	21.258	58,4%
ServiRed/Maestro	8.743	32,4%	6.428	67,9%	15.171	41,6%
Total	**26.959**	**100,0%**	**9.469**	**100,0%**	**36.428**	**100,0%**

IMPORTES	Compras	% s/ total	Anticipos	% s/ total	Volumen de Ventas	% s/ total
ServiRed/MasterCard	529.140	64,3%	318.038	39,0%	847.178	51,7%
ServiRed/Maestro	294.042	35,7%	496.582	61,0%	790.624	48,3%
Total	**823.182**	**100,0%**	**814.620**	**100,0%**	**1.637.802**	**100,0%**

GASTOS POR TARJETA

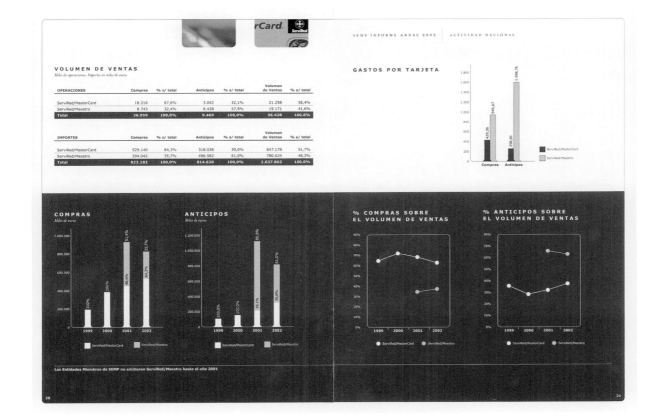

Las Entidades Miembros de SEMP no emitieron ServiRed/Maestro hasta el año 2001

Statistik 2003 — **Telefonseelsorge Notruf 142**

Anrufe gesamt: 11.909

Anrufe

26 %	Männer	••••••••••••
74 %	Frauen	•••••••••••••••••••••••••••••••••••
60 %	Anonym	••••••••••••••••••••••••••••
40 %	Namentlich	•••••••••••••••••••
22 %	ErstanruferInnen *	•••••••••••
78 %	MehrfachanruferInnen *	•••••••••••••••••••••••••••••••••••••••

Alter *

38 %	0 – 19 Jahre	•••••••••••••••••••
11 %	20 – 39 Jahre	••••••
15 %	40 – 59 Jahre	••••••••
3 %	60 – 79 Jahre	••
1 %	über 80 Jahre	•
32 %	nicht erfasst	•••••••••••••••••

* Konnte nur zum Teil oder ungenau erhoben werden.

Lebensform

15 %	Alleinlebend	••••••••
3 %	In Partnerschaft	••
4 %	Alleinerzieher	••
20 %	Familie	••••••••••
1 %	Heim/WG	•
57 %	nicht erfasst	••••••••••••••••••••••••••••

Problembereich

23 %	Psychische Themen	••••••••••••
25 %	Partnerschaft, Familie	•••••••••••••
16 %	Soziales Umfeld	••••••••
36 %	sonstige Themen	••••••••••••••••••

Tagesbereich

17 %	Vormittag	•••••••••
37 %	Nachmittag	••••••••••••••••••
34 %	Abend	•••••••••••••••••
12 %	Nacht	••••••

Statistik 2003 — **Details Jugendliche**

Anrufe gesamt: 4.618

Anrufe

39 %	Burschen	•••••••••••••••••••
61 %	Mädchen	••••••••••••••••••••••••••••••
87 %	Anonym	•••
13 %	Namentlich	•••••••
28 %	ErstanruferInnen *	••••••••••••••
72 %	MehrfachanruferInnen *	••••••••••••••••••••••••••••••••••••

Alter *

4 %	0 – 10 Jahre	••
68 %	11 – 15 Jahre	••••••••••••••••••••••••••••••••••
28 %	16 – 20 Jahre	••••••••••••••

Anlässe für Anrufe

8 %	Familienprobleme	••••
22 %	Freundschaft, Liebe	•••••••••••
5 %	Probleme mit Gruppen	•••
2 %	Probleme in der Schule	•
3 %	Gewalt	••
2 %	Sucht	•
6 %	Psychische Probleme	•••
5 %	Lebenssituation	•••
9 %	Fachauskünfte	•••••
35 %	Anrufe ohne spezielles Thema	•••••••••••••••••
1 %	Schweigeanrufe	•

Tagesbereich

14 %	Vormittag	•••••••
44 %	Nachmittag	••••••••••••••••••••••
35 %	Abend	•••••••••••••••••••
7 %	Nacht	••••

Telefonseelsorge
Vorarlberg
Jahresbericht 2003

Graphs showing details and statistics on telephone calls received by hotline services.
The title of the annual report is : "Listening—The ear is the way to the heart," so the color red is chosen as it symbolizes the heart.

ホットライン・サービスが受けた電話相談の詳細と統計を示すグラフ。アニュアル・レポートのタイトルが「聴くこと：耳は心に通じる道」であるので、「心」を象徴する色として赤を使用している。

Austria　2004
AD, D: Peter Felder　CW: Dr. Albert Lingg　DF, S: Felder Grafikdesign　CL: Telefonseelsorge Vorarlberg (the samaritans on phone Vorarlberg)

Statistik

	Notruf 142	Internet-Beratung www.142online.at
Männer	22 %	24 %
Frauen	60 %	76 %
Unbekannt	18 %	
Anonym	58 %	35 %
Namentlich	42 %	65 %
ErstanruferInnen*	24 %	54 %
MehrfachanruferInnen*	76 %	46 %

Alter*		Notruf 142	Internet-Beratung
	00 – 19 Jahre	31 %	31 %
	20 – 39 Jahre	13 %	21 %
	40 – 59 Jahre	15 %	07 %
	60 – 79 Jahre	03 %	
	über 80 Jahre	01 %	
	unbekannt	37 %	41 %

Lebensform*			
	Alleinlebend	15 %	07 %
	In Partnerschaft	03 %	03 %
	Alleinerziehend	04 %	03 %
	Familie	16 %	32 %
	Heim	01 %	01 %
	unbekannt	61 %	54 %

Problembereiche			
	Psychische Themen	23 %	30 %
	Partnerschaft/Familie	21 %	47 %
	Soziales Umfeld	07 %	10 %
	Sonstige Themen	49 %	13 %

Tagesbereich			
	Vormittag	17 %	20 %
	Nachmittag	39 %	30 %
	Abend	24 %	30 %
	Nacht	20 %	20 %

Anrufe: Anzahl gesamt: 13.441   Mailberatung: 159

* Konnte nur zum Teil oder
ungenau erhoben werden.

Bar graphs from an annual report show details and statistics on telephone calls received by hotline services. Each diagram is depicted in different colors depending on the topic.

アニュアル・レポートから抜粋した、ホットライン・サービスが受けた相談電話の詳細と統計を示す棒グラフ。それぞれテーマごとに色分けされている。

Austria 2002
AD, D: Peter Felder   D: René Dalpra   CW: Elisabeth Tos / Sepp Grofler   DF, S: Felder Grafikdesign   CL: Telefonseelsorge Vorarlberg (the samaritans on phone Vorarlberg)

GRAPHS & TABLES

SYSTEM & PROCESS CHARTS

MAPS & PICTOGRAMS

ILLUSTRATIVE DIAGRAMS

FINANCIAL HIGHLIGHTS

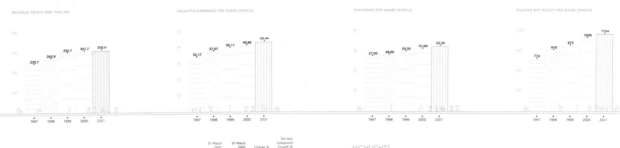

REVENUE PROFIT (PRE-TAX) £M — 235.7 (1997), 265.9 (1998), 292.7 (1999), 301.7 (2000), 308.9 (2001)

ADJUSTED EARNINGS PER SHARE (PENCE) — 33.17 (1997), 37.07 (1998), 39.11 (1999), 40.86 (2000), 43.44 (2001)

DIVIDENDS PER SHARE (PENCE) — 27.00 (1997), 28.00 (1998), 29.50 (1999), 31.00 (2000), 32.50 (2001)

DILUTED NET ASSETS PER SHARE (PENCE) — 774 (1997), 930 (1998), 975 (1999), 1090 (2000), 1154 (2001)

	31 March 2001	31 March 2000	Change %	Ten Year Compound Growth %
NET PROPERTY INCOME	£497.5m	£457.2m	+8.8	+4.6
*REVENUE PROFIT (PRE-TAX)	£308.9m	£301.7m	+2.4	+3.7
PRE-TAX PROFIT	£314.6m	£327.7m	−4.0	+3.5
*ADJUSTED EARNINGS PER SHARE	43.44p	40.86p	+6.3	+3.5
EARNINGS PER SHARE	44.57p	45.44p	−1.9	+3.5
DIVIDENDS PER SHARE	32.50p	31.00p	+4.8	+5.1
*ADJUSTED DIVIDEND COVER (times)	1.34	1.37		
DIVIDEND COVER (times)	1.37	1.52		
DILUTED NET ASSETS PER SHARE	1154p	1090p	+5.9	+5.6
PROPERTIES	£8,229.0m	£7,453.7m		
BORROWINGS	£1,757.1m	£1,556.3m		
EQUITY SHAREHOLDERS' FUNDS	£6,150.9m	£5,781.8m		
†GEARING (net)	28.1%	24.5%		
†INTEREST COVER (times)	3.04	3.11		

*Excludes results of property sales and bid costs.
†See glossary (page 72).

HIGHLIGHTS

- concluded our strategic review and restructured the Group into Portfolio Management and Development business units
- completed the acquisition of Trillium and created our Total Property Services business unit
- broadened our skill base by appointing three new executive directors
- invested £577.8m on acquisitions and developments for the investment property business
- increased the development programme spend to £2bn
- accelerated the portfolio rationalisation by selling 72 properties for £431.2m
- appointed preferred bidder for BBC property partnership contract

Since the year end

- appointed preferred bidder for BT property partnership contract
- completed acquisition of Whitecliff Properties for £63.4m

2

3

PORTFOLIO MANAGEMENT SHOPS AND SHOPPING CENTRES

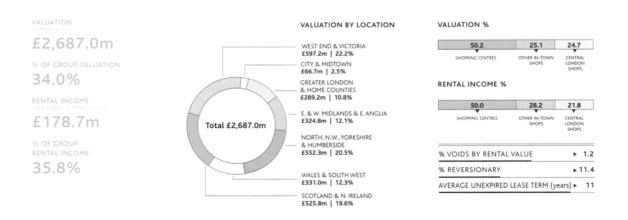

VALUATION
31 MARCH 2001
£2,687.0m

% OF GROUP VALUATION
34.0%

RENTAL INCOME
YEAR ENDED 31 MARCH 2001
£178.7m

% OF GROUP RENTAL INCOME
35.8%

VALUATION BY LOCATION

Total £2,687.0m

WEST END & VICTORIA
£597.2m | 22.2%

CITY & MIDTOWN
£66.7m | 2.5%

GREATER LONDON & HOME COUNTIES
£289.2m | 10.8%

E. & W. MIDLANDS & E. ANGLIA
£324.8m | 12.1%

NORTH, N.W., YORKSHIRE & HUMBERSIDE
£552.3m | 20.5%

WALES & SOUTH WEST
£331.0m | 12.3%

SCOTLAND & N. IRELAND
£525.8m | 19.6%

VALUATION %

50.2	25.1	24.7
SHOPPING CENTRES	OTHER IN-TOWN SHOPS	CENTRAL LONDON SHOPS

RENTAL INCOME %

50.0	28.2	21.8
SHOPPING CENTRES	OTHER IN-TOWN SHOPS	CENTRAL LONDON SHOPS

% VOIDS BY RENTAL VALUE	▶ 1.2
% REVERSIONARY	▶ 11.4
AVERAGE UNEXPIRED LEASE TERM (years) ▶	11

Bar charts explaining the financial highlights of Land Securities between 1997 and 2001, and diagrams indicating the portforio valuation by location. From an annual report.

Land Securities社の1997年から2001年までの業績の推移を説明する棒グラフと、土地別の資産評価を示すダイアグラム。アニュアル・レポートより。

UK 2001
CD: Gilmar Wendt / Nick Austin　AD, D, I: Mike Hall　P: Chris Mouse / Marcus Lyon　DF, S: SAS　CL: Land Securities

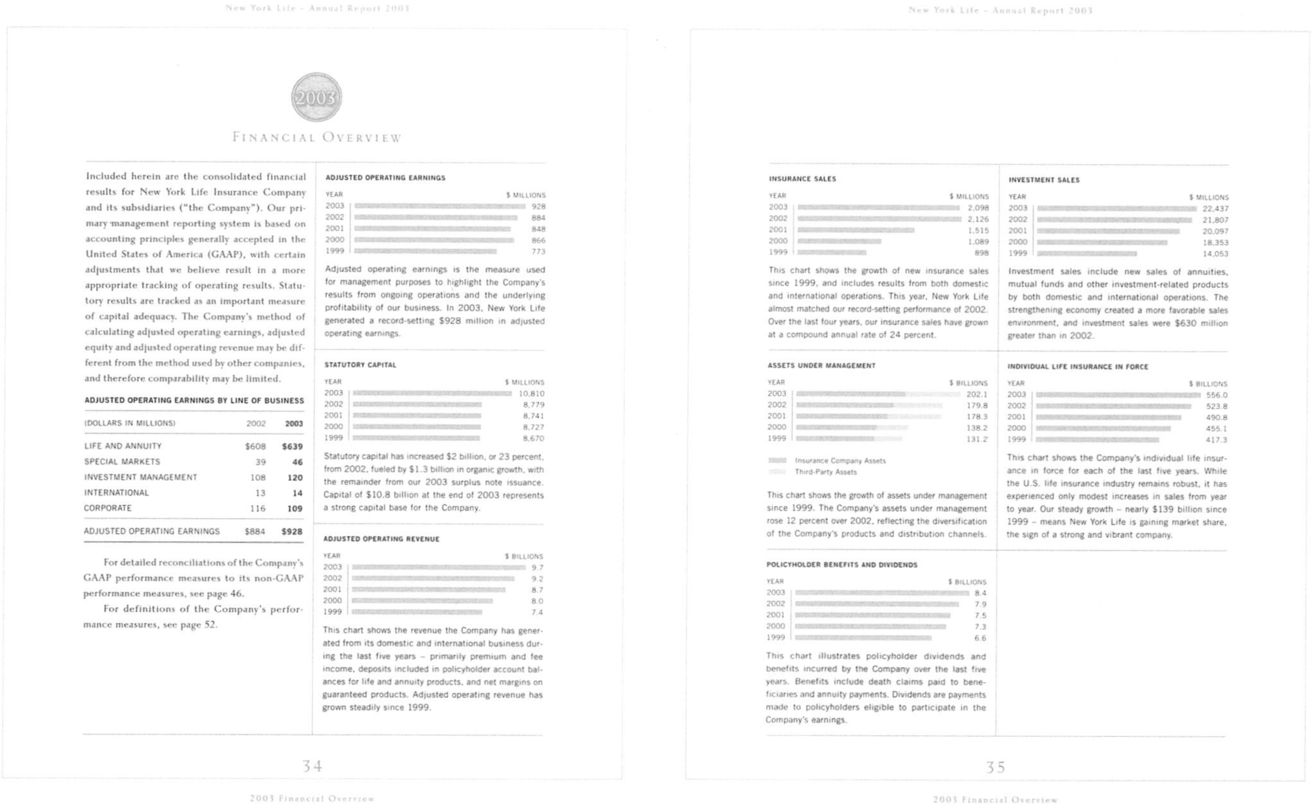

a

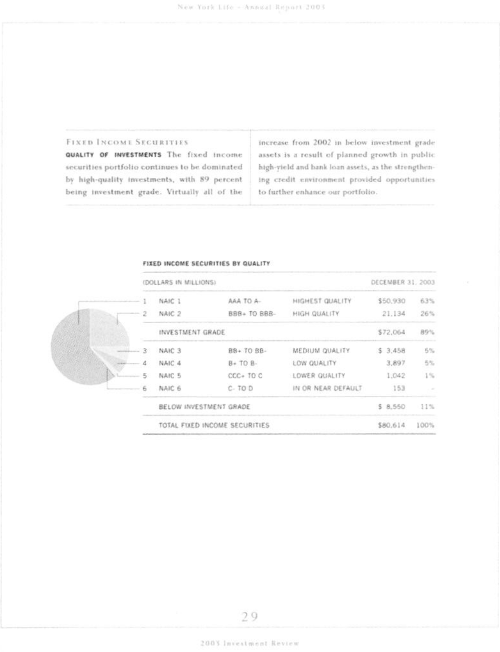

b

Graphs showing the financial overview in easily understandable way. From an annual report of an insurance mutual company. (a)
A pie chart illustrates percentage investment of fixed income securities by quality. (b)

決算の概要を簡単に分かりやすく表したグラフ。保険相互会社のアニュアル・レポートより。 (a)
確定所得証券への投資額のランク別内訳を示した円グラフ。 (b)

Canada 2004
CD, AD: Frank Viva   D: Sarah Wu   P: Christopher Wahl / Gloria Baker   I: Mark Summers / Ken Perkins   CW: Paul Goldman
DF, S: Viva Dolan Communications & Design Inc.   CL: New York Life Insurance Company

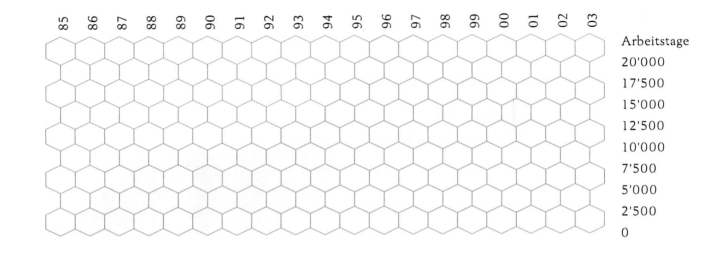

85 86 87 88 89 90 91 92 93 94 95 96 97 98 99 00 01 02 03

Arbeitstage

20'000

17'500

15'000

12'500

10'000

7'500

5'000

2'500

0

From an annual report for an environmental protection foundation. Diagrams describe how the foundation helps to maintain the high altitude meadows and farmland by fighting erosion and growing bush land.

環境保護団体のアニュアル・レポートより。高地にある牧草地や農地を侵食や増大する低木地から守るという財団の活動を説明するダイアグラム。

Switzerland 2004
CD, AD, D: Heinz Wild　D: Dan Petter　P: Pascal Wüest　I: Dan Petter　CW: Christine Loriol / Marianne Hassenstein / Christoph Müller
DF, S: Heinz Wild Design　CL: Stiftung Umwelt-Einsatz Schweiz SUS

As of March 31, 2003
Units in Millions

Outside Japan

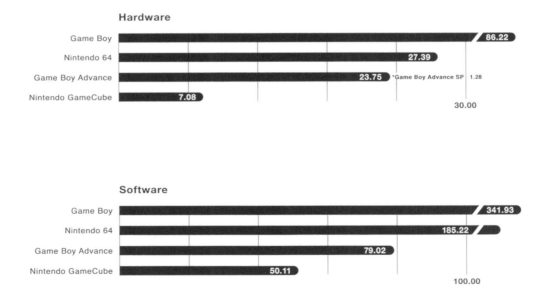

Hardware

Game Boy	86.22
Nintendo 64	27.39
Game Boy Advance	23.75　*Game Boy Advance SP　1.28
Nintendo GameCube	7.08

30.00

Software

Game Boy	341.93
Nintendo 64	185.22
Game Boy Advance	79.02
Nintendo GameCube	50.11

100.00

A graph showing the consolidated total units of Nintendo hardware and software sold in abroad.

国外における任天堂のハードウェアとソフトウェアの連結累計販売台数を表すグラフ。

Japan 2003
CD: Shin Kojo　AD, D: Takashi Maeda　CL, S: Nintendo Co., Ltd.

Der Mittelstand – eine Säule der deutschen Wirtschaft

ANTEIL MITTELSTAND AN DER GESAMTWIRTSCHAFT, 2000

43,2 %
Umsatz*

37,2 %
Bruttoinvestitionen

48,8 %
Bruttowertschöpfung

72,2 %
Beschäftigung von Erwerbstätigen**

83 %
Ausbildung von Lehrlingen

99,7 %
Anzahl Unternehmen***

* MwSt.-pflichtiger Umsatz. ** Vollzeitkräfte. *** Mindestens 16,6 Tsd. Euro steuerpflichtiger Jahresumsatz.
Quelle: IfM Bonn, Presseartikel, McKinsey

Eigenkapitalquote im Vergleich

DURCHSCHNITTLICHE EIGENKAPITALQUOTE DES DEUTSCHEN MITTELSTANDES / in Prozent der Bilanzsumme

INTERNATIONAL*

USA	45 %
Spanien	41 %
Großbritannien	40 %
Frankreich	34 %
Italien	22 %
Japan	22 %
Deutschland **	21 %

NATIONAL

TecDax	50 %
M-Dax	29 %
Dax	23 %
Mittelstand **	20 %

* Durchschnitt 1995–1999 (EU bis 40 Mio. Euro Umsatz, USA bis 25 Mio. US-Dollar)   ** Deutschland / Mittelstand: 2,5–50 Mio. Euro Umsatz
Quelle: Deutsche Bundesbank, Europäische Kommission, McKinsey

These graphs showing the economic situation. From a corporate magazine of Sal. Oppenheim, one of leading private banks in Europe.

経済状況を示すグラフ。ヨーロッパでも有数の個人銀行、Sal. Oppenheim社のコーポレイト・マガジンより。

Germany 2003
AD, D: Bernd Vollmöller   D: Volker Weinmann   CW: Ulrich Mattwer   DF, S: Simon & Goetz Design   CL: SAL, Oppenheim jr. & Cie. KGaA

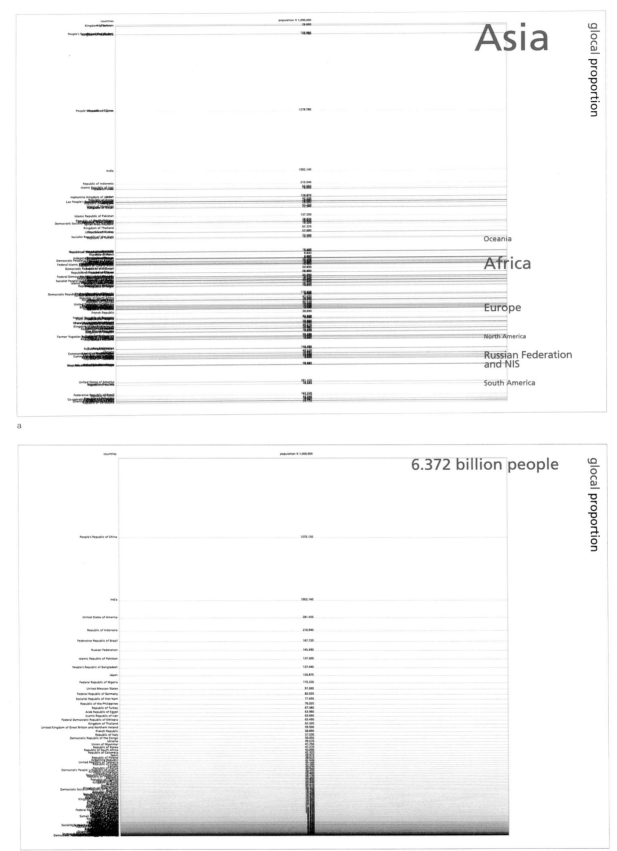

a

b

Number of countries graphed geometrically by continent according to population. (a)
Number of countries graphed geometrically according to population. (b)

人口順、大陸別に国の数を幾何学的にグラフ化。 (a)
人口順に国の数を幾何学的にグラフ化。 (b)

Japan   2003
AD, D: Shinnoske Sugisaki   DF, S: Shinnoske Inc.   CL: Inter Medium Institute

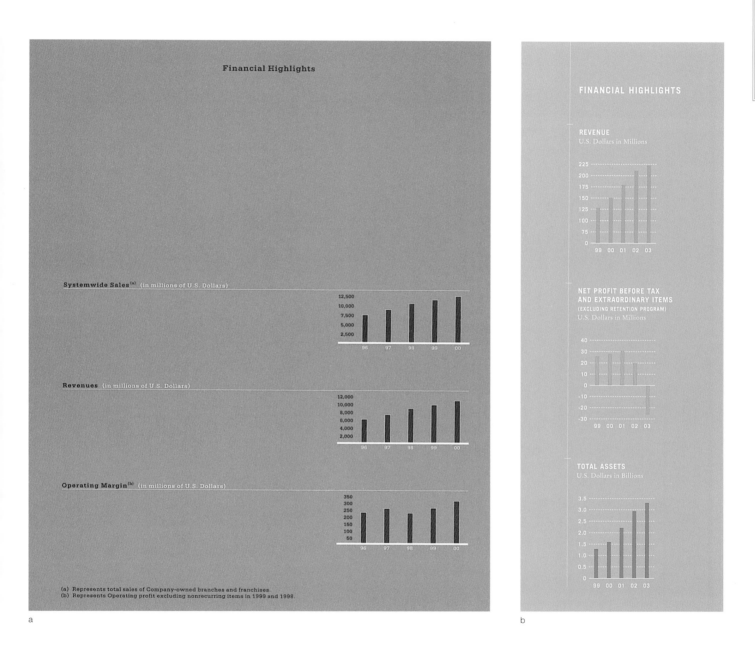

a

b

From the 2000 annual report of Manpower Inc.
Graphs showing financial highlights (Sales, revenues, operating margin). (a)

Manpower社の2000年度のアニュアル・レポートより。
グラフは主な財政状況（売上、収益、営業利益率）を示している。 (a)

USA 2001
CD, AD: Greg Samata   D: Beth May   CW: Tracy Shilobrit   DF, S: Samata Mason
CL: Manpower, Inc.

Graphs for the annual report of an airplane leasing company. (b)

航空機リース会社のアニュアル・レポートのためのグラフ。 (b)

USA 2004
AD: Jack Anderson   AD, D: Katha Dalton   D, I: Holly Craven / Michael Brugman
P: Jeff Corwin   CW: John Koval   DF, S: Hornall Anderson Design Works, Inc.
CL: Boullioun Aviation Services

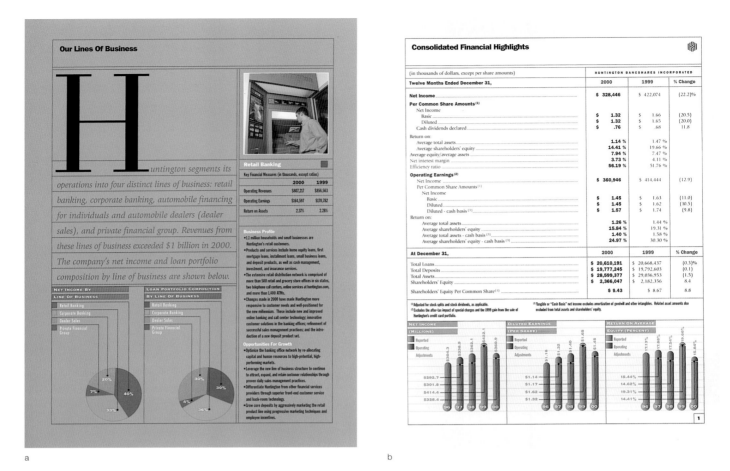

a

b

Pie charts illustrate the bank's net income and loan portforio composition by line of business. (a)
Graphs show revenues of a banking company over the past 5 years. From an annual report. (b)

銀行の純利益と貸出債権の内訳を業務別に示した円グラフ。 (a)
銀行の過去5年間の収益を示すグラフ。アニュアル・レポートより。 (b)

USA 2001
CD, AD, D: Eric Rickabaugh　P: George Anderson / Stock　CW: Nancy Flynn　DF, S: Rickabaugh Graphics　CL: Huntington Banks

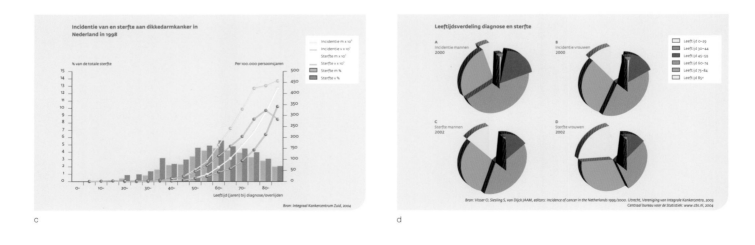

c

d

Graphs showing the diagnosis and mortaliy of the large intestine cancer by age. (c, d)

年齢別の大腸癌の診断と死亡率を示すグラフ。 (c, d)

Netherlands 2004
CD: Annemieke Later　D: René de Jong　DF, S: TelDesign　CL: KWF-Kankerbestrijding

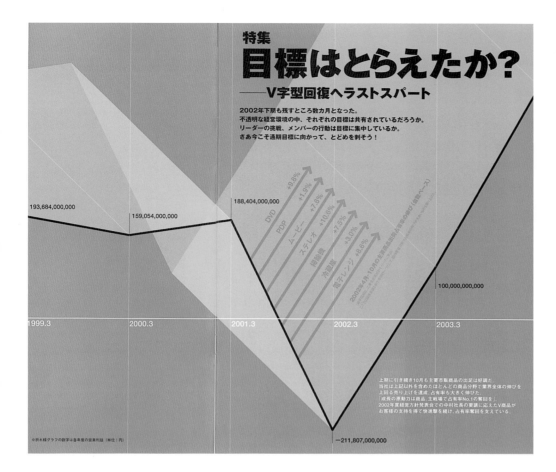

Graph showing the growth of businness profit
and market share of primary goods shipment.

営業利益と主要商品出荷占有率の伸びを表すグラフ。

Japan 2002-2003
AD, D: Shinnoske Sugisaki　D: Jun Itadani　DF, S: Shinnoske Inc.
CL: Matsushita Electric Industrial Co., Ltd.

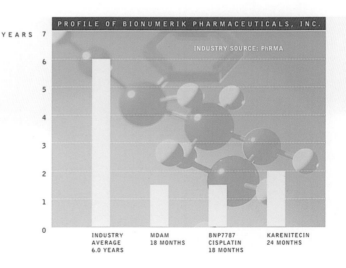

The graph explaining the power of a pharmaceutical company's approach.

製薬会社の開発力を表すグラフ。

USA 2000
CD, AD, D: Wing Chan　I: Jared Schneidman (JSD)
DF, S: Wing Chan Design, Inc.　CL: BioNumerik Pharmaceuticals, Inc.

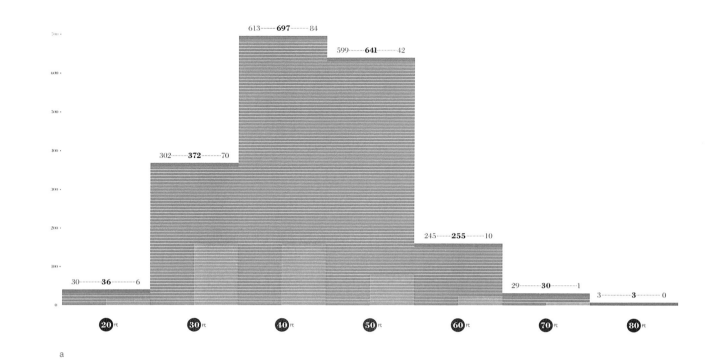

a

JAGDA地区・地域別正会員総数 —— 2,034人

b

A bar graph expressing number of members by area and region. The graph as a whole forms a map of Japan. (a)
A graph showing male-female ratio of members by age. (b)

年代別の会員数を男女比で構成したグラフ。 (a)
地区、地域別会員数を棒グラフで表現。グラフ全体が日本地図にもなっている。 (b)

Japan 2000
CD, AD, D, S: Tetsuya Ota   CL: JAGDA

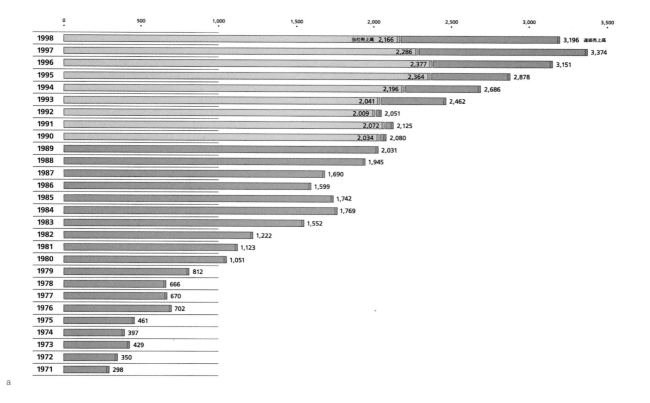

a

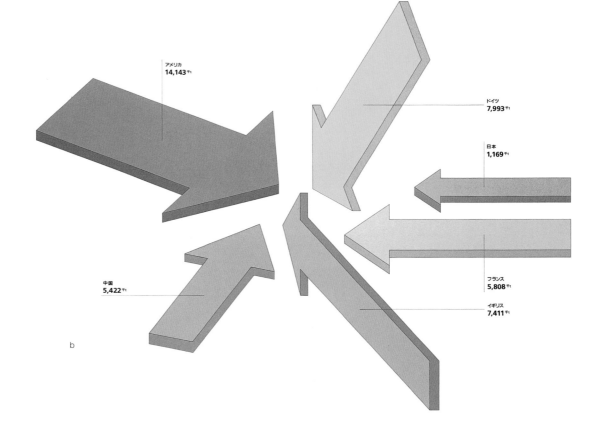

b

Sales statistics expressed as a bar graph. (a)
Paper imports of major world nations shown in an arrow bar graph. (b)

売上高の推移を棒グラフで表現。 (a)
世界主要国の紙の輸入高を矢印の棒グラフで表現。 (b)

Japan   1999
CD, AD, D, S: Tetsuya Ota   CL: Nippon Electric Glass (a) / Nippon Paper Industries (b)

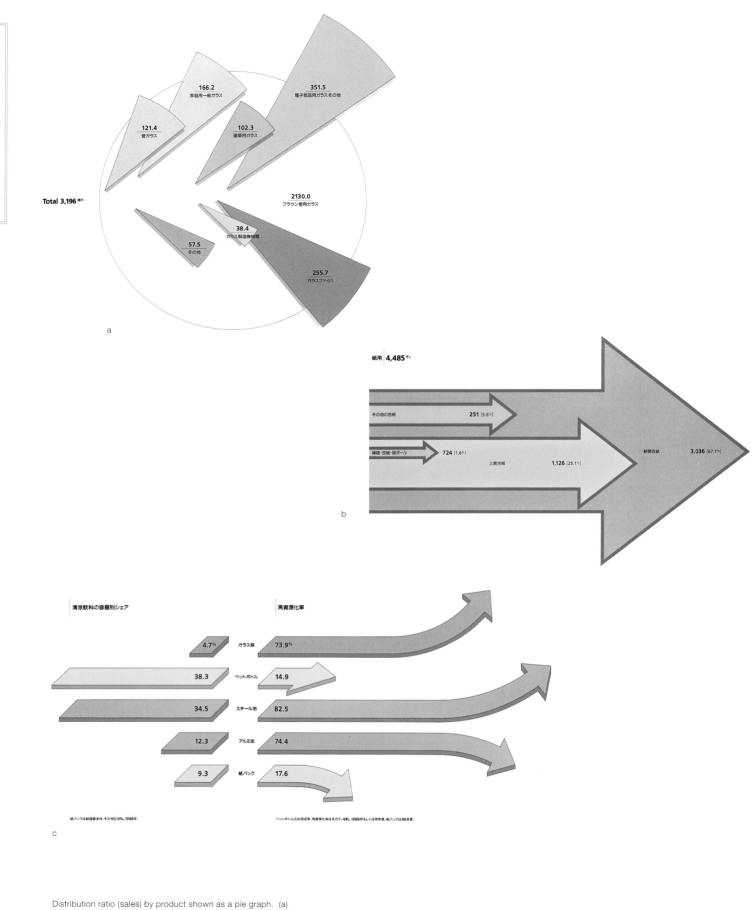

a

Total 3,196 億円

121.4
管ガラス

166.2
家庭用一般ガラス

102.3
建築用ガラス

351.5
電子部品用ガラスその他

2130.0
ブラウン管用ガラス

38.4
ガラス製造機械類

57.5
その他

255.7
ガラスファイバ

紙用 **4,485** 千t

その他の古紙　　　251 [5.6%]

雑誌・古紙・段ボール　724 [1.6%]

上質古紙　　1,126 [25.1%]

新聞古紙　　3,036 [67.7%]

b

清涼飲料の容器別シェア

再資源化率

4.7%　ガラス瓶　73.9%

38.3　ペットボトル　14.9

34.5　スチール缶　82.5

12.3　アルミ缶　74.4

9.3　紙パック　17.6

紙パックは紙容器全体。その他0.9%。1998年

'ペットボトルのみ回収率。再資源化率はその7〜8割。1998年もしくは同年度、紙パックは96年度

c

Distribution ratio (sales) by product shown as a pie graph.　(a)
Market share of soft drinks by container and recycling ratio expressed as a bar graph using arrows.　(b)
The use of arrow-like forms to express a comparison by paper grade of used paper consumption creates a dynamic visual effect.　(c)

製品別構成比（売上）を円グラフでみせる。　(a)
清涼飲料の容器別シェアと再資源化率を、矢印を用いた棒グラフで表現。　(b)
主要古紙の紙別消費高の量の比較を相似形の矢印で動きのある視覚的効果で表現。　(c)

Japan　1999
CD, AD, D, S: Tetsuya Ota　CL: Nippon Electric Glass (a) / Asahi Shinbun (b) / Japan Paper Association (c)

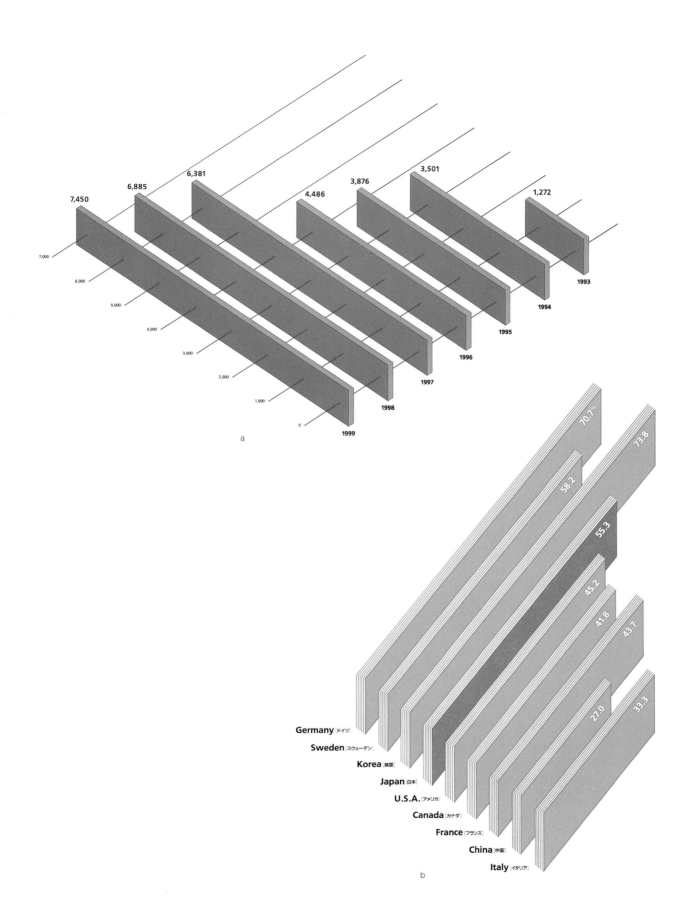

a

b

Oblique bar graph emphasizing fluctuations in company sales. (a)
A bar graph imaged after paper, expressing paper-recycling ratios of nine countries. (b)

斜め棒グラフで企業の売上の変化を強調。 (a)
世界9カ国の古紙の回収率を棒グラフで紙をイメージして作成。 (b)

Japan 1999
CD, AD, D, S: Tetsuya Ota   CL: NTT-DO (a) / Nippon Paper Industries (b)

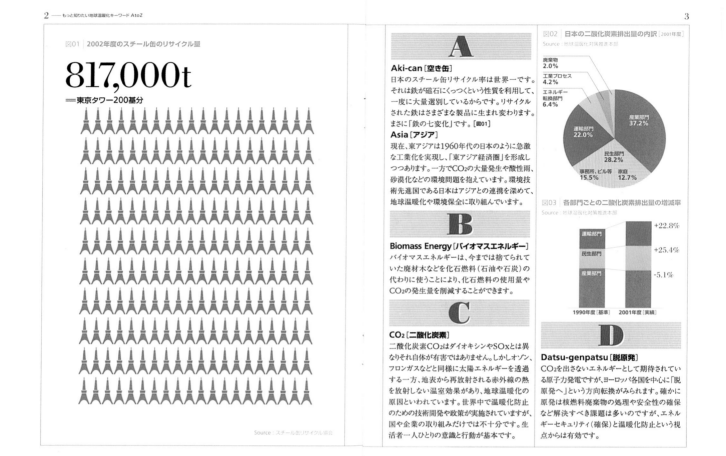

図01 | 2002年度のスチール缶のリサイクル量

817,000t

=東京タワー200基分

Source：スチール缶リサイクル協会

A

Aki-can [空き缶]

日本のスチール缶リサイクル率は世界一です。それは鉄が磁石にくっつくという性質を利用して、一度に大量選別しているからです。リサイクルされた鉄はさまざまな製品に生まれ変わります。まさに「鉄の七変化」です。[図01]

Asia [アジア]

現在、東アジアは1960年代の日本のように急激な工業化を実現し、「東アジア経済圏」を形成しつつあります。一方でCO2の大量発生や酸性雨、砂漠化などの環境問題を抱えています。環境技術先進国である日本はアジアとの連携を深めて、地球温暖化や環境保全に取り組んでいます。

B

Biomass Energy [バイオマスエネルギー]

バイオマスエネルギーは、今までは捨てられていた廃材木などを化石燃料（石油や石炭）の代わりに使うことにより、化石燃料の使用量やCO2の発生量を削減することができます。

C

CO2 [二酸化炭素]

二酸化炭素CO2はダイオキシンやSOxとは異なりそれ自体が有害ではありません。しかしオゾン、フロンガスなどと同様に太陽エネルギーを透過する一方、地表から再放射される赤外線の熱を放射しない温室効果があり、地球温暖化の原因といわれています。世界中で温暖化防止のための技術開発や政策が実施されていますが、国や企業の取り組みだけでは不十分です。生活者一人ひとりの意識と行動が基本です。

図02 | 日本の二酸化炭素排出量の内訳 [2001年度]

Source：地球温暖化対策推進本部

廃棄物 2.0%
工業プロセス 4.2%
エネルギー転換部門 6.4%
産業部門 37.2%
運輸部門 22.0%
民生部門 28.2%
事務所、ビル等 15.5%
家庭 12.7%

図03 | 各部門ごとの二酸化炭素排出量の増減率

Source：地球温暖化対策推進本部

運輸部門 +22.8%
民生部門 +25.4%
産業部門 -5.1%

1990年度 [基準] 2001年度 [実績]

D

Datsu-genpatsu [脱原発]

CO2を出さないエネルギーとして期待されている原子力発電ですが、ヨーロッパ各国を中心に「脱原発へ」という方向転換がみられます。確かに原発は核燃料廃棄物の処理や安全性の確保など解決すべき課題は多いのですが、エネルギーセキュリティ（確保）と温暖化防止という視点からは有効です。

もっと知りたい地球温暖化キーワード

A to Z

From a pamphlet on global warming. 38 key words defined using easy-to-understand comments and illustrations.

地球温暖化に関するパンフレットより。38のキーワードを分かりやすい解説と図で説明。

Japan   2004

CD: Reiji Oshima   AD: Kenzo Nakagawa   D: Satoshi Morikami / Infogram   I: Kumiko Nagasaki   CW: Yasuko Seki   DF, S: NDC Graphics Inc.
CL: The Japan Iron and Steel Federation

図10 | 国別のエネルギー起源二酸化炭素排出量

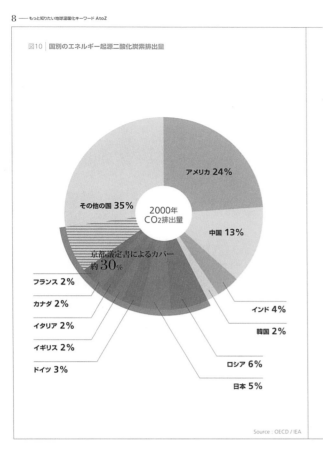

アメリカ 24%

その他の国 35%

2000年
CO₂排出量

中国 13%

京都議定書によるカバー
約30%

フランス 2%
カナダ 2%
イタリア 2%
イギリス 2%
ドイツ 3%

インド 4%
韓国 2%
ロシア 6%
日本 5%

Source : OECD / IEA

図12 | 製鉄所内の緑化総面積

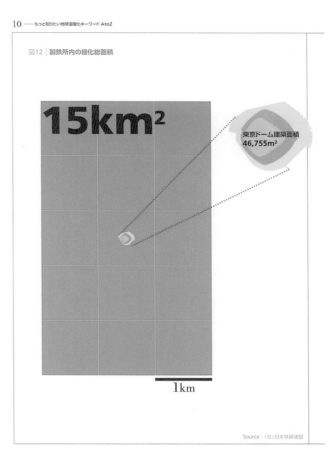

15km²

東京ドーム建築面積
46,755m²

1km

Source : (社)日本鉄鋼連盟

図13 | コークス炉ガスの改質による水素増幅

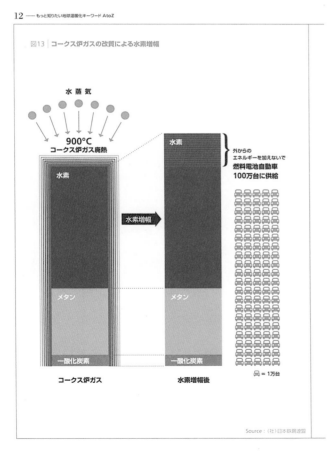

水 蒸 気

900°C
コークス炉廃熱

水素

水素増幅

メタン

一酸化炭素

コークス炉ガス

水素

メタン

一酸化炭素

水素増幅後

外からの
エネルギーを加えないで
燃料電池自動車
100万台に供給

🚗 = 1万台

Source : (社)日本鉄鋼連盟

図15 | 鉄鋼業のエネルギー消費量削減目標

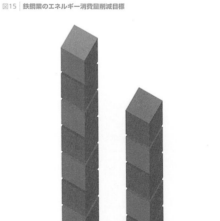

-10%

1990年

2010年 [目標]

Source : (社)日本鉄鋼連盟

数字で見るインターネットの最新動向

N^et Impre^ssions | Volume 02

Edited by 小橋 昭彦 ＋ インターネットマガジン 編集部　Designed by © Infogram

電子商取引市場［BtoC］のセグメント構成変化

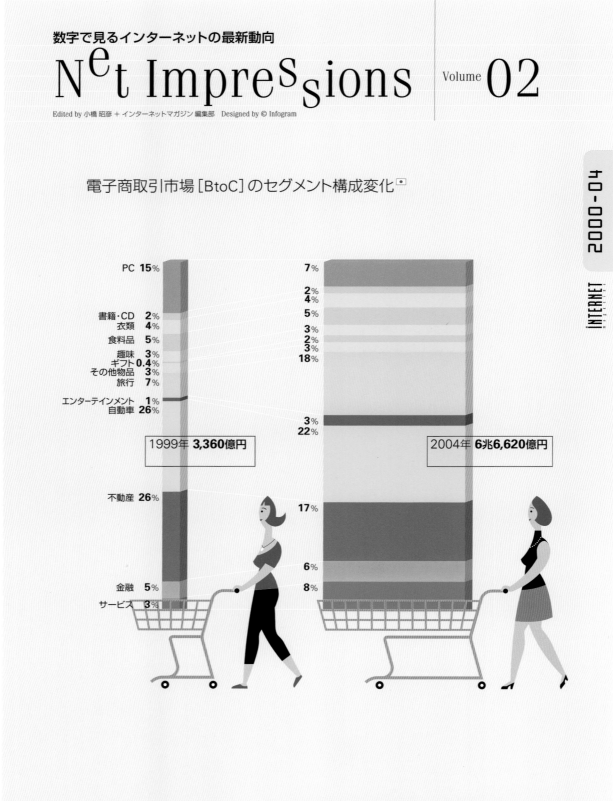

PC **15**%

書籍・CD **2**%
衣類 **4**%
食料品 **5**%
趣味 **3**%
ギフト **0.4**%
その他物品 **3**%
旅行 **7**%

エンターテインメント **1**%
自動車 **26**%

1999年 **3,360**億円

不動産 **26**%

金融 **5**%
サービス **3**%

7%
2%
4%
5%
3%
2%
3%
18%

3%
22%

2004年 **6兆6,620**億円

17%

6%
8%

Source:「日本の消費者向け（BtoC）電子商取引市場」電子商取引実証推進協議会・アンダーセン コンサルティング

From "Internet magazine", graphs showing results of a survey on internet user trends.

『インターネットマガジン』より。インターネット利用者の動向調査結果をグラフで表している。

Japan　2000-2002
AD: Kenzo Nakagawa / Akiyuki Okada　D: Satoshi Morikami / Norika Nakayama / Infogram　I: Hiroyasu Nobuyama　DF, S: NDC Graphics Inc.
CL: Impress Corporation

数字で見るインターネットの最新動向
Net Impressions　Volume 05

Edited by 小橋 昭彦 + インターネットマガジン 編集部　Designed by © Infogram

主な耐久消費財の普及状況

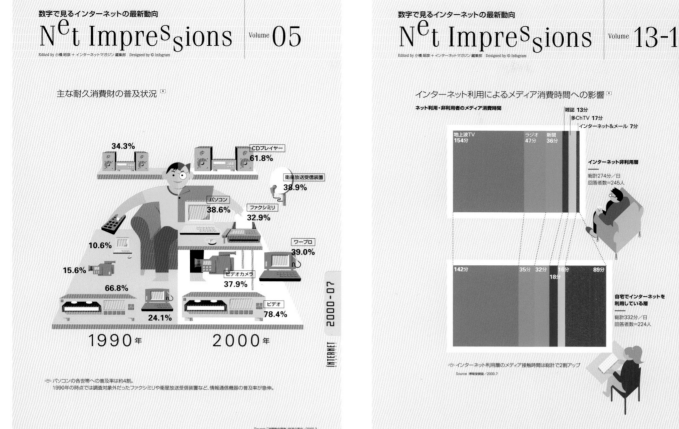

34.3%
CDプレイヤー 61.8%
衛星放送受信装置 38.9%
パソコン 38.6%
ファクシミリ 32.9%
10.6%
ワープロ 39.0%
15.6%
ビデオカメラ 37.9%
66.8%
24.1%
ビデオ 78.4%

1990年　2000年

INTERNET 2000-07

※パソコンの各世帯への普及率は約4割。
1990年の時点では調査対象外だったファクシミリや衛星放送受信装置など、情報通信機器の普及率が急伸。

Source『消費動向調査』(経済企画庁)／2000.3

数字で見るインターネットの最新動向
Net Impressions　Volume 13-1

インターネット利用によるメディア消費時間への影響

ネット利用・非利用者のメディア消費時間

雑誌 13分
多ChTV 17分
インターネット&メール 7分

地上波TV 154分　ラジオ 47分　新聞 36分

インターネット非利用層
総計274分／日
回答者数=245人

142分　35分　32分　18分　16分　89分

自宅でインターネットを利用している層
総計332分／日
回答者数=224人

※インターネット利用層のメディア接触時間は総計で2割アップ

Source 博報堂調査／2000.7

INTERNET 2001-03

数字で見るインターネットの最新動向
Net Impressions　Volume 10-1

Edited by 小橋 昭彦 + インターネットマガジン 編集部　Designed by © Infogram

インターネット利用者の情報源

各メディアから得る情報［ネット利用者］

テレビ　　　　　　　インターネット

項目	テレビ	インターネット
趣味に関する情報	25.8%	59.3%
映画・演劇・音楽についての情報	43.5%	24.6%
商品や物品についての情報	43.5%	22.2%
スポーツについての情報	68.5%	10.5%
天気予報	85.5%	8.5%
経済・株価の動き	42.3%	6.9%
事件・事故	87.1%	5.6%
交通情報	37.1%	4.4%

INTERNET 2000-12

※社会情勢や経済情報はテレビで、趣味や教養に関する情報はネットで仕入れている

Source『MCR（Media Contact Report）』(株)ビデオリサーチ／1999.6

数字で見るインターネットの最新動向
Net Impressions　Volume 14-2

Edited by 衣袋 宏美［ネットレイティングス株式会社］＋インターネットマガジン 編集部　Designed by © Infogram

Powered by Nielsen//NetRatings

携帯電話からのウェブ利用者、900万人規模に

インターネット利用可能携帯電話の所有者数とウェブ利用者数

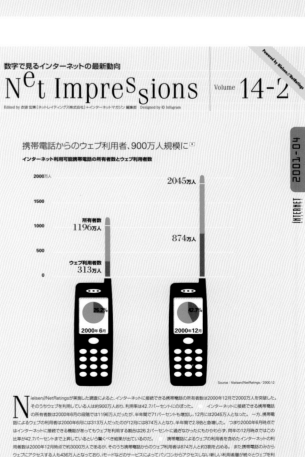

2000万人
1500
1000
500
0

2045万人

所有者数 1196万人

874万人

ウェブ利用者数 313万人

26.2% 2000年6月
42.7% 2000年12月

Source：Nielsen//NetRatings／2000.12

Nielsen//NetRatingsが実施した調査によると、インターネットに接続できる携帯電話の所有者数は2000年12月で2000万人を突破した。　そのうちウェブを利用している人は約900万人おり、利用率は42.7パーセントにのぼった。　インターネットに接続できる携帯電話による所有者数は2000年6月の段階では1196万人だったが、半年間で71パーセントも増加し、12月には2045万人となった。一方、携帯電話によるウェブの利用者は2000年6月には313万人だったのが12月には874万人となり、半年間で2.8倍と急増した。つまり2000年6月時点ではインターネットに接続できる機能があってもウェブを利用する割合は26.2パーセントに過ぎなかったにもかかわらず、同年12月時点ではこの比率が42.7パーセントまで上昇しているという驚くべき結果が出ているのだ。　携帯電話によるウェブの利用者を含めたインターネットの利用者数は2000年12月時点で約3000万人であるが、そのうち携帯電話からのウェブ利用者は874万人と約3割を占める。また携帯電話のみからウェブにアクセスする人も436万人となっており、iモードなどのサービスによってパソコンからアクセスしない新しい利用者層が続々とウェブを利用するようになっていることを象徴している。

Nielsen//NetRatingsは、全世界最大のインターネット利用者行動を継続的に把握する調査会社です。本調査はパソコンによるインターネット利用者数を示したものです。本コラムの数字はインターネット利用可能携帯電話の所有者数およびウェブ利用者数です。

INTERNET 2001-04

2000-03

INTERNET

数字で見るインターネットの最新動向

N^et Impre^ssions | Volume 01

Edited by 小橋 昭彦 + インターネットマガジン 編集部   Designed by © Infogram

インターネットの普及率と英語能力

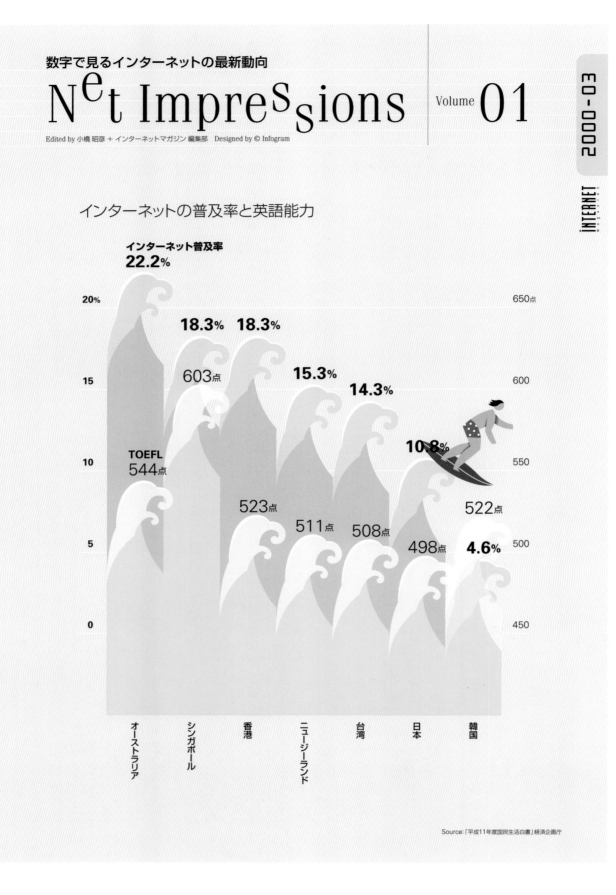

インターネット普及率
22.2%

20%   650点

18.3% 18.3%   15

603点   **15.3%**
14.3%   600

TOEFL   **10.8%**
544点

523点   522点
511点   508点
498点   **4.6%**

オーストラリア   シンガポール   香港   ニュージーランド   台湾   日本   韓国

Source:「平成11年度国民生活白書」経済企画庁

From "Internet magazine", graphs showing results of a survey on internet user trends.

『インターネットマガジン』より。インターネット利用者の動向調査結果をグラフで表している。

Japan 2000-2002
AD: Kenzo Nakagawa / Akiyuki Okada   D: Satoshi Morikami / Norika Nakayama / Infogram   I: Hiroyasu Nobuyama   DF, S: NDC Graphics Inc.
CL: Impress Corporation

数字で見るインターネットの最新動向

N^{e}t Impre^{s}sions　Volume 15-1

Edited by 小橋 昭彦 + インターネットマガジン 編集部　Designed by © Infogram

INTERNET 2001-05

電子商取引市場規模

モバイルコマースの市場規模

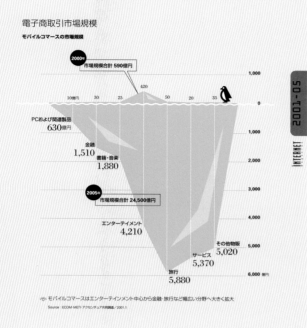

2000年　市場規模合計 590億円

1,000 / 10億円 30 25 420 50 20 35 0

PCおよび関連製品 630億円

金融 1,510
書籍・音楽 1,880

2005年　市場規模合計 24,500億円

1,000 / 2,000 / 3,000 / 4,000 / 5,000 / 6,000 億円

エンターテイメント 4,210
その他物販 5,020
サービス 5,370
旅行 5,880

- モバイルコマースはエンターテインメント中心から金融・旅行など幅広い分野へ大きく拡大

Source : ECOM・METI・アクセンチュア共同調査／2001.1

数字で見るインターネットの最新動向

N^{e}t Impre^{s}sions　Volume 14-1

Edited by 小橋 昭彦 + インターネットマガジン 編集部　Designed by © Infogram

INTERNET 2001-04

起業家精神ランキング

現在、会社設立中ないしは設立後42か月以内の会社運営に携わっている人の割合

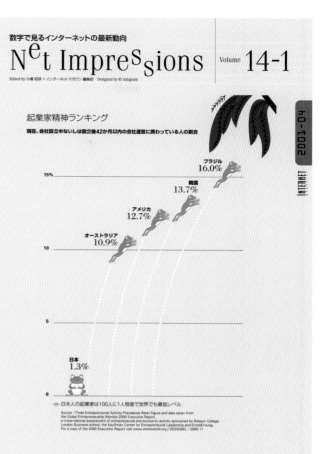

15% / ブラジル 16.0%
韓国 13.7%
アメリカ 12.7%
10 / オーストラリア 10.9%
5
日本 1.3%
0

- 日本人の起業家は100人に1人程度で世界でも最低レベル

Source : 「Total Entrepreneurial Activity Prevalence Rate」Figure and data taken from
the Global Entrepreneurship Monitor 2000 Executive Report,
a cross-national assessment of entrepreneurial and economic activity sponsored by Babson College,
London Business school, the Kauffman Center for Entrepreneurial Leadership and Ernst&Young.
For a copy of the 2000 Executive Report visit www.entreworld.org / GEM2000../ 2000.11

数字で見るインターネットの最新動向

N^{e}t Impre^{s}sions　Volume 18-2

Powered by Nielsen//NetRatings

Edited by 衣袋 宏美「ネットレイティングス株式会社」+ インターネットマガジン 編集部　Designed by © Infogram

INTERNET 2001-08

自宅以外のPCユーザーのネット接続比率は関東が約5割

自宅以外でのパソコン利用率｜インターネット利用率[地域別]

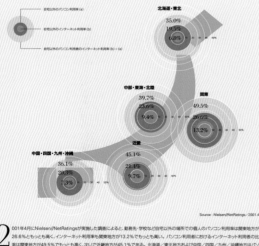

自宅以外のパソコン利用率 (a)
自宅以外のインターネット利用率 (b)
自宅以外のパソコン利用者のインターネット利用率 (b)÷(a)

北海道・東北
35.0%
19.5%
6.8%

中部・東海・北陸
39.7%
23.6%
9.4%

関東
49.5%
26.6%
13.2%

近畿
45.1%
21.4%
9.7%

中国・四国・九州・沖縄
36.1%
20.3%
7.3%

Source : Nielsen//NetRatings／2001.4

2001年4月にNielsen//NetRatingsが実施した調査によると、勤務先・学校など自宅以外の場所での個人のパソコン利用率は関東地方が26.6%でもっとも高く、インターネット利用率も関東地方が13.2%でもっとも高い。パソコン利用者におけるインターネット利用者の比率は関東地方が49.5%でもっとも高く、次いで近畿地方が45.1%である。北海道／東北地方および中国／四国／九州／沖縄地方はパソコン利用率、インターネット利用率、パソコン利用者のインターネット利用率のいずれも相対的には低い水準にある。一方、利用場所が自宅の場合、パソコンの世帯所有率は関東地方が51.7%ともっとも高く、続いて中部／東海／北陸地方の46.8%、近畿地方の46.3%となっている。世帯のインターネット利用率も関東地方が37.1%でもっとも高く、近畿地方の34.4%、中部／東海／北陸地方の29.2%と続いている。パソコン利用世帯におけるインターネット利用率は自宅よりも相対的に高く、どの地方でも50%以上を超える水準にある。また近畿地方が74.2%と関東地区の71.8%を上回っているのも特徴だ。北海道／東北地方および中国／四国／九州／沖縄地方は自宅外と同様、パソコン利用率、インターネット利用率自体がまだ相対的には低い水準である。

Nielsen//NetRatingsは毎月定点調査をインターネットの利用動向の調査を実施し、本調査をもとにした月刊インターネットの発表を行っている。また本調査の詳細はインターネット小委調査員レポートにまとめ、毎月発行している。今回は2001年4月に実施した調査データとした。

数字で見るインターネットの最新動向

N^{e}t Impre^{s}sions　Volume 07

Edited by 小橋 昭彦 + インターネットマガジン 編集部　Designed by © Infogram

INTERNET 2000-09

世界におけるデジタルデバイド

地域別インターネット普及率

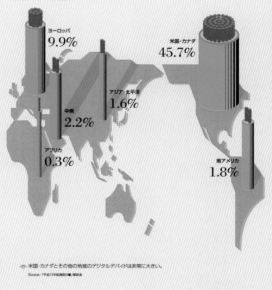

ヨーロッパ 9.9%
米国・カナダ 45.7%
中東 2.2%
アジア・太平洋 1.6%
アフリカ 0.3%
南アメリカ 1.8%

- 米国・カナダとその他の地域のデジタルデバイドは非常に大きい。

Source : 「平成12年版通信白書」解説編

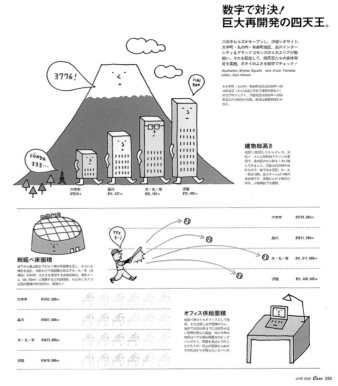

Comparative graphs related to Tokyo's urban development expressed with illustrations.

東京の都市開発についての各種比較グラフをイラストレーションで表した。

Japan 2003

AD: Yasushi Fujimoto(Cap)　D: Youichi Iwamoto　I: Shuhei Eguchi　S: Magazinehouse, Ltd.

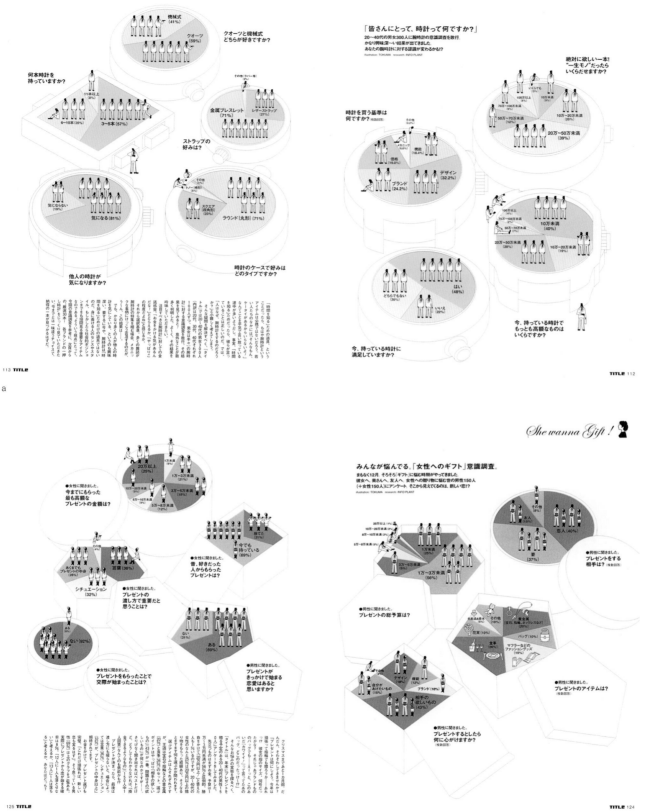

a

b

An opinion poll of 300 men and women aged 20 through 50 on wrist watches from the magazine "TITLe." (a)
An opinion poll of 150 men aged 20 through 50 on gifts for women from the magazine "TITLe." (b)

雑誌『TITLe』より。20代～40代の男女300人の、腕時計に対する意識調査。 (a)
雑誌『TITLe』より。20代～40代の男性150人の女性へのギフトに対する意識調査。 (b)

Japan 2003
AD: Tetsushi Kawamura   I: Tokuma   DF: Atomosphere, Ltd.   CL: Bungeishunju Ltd.   S: bowlgraphics

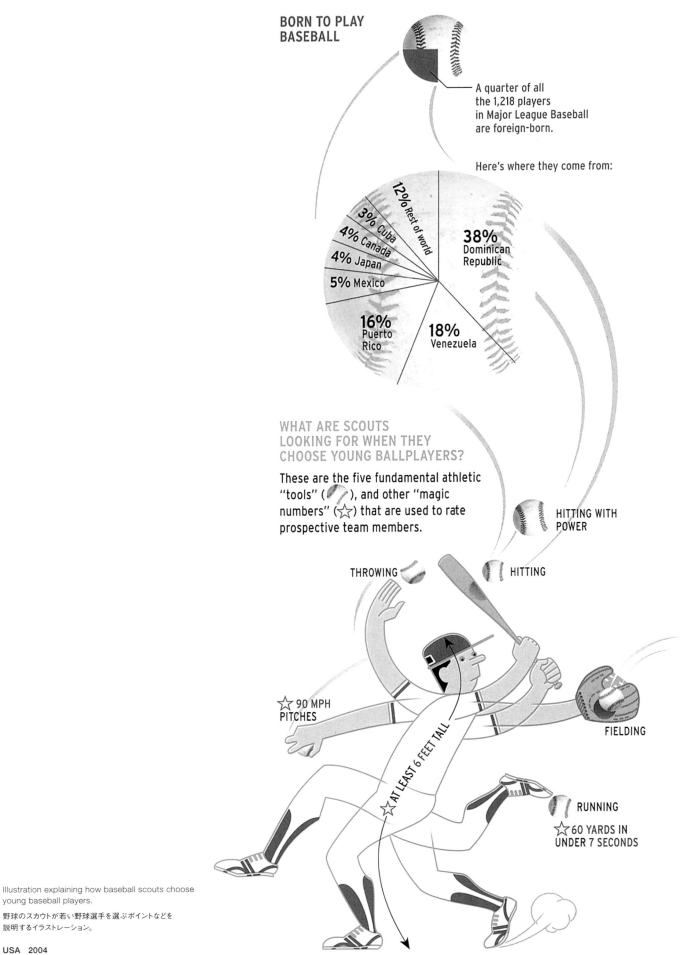

BORN TO PLAY BASEBALL

A quarter of all the 1,218 players in Major League Baseball are foreign-born.

Here's where they come from:

12% Rest of world

3% Cuba

4% Canada

4% Japan

5% Mexico

16% Puerto Rico

18% Venezuela

38% Dominican Republic

WHAT ARE SCOUTS LOOKING FOR WHEN THEY CHOOSE YOUNG BALLPLAYERS?

These are the five fundamental athletic "tools" ( ), and other "magic numbers" (☆) that are used to rate prospective team members.

HITTING WITH POWER

HITTING

THROWING

☆ 90 MPH PITCHES

AT LEAST 6 FEET TALL

FIELDING

RUNNING

☆ 60 YARDS IN UNDER 7 SECONDS

Illustration explaining how baseball scouts choose young baseball players.

野球のスカウトが若い野球選手を選ぶポイントなどを説明するイラストレーション。

USA   2004
AD: Holly Holliday   D, I, S: Nigel Holmes
DF: Explanation Graphics   CL: Attaché Magazine

7.700 Gigawattstunden

8.690 Gigawattstunden

9.180 Gigawattstunden
ohne Aktionsplan

8.670 Gigawattstunden
mit Aktionsplan

Energieverbrauch
Vorarlberg 1990

Energieverbrauch
Vorarlberg 2000

Energieverbrauch
Vorarlberg 2010

1 Gigawattstunde = 1 Million Kilowattstunden

Graphs showing the government's plan of energy consumption, CO2 sources, etc. up through 2010.
2010年までのエネルギーの消費量やCO2の放出量などに関する政府の計画を示すグラフ。

Austria 2001
CD, AD: Sigi Ramoser   D, P, I: Klaus Österce   CW: Elke Burtscher   DF, S: Sägenvier   CL: Land Vorarlberg

Graphs explaining financial highlights,
dividend per share,
operating profits, and so on.

財務概要、1株当たりの配当金、
営業利益などを説明するグラフ。

UK 2002
CD: David Stocks   AD, D: Gilmar·Wendt
I: Emma Slater / Roger Taylor
DF, S: SAS   CL: MFI Group

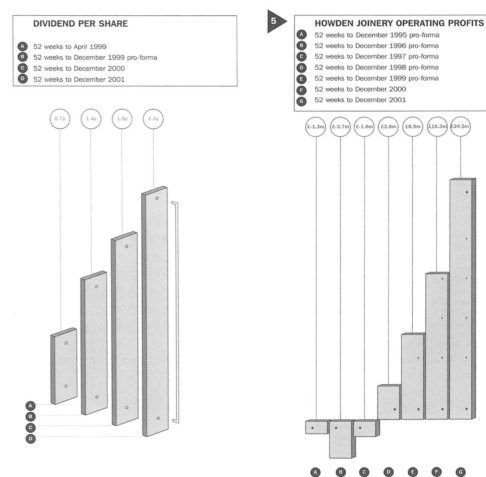

DIVIDEND PER SHARE

- A 52 weeks to April 1999
- B 52 weeks to December 1999 pro-forma
- C 52 weeks to December 2000
- D 52 weeks to December 2001

0.7p 1.4p 1.9p 2.5p

HOWDEN JOINERY OPERATING PROFITS

- A 52 weeks to December 1995 pro-forma
- B 52 weeks to December 1996 pro-forma
- C 52 weeks to December 1997 pro-forma
- D 52 weeks to December 1998 pro-forma
- E 52 weeks to December 1999 pro-forma
- F 52 weeks to December 2000
- G 52 weeks to December 2001

£-1.3m £-3.7m £-1.6m £3.6m £8.9m £15.3m £24.5m

A B C D E F G

Growing profits
The chart below shows the contribution of gross profits from biotechnology products (PiICmara™) to the Company's gross profits over the last three years.

2000 £0.2m   2001 £2.1m   2002 £3.2m

APPLYING BIOTECHNOLOGY PROMOTES GROWTH

Graph showing the growth of profits from biotechnology products over the last three years.

バイオテクノロジー製品に関する過去3年間での利益の伸びを示すグラフ。

UK 2002
CD: Tor Pettersen   AD, D, CW: David Brown   D: Craig Johnson
DF, S: Tor Pettersen & Partners   CL: Sygen International

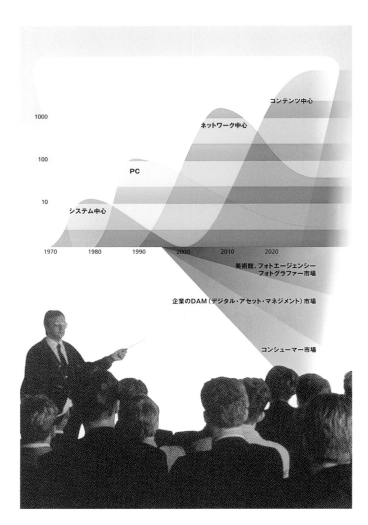

Above, the movement and numbers centered around the computer market;
below, the market share and market Celartem Technology has expanded.

上はコンピュータ市場の中心の動きとその数、
下はセラーテムテクノロジー社が広げてきた販売シェア数と市場を表している。

Japan 2001
AD: Shinnoske Sugisaki   D: Chiaki Okuno / Shinsuke Suzuki
/ Seiji Minato (CID Lab. Inc.)   CW: Hiroshi Iida (NCP Agency)
DF, S: Shinnoske Inc.   CL: Celartem Technology Inc.

transfor ming
our costs...

Kingfisher is a customer-driven business with a simple aim – to give people the inspiration, confidence and product solutions with which they can create better homes.

The booming popularity of home improvement has coincided with a fundamental shift in the customer profile – fewer families, more female shoppers, more time-pressured, more affluent, highly value-conscious.

Group brands now offer products that are easier to use, with more comprehensive instruction and less preparation and finishing. Products with detailed explanation and a greater focus on colour, design and the end result. Ranges combining leading edge design with seasonal flexibility.

Kingfisher has also pursued new and innovative ways of delivering exceptional value for money. EDLP – 'every day low pricing' – was launched in 1998 and it quickly became clear that low retail prices every day required low supplier costs every day.

The Cost Price Reduction Programme (CPR) was created specifically to deliver a reduction in the cost of goods and drive the bottom line. The programme aims to forge mutually-beneficial long term partnerships with key suppliers – relationships that benefit both sides of the retailer supplier equation. For Kingfisher, lower product costs and commonality where the real benefit lies – at the product, component or formulation level.

For suppliers, growing volumes and the associated opportunity to reduce costs and invest in their operations. Today, an increasing number of suppliers are transforming their business and driving long term profit growth through partnership with Kingfisher.

CPR was introduced in Castorama France towards the end of 2002. Initial results have been encouraging and the programme will underpin delivery of this year's targeted integration benefits. It will create similar opportunities for long term partnerships, including suppliers working across the Group with both B&Q and Castorama.

Today, Kingfisher is working with suppliers to longer time horizons than ever before – three, five, even seven years – with agreement on capacity, cost reduction and product innovation. This is creating a truly world class supplier base.

4 For more information on Kingfisher visit www.kingfisher.com

No other home improvement retailer in the world operates a comparable, systematic programme of cost reduction with such significant benefits for the business, its shareholders, suppliers and, of course, customers. CPR is entirely customer focused – the people who shop at Kingfisher's Home Improvement brands experience the CPR saving as lower prices, improved service and more and better stores.

...and our prices

Driving down the cost of home improvement B&Q's 'Price Reverse' campaign – an initiative enabled by CPR – has reduced the price of many products to levels lower than ten years ago.

1992

Crown Emulsion Matt White 5 litres	£13.98
Gainsborough 9.5kw Shower 1000X	£159.99
Bacho 244 Saw	£11.49
B&Q Value Silk Magnolia Paint 5 litres	£20.96
Dehumidifier WDH-101P	£219.00
Avon 6 Panel Door	£34.95
TOTAL	£460.37

THANK YOU FOR SHOPPING WITH B&Q

2002*

Crown Emulsion Matt White 5 litres	£6.98
Gainsborough 9.5kw Shower 1000X	£89.98
Bacho 244 Saw	£6.88
B&Q Value Silk Magnolia Paint 10 litres	£8.98
Dehumidifier WDH-101P	£99.00
Avon 6 Panel Door	£16.94
TOTAL	£228.76

THANK YOU FOR SHOPPING WITH B&Q

*Note: actual prices, not adjusted for inflation. RPI over the period was 26.5%.

A comparative table in the form of two checkout receipts showing the cost saving on home improvement products over 10 years from B&Q stores.

2枚のレシートの形をした比較表。B&Qの店舗において日曜大工関連の製品の価格がここ10年間でどの程度下がったかを表している。

UK 2003
CD: Tor Pettersen   AD, D: Jeff Davis   D: Nick Kendall   DF, S: Tor Pettersen & Partners   CL: Kingfisher plc

BAYER'S HEADACHE
Some investors want Bayer to focus on one or two business areas and sell the rest to boost profitability.

Bayer's sales, 2002

Polymers: **38.3%**
Health care: **33.3**
Pesticides, herbicides: **16.7**
Chemicals: **11.7**

Total sales: €28.2 billion

Sales figures based on 2002 total external sales outside corporation of €28.2 billion. Source: Bayer

a

Hermès sales, 2002: €1.2 billion

Leather goods: **31%**
Ready-to-wear: **14**
Art of Living*: **12**
Watches: **9**
Silk scarves: **7**
Perfumes: **5**
Other: **22**

*Lifestyle and home products. Source: Hermès

Clothes horse Analysts say Gaultier's designs should boost ready-to-wear, Hermès's second-biggest category.

b

Pie chart illustrating Bayer's sales by category. (a)
Pie chart illustrating Hermes' sales by category. (b)

バイエル社の業務別の売上を示す円グラフ。 (a)
エルメスの商品別の売上を示す円グラフ。 (b)

USA 2003 (a) / **2004** (b)
AD: Carol Macrini   D, I, S: Eliot Bergman   CL: Bloomberg Markets Magazine

BUND
CA. 245 000 WOHNEINHEITEN

BUNDESLÄNDER
CA. 340 000 WOHNEINHEITEN

KOMMUNEN
CA. 2 200 000 WOHNEINHEITEN

Wohnungsvermögen im Eigentum der öffentlichen Hand
QUELLE: BUNDESMINISTERIUM FÜR VERKEHR, BAU- UND WOHNUNGSWESEN

555.7   1.117,9   5.392,4   22.480,0*
1991   1994   1997   2000

Gesamtprivatisierungserlöse des Bundes in Millionen DM
QUELLE: BUNDESMINISTERIUM FÜR FINANZEN

VERKEHRSBETRIEBE

ENERGIEVERSORGUNG   SCHULEN

KRANKENHÄUSER   WOHNUNGSBAU

Die Privatisierungspotenziale der Städte und Gemeinden

Diagrams show the potentials of privatization within cities and communities in Germany.
The pictures of flowers represent the prosperous economic development due to privatization.

ドイツの町とコミュニティの民営化の可能性を示すダイアグラム。花の写真で、民営化による将来的な経済発展を表現している。

Germany 2004
AD, D: Bernd Vollmöller   DF, S: Simon & Goetz Design   CL: Sal. Oppenheim jr. & Cie. KGaA

Educação
Education

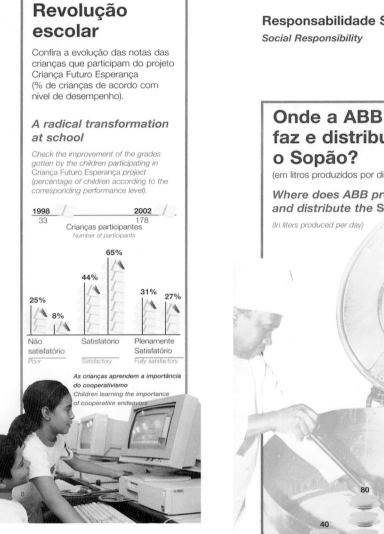

Revolução escolar

Confira a evolução das notas das crianças que participam do projeto Criança Futuro Esperança (% de crianças de acordo com nível de desempenho).

A radical transformation at school

Check the improvement of the grades gotten by the children participating in Criança Futuro Esperança project (percentage of children according to the corresponding performance level).

1998	2002
33	178

Crianças participantes
Number of participants

25% 8% 44% 65% 31% 27%

Não satisfatório — *Poor*
Satisfatório — *Satsfactory*
Plenamente Satisfatório — *Fully satsfactory*

As crianças aprendem a importância do cooperativismo
Children learning the importance of cooperative endeavors

a

Responsabilidade Social
Social Responsibility

Onde a ABB faz e distribui o Sopão?

(em litros produzidos por dia)

Where does ABB prepare and distribute the Sopão?

(In liters produced per day)

200
80
40
20

Blumenau   Betim   Osasco   Guarulhos

b

Saúde
Health

Quem deixou de fumar?

(entre aqueles que participaram do programa em cada ano, em %)

Percentage of those who have quit smoking

(% of ABB employees that stopped smoking)

15% 20% 12% 10%

1999   2000   2001   2002

c

Graphs showing improvement of the grades achieved by the children participating in the project. (a)
Graphs indicating the amount of a product produced per a day. (b)
Graphs showing the percentage of those who have quit smoking. (c)

プロジェクトに参加した児童の成績の向上を示すグラフ。(a)
一日に生産される製品の量を示すグラフ。(b)
タバコをやめた人のパーセンテージを示すグラフ。(c)

Brazil   2003
CD: Meire Kanno   AD: Vanessa Soares   DF, S: Azul Publicidade e Propaganda   CL: ABB Ltda.

SCALE

Size matters. In distribution.

In production. In marketing.

Indeed, in just about every single link in the food processing chain.

Which means that growth is no longer just an option for your cooperative: it has become an imperative.

1995

In 1995 sales of the top 10 food retailer chains represented 31% of all food sales at retail.

Total grocery store sales:
$391,312,000,000

1999

By 1999 Costco and SAM's Club, Ahold USA and Delhaize America had broken into the ranks of the top 10, and the top 10 chains' share of food sales had rocketed to 54%.

Total grocery store sales:
$441,300,000,000

Source for Top Ten Marketing Guidebook 2001; Progressive Grocer/Supermarket Business. Source for Food and Beverage US retail Store Sales; US Census Bureau NAICS 445 Tseries

In 2000, food and beverage giants reacted to the new world of fewer, mightier retail chains by making huge acquisitions of their own.

General Mills acquired Pillsbury for $10.5B, becoming 3rd largest U.S. food producer.

Pepsi won Gatorade when it bought Quaker Oats for $12.4B.

Unilever doubled its brands by buying Best Foods for $24B.

Phillip Morris/Kraft purchased Nabisco for $19B.

Buying Snapple for $1.5B kept Cadbury Schweppe's in the beverage big leagues.

Source: Wall Street reports

Illustrated charts and graphs using a warm palette to soften the news of tough industry trends in a straightforward, appealing way.
From an apple juice company's annual report.

アップルジュース・メーカーのアニュアル・レポートより。イラストを使用したチャートやグラフ。温かみのある色を使うことで具体的な数値の印象をやわらげた。
業界の厳しい動向に関するニュースを率直に訴えている。

USA 2001
AD, D: Katha Dalton   D: Jana Nishi / Michael Brugman   I: Rodica Prato   CW: Evelyne Rozner   DF, S: Hornall Anderson Design Works, Inc.   CL: Tree Top

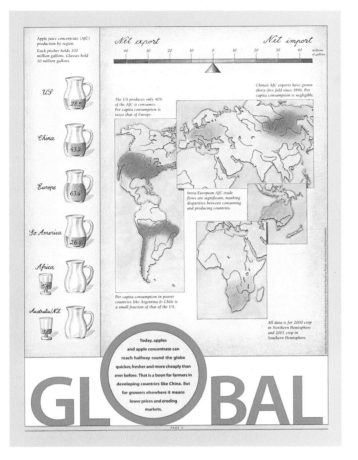

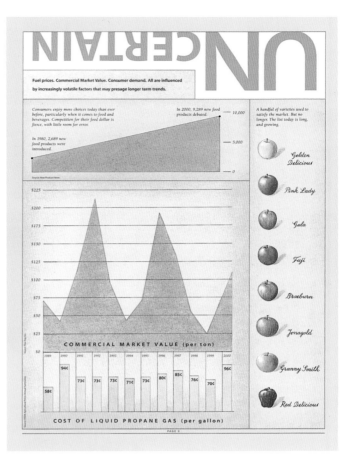

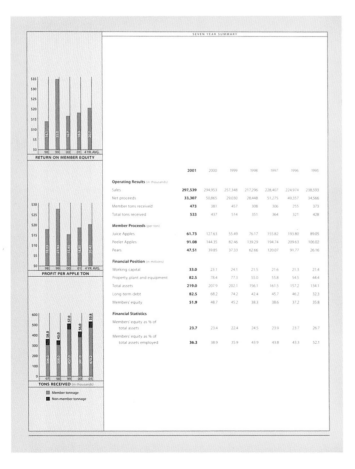

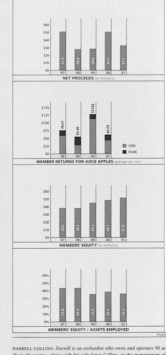

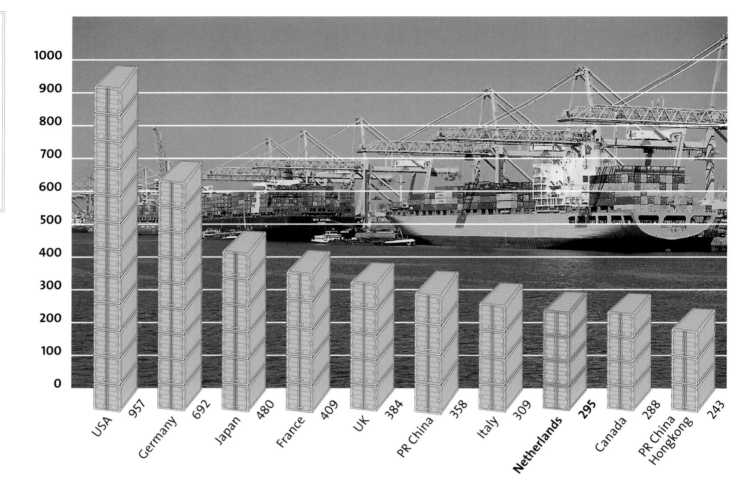

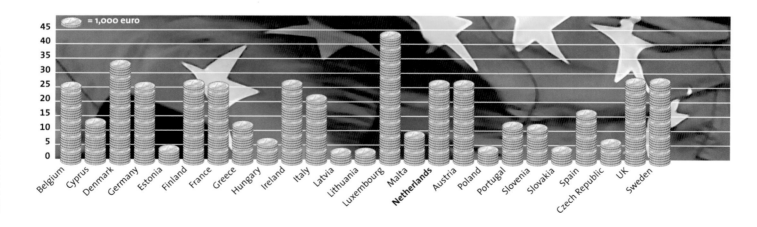

Graphs from a book on the Netherlands providing various data.

オランダを紹介する本より。様々なデータを表すグラフ。

Netherlands   2004
CD: Paul Vermijs   D: Toon Tesser   DF, S: TelDesign   CL: Ministry of Foreign Affairs

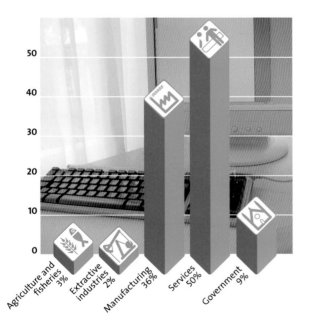

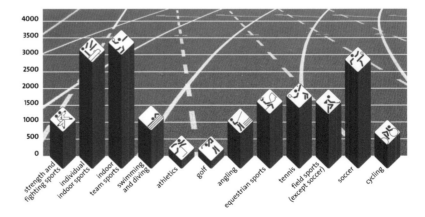

A Graph indicating statistical figures of black people in Salvador city, Brazil.

ブラジルのサルバドルに住む黒人に関する統計的数値を示すグラフ。

Brazil 2003
D, S: Douglas Okasaki   P: Cassio Alves   CW: Nadja Vladi
CL: A Tarde Newspaper

REVENUE (in millions)

$41.7

$29.0

$9.4

1998   1999   2000

A Graph shows the revenue of a consulting company. From an annual report.

コンサルティング会社の収益を示すグラフ。アニュアル・レポートより。

USA 2000
CD, AD, D: Gordon Mortensen   D: Michael McDaniel   I: Jonathan Carlson   CW: Words By Design
DF, S: Mortensen Design Inc.   CL: Zamba Corporation

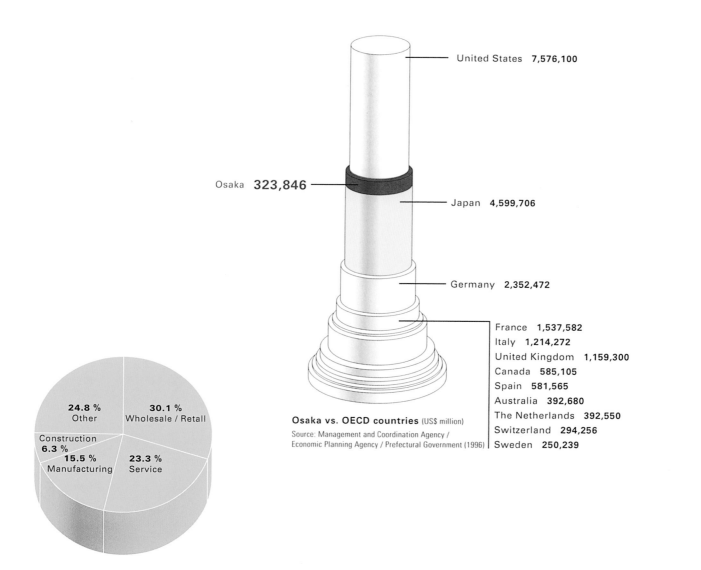

United States **7,576,100**

Osaka **323,846**

Japan **4,599,706**

Germany **2,352,472**

France **1,537,582**
Italy **1,214,272**
United Kingdom **1,159,300**
Canada **585,105**
Spain **581,565**
Australia **392,680**
The Netherlands **392,550**
Switzerland **294,256**
Sweden **250,239**

Osaka vs. OECD countries (US$ million)

Source: Management and Coordination Agency /
Economic Planning Agency / Prefectural Government (1996)

24.8 %
Other

30.1 %
Wholesale / Retail

Construction
6.3 %

15.5 %
Manufacturing

23.3 %
Service

Percentage of businesses by industry sector

Source: Annual Report of Prefectural Accounts 1996 (Economic Research Institute, Economic Planning Agency) /
Establishment Census (Statistics Bureau, Management and Coordination Agency) /
Report of Number of Establishments (Osaka Prefectural Government) (1996)

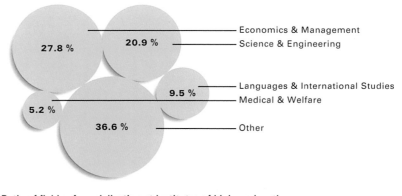

27.8 %

20.9 %

Economics & Management
Science & Engineering

9.5 %

Languages & International Studies
Medical & Welfare

5.2 %

36.6 %

Other

Ratio of fields of specialization at institutes of higher education

Source: School Basic Survey, conducted by the Ministry of Education (1998)

Diagrams used in a pamphlet to attract foreign business to Osaka expressing the GDP of different countries and the employment and schooling categories in Osaka.

大阪への海外企業誘致のためのパンフレットに使用されたダイアグラム。それぞれ各国のGDP、大阪での就業・就学カテゴリーを表現している。

Japan 2000
AD: Shinnoske Sugisaki   D: Chiaki Okuno / Reika Kusaka   DF, S: Shinnoske Inc.   CL: Osaka Prefecture

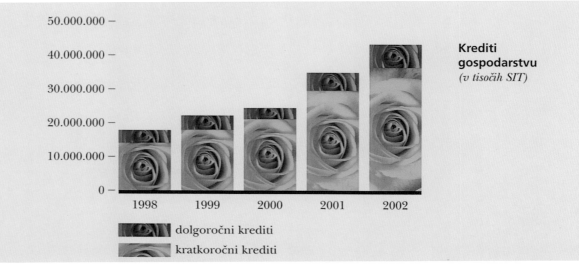

**Krediti
gospodarstvu**
(v tisočih SIT)

dolgoročni krediti

kratkoročni krediti

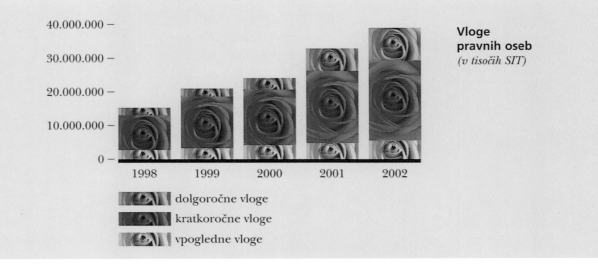

**Vloge
pravnih oseb**
(v tisočih SIT)

dolgoročne vloge

kratkoročne vloge

vpogledne vloge

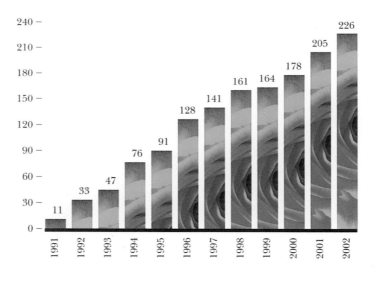

**Število zaposlenih
v banki na dan 31. 12.**

Bar graphs displaying the growth of financial services from 1998 to 2002.

1998年から2002年までの金融サービスの伸びを表した棒グラフ。

Slovenia   2003
AD, D, S: Edi Berk   P: Dragan Arrigler   DF: KROG, Ljubljana   CL: Probanka, Maribor

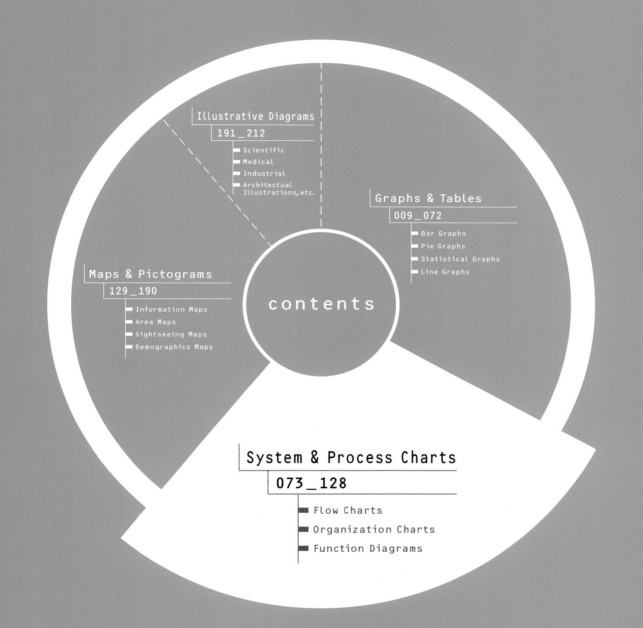

contents

GRAPHS & TABLES · SYSTEM & PROCESS CHARTS · MAPS & PICTOGRAMS · ILLUSTRATIVE DIAGRAMS

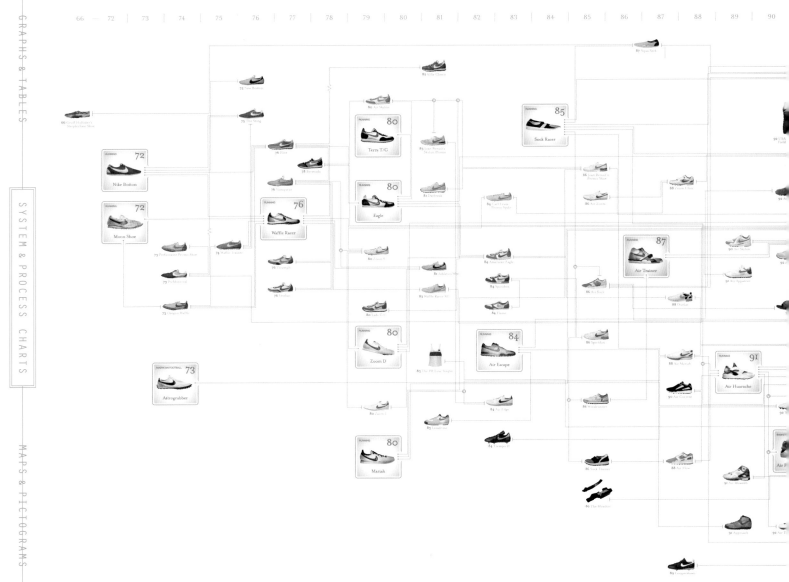

Genealogy of **Speed**
1966–

Speed is our obsession. Since the mid '60s, we have been designing and creating products specifically for speed. Designs from one have contributed to another – racing flats have influenced basketball, football has influenced cycling and sprinting has helped shape speed skating. Along the way, we enlisted the help of some of the greatest athletes in the world. We have analyzed how their feet work, scrutinized their old shoes, probed their minds, studied their bodies for any hint of how to make them go faster by fractions of a second. We have dug into our archives, interviewed our designers, uncovered the stories you see here. They are the stories that make us who we are. This is our family history. This is our genealogy of speed.

A genealogical expression of the many products developed as a collaboration between Nike technology and the world's top athletes in pursuit of "Speed."

「Speed」を追求するために、ナイキ社の持つ最高の技術と世界トップレベルのアスリートの協力により開発された数々のプロダクトを家系図化したもの。

Japan   2004
CD: Paul Tew   AD: Jeff Dey   CW: Dennie Wendt   DF: Big Giant   S, CL: NIKE, Inc.

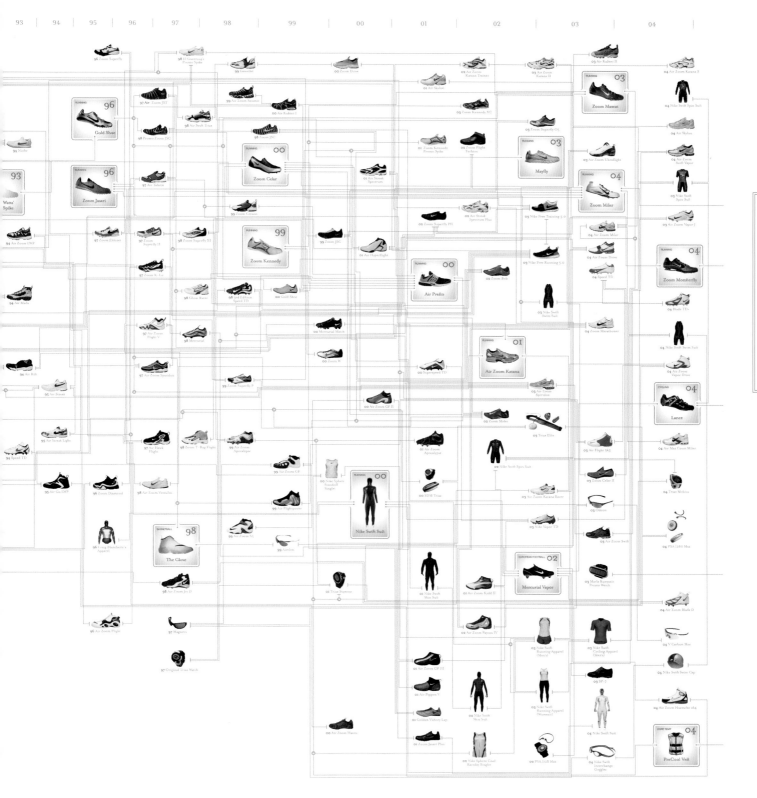

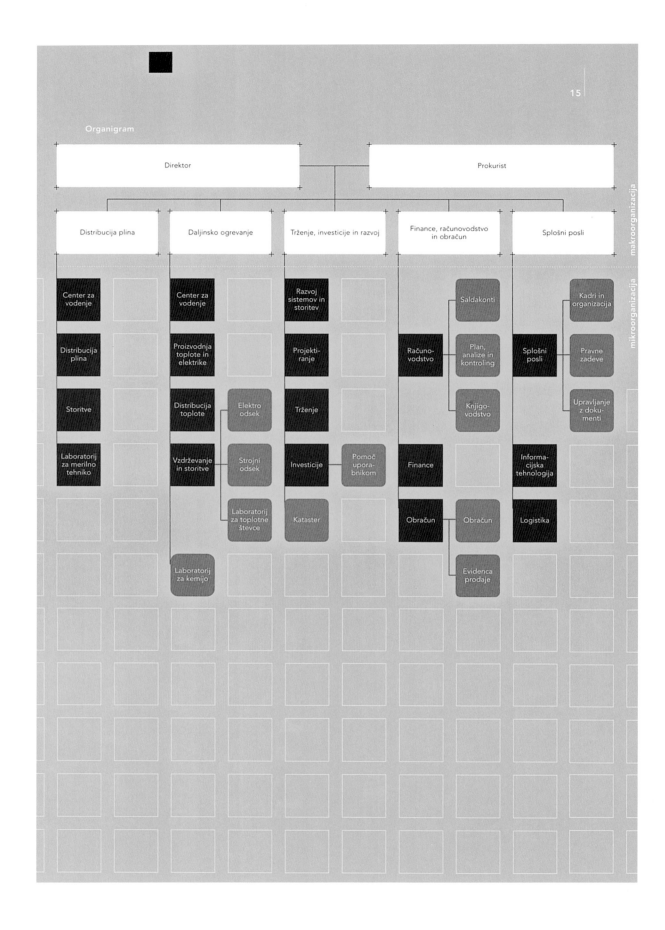

Organaization chart of the Energetika Ljubljana, a public-service company in Slovenia.

スロベニアの公共事業、Energetika Ljubljana社の組織図。

Slovenia 2002
CD: Ladeja Godina Kosir   AD, D: Sašo Urukalo   P: Klemen Lajevec   I: Arhiv E.L. / Tadej Brate   CW: Medeja Lončar / Jana Bogdanovski / Tadeja Bular
DF, S: Agencija Imelda   CL: Energetika Ljubljana

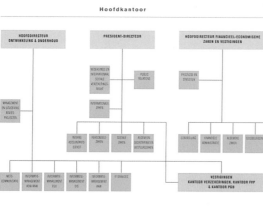

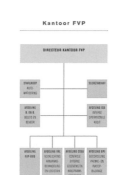

14

15

Organizational charts of a bank. From an annual report.

銀行の組織図。アニュアル・レポートより。

Netherlands 2001
CD, AD, D, P: Wout De Vringer   CD, AD: Bob Van Dijk   CW: Corporate Communication / SVB   DF, S: Faydherbe / De Vringer   CL: SVB (Sociale Verzekerings Bank)

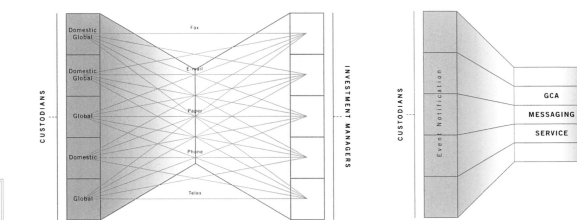

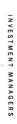

Charts explain the complex communications connections between parties communicating vital corporate financial information.

重要な企業の財政情報をやりとりする際の複雑なコミュニケーション関係を説明するチャート。

USA 2004
CD: Steve Ferrari   D, I: Kurt Finkbeiner   DF, S: Graphic Expression, Inc.   CL: Depository Trust & Clearing Corp.

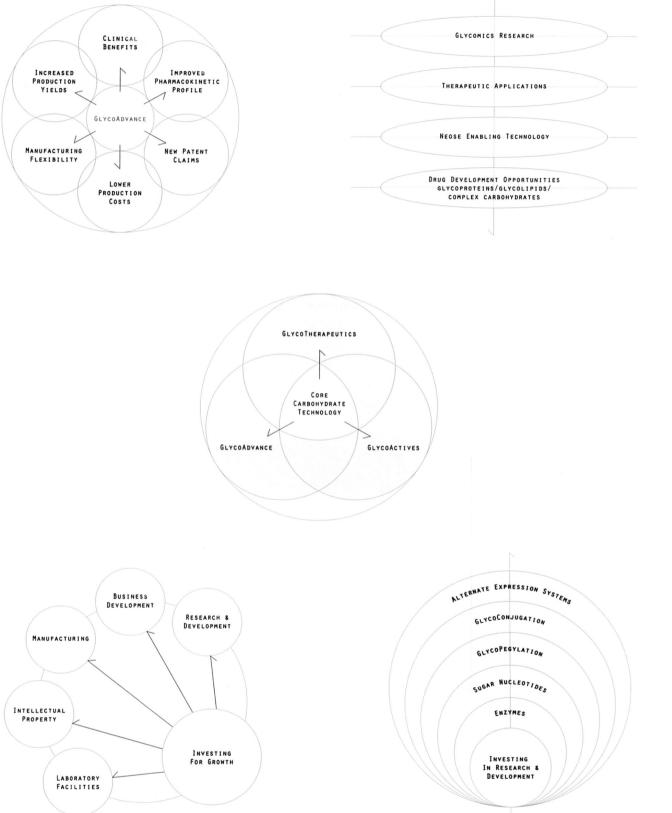

Charts illustrating the relationship between Neose's technology and its products and business strategy.

Neose社のテクノロジーと同社の製品やビジネス戦略の関連性を表したチャート。

USA 2001

CD: Steve Ferrari   D, I: Kurt Finkbeiner   DF, S: Graphic Expression, Inc.   CL: Neose Technologies, Inc.

Ruimte en technologie

Door de eeuwen heen is de mens op zoek geweest naar nieuwe mogelijkheden om zichzelf en zijn spullen te verplaatsen. Een drang die voortspruit uit de behoefte nieuwe gebieden te ontdekken, producten naar de markt te brengen, pelgrimstochten te ondernemen, enzovoorts. Naarmate de mens meer greep krijgt op de natuurwetenschappen worden dieren ingeruild voor machines.

Nieuwe technologie beïnvloedt het ruimtegebruik. Ondanks alle vooruitgang blijkt nieuwe technologie toch steeds weer beperkingen te hebben. Een aardig voorbeeld vormen de vroegere zeezeilschepen. Ze voeren langs de kusten van Europa, maar hadden een beperkte actieradius. Goederen die toch verder moesten, werden gestapeld in tussenhavens. Daar werden ze opgepakt en verder

vervoerd. Op deze wijze ontstonden er stapelhavens langs de Europese kusten, waarvan de haven van Amsterdam (en Zaandam) een bekend voorbeeld is. Rond zo'n stapelhaven ontstond nieuwe industrie om de gestapelde goederen te bewerken. Later werden deze beperkingen overwonnen. Zo ontwikkelden de vikings hun drakars, waarmee ze aanzienlijk grotere afstanden konden afleggen. Met de rooftochten die volgden over heel Europa, werd de basis gelegd voor nieuwe handelsroutes en bijbehorende havens. Overigens was het stapelen van goederen niet alleen een gevolg van technische beperkingen. Landheren gunden aan steden stapelrechten zodat deze zich economisch konden ontwikkelen. Bekende voorbeelden zijn Dordrecht en Brugge. De stapelrechten hadden als gevolg dat de transportsystemen zich in de richting

van deze steden gingen ontwikkelen. Ten tijde van de renaissance verbeterde het zeilschip, zodat ook oceanen konden worden overgestoken. Later volgden de stoomschepen en de schepen gestookt op gasolie. Het oude netwerk van kustvaartroutes werd nu aangevuld met oceaanroutes. Het centrum hiervan lag eerst in Zuidwest-Europa (Spanje en Portugal) en verschoof later naar Noordwest-Europa (Engeland, Frankrijk, Nederland). Overigens werden de handelsexpedities niet alleen mogelijk gemaakt door verbeterde scheepvaarttechnieken. Ook de kredietservice van de banken verbeterde. De handelsexpedities moesten tenslotte ook worden gefinancierd. Vanaf de napoleontische tijd werd het continentale vervoer sterk gestimuleerd door forse uitbreiding van het vaarwegennet en later door

aanleg van de spoorwegen. [...] tijd werd de nieuwe stoomte[...] gebruikt voor industrialisatie[...] door ontstonden in het binn[...] industriecentra voor textielp[...] verwerking van landbouwpr[...] verwerking van ijzererts en [...] productie, enzovoorts. Een [...] als die van Rotterdam verar[...] van opslagplaats (stapel) in [...] haven, vooral door de sterke[...] mische groei in het Duitse a[...] en de goede achterlandverb[...] Zowel productie als transpo[...] kenmerkte zich door bulkho[...] heden van materialen en pr[...] Dit werd later een beperking[...] nieuwe industrie zich meer [...] ten op het vervoer van relat[...] volumes die snel moesten v[...] afgeleverd dan op grote hoe[...] halfproducten, en mensen z[...] zowel zakelijk als privé op e[...] groter gebied gingen oriënte[...]

```
                                                    1897 TAXI
                                                1886 DAIMLER OP PETROLEUM
                                               1881 ELEKTRISCHE TRAM (BERLIJN)
                                              1867 EERSTE MOTORFIETS
                                             1865 'DE REIS NAAR DE MAAN IN 28 DAGEN EN 12 UUR'
                                            1863 METRO (LONDEN)
                                           1862 OTTOMOTOR
                                          1861 VELOCIPEDE (ERNEST MICHAUX)
                                         1860 GASMOTOR
                                        1849 ZWEEFVLIEGTUIG (CAYLEY)
                                       1839 DE FIETS MET ACHTERWIELAANDRIJVING (KIRCKPATRICK MACMILLAN)
                                      1827 OMNIBUS RIJDT OVER BROADWAY
                                     1817 LOOPFIETS DRAISINE (BARON KARL DRAIS)
                                    1814 STOOMAANGEDREVEN LOCOMOTIEF (GEORGE STEPHENSON)
                                   1801 ONDERZEEBOOT NAUTILUS (ROBERT FULTON)
                                  1787 STOOMBOOT (JOHN FITCH)
                                 1783 PARACHUTE
                                1783 HETELUCHTBALLON
                               1620 ONDERZEEBOOT (CONELIS DREBBEL)
                              1492 ORNITHOPTER (LEONARDO DA VINCI)
                             1450 RIJTUIG
                            770 HOEFIJZER
                           181-234 KRUIWAGEN
                          100 VC AEOLIPILE (HERO VAN ALEXANDRIA)
                         300 VC ROMEINSE STRIJDWAGEN
                        400 VC VLIEGER (CHINA)
                       2000 VC PAARDEN WORDEN GETEMD
                      3500 VC KAR
```

Diagram indicating the development of mobility from 3500 B.C. till 2004.

紀元前3500年から2004年までの移動手段の発達を示すチャート。

Netherlands 2003
CD, AD: André Toet   CD: Jan Sevenster   D: Bas Meulendijks   CW: Paul Van Koningsbruggen
DF, S: Samenwerkende Ontwerpers   CL: Grafische Cultuurstichting

```
                                                               2004 ?
                                                           1994 CHUNNEL
                                                       1983 TGV
                                                   1981 SPACE SHUTTLE
                                                   1981 VLIEGTUIG OP ZONNEENERGIE
                                               1970 JUMBOJET
                                           1969 BEMANDE MAANMISSIE APOLLO
                                       1968 SUPERSONIC TRANSPORT (SST)
                                   1964 BULLET TRAIN
                               1963 VALENTINA TERESJKOVA EERSTE VROUW IN DE RUIMTE
                           1961 JOERI GAGARIN EERSTE MAN IN DE RUIMTE
                       1958 REGENDRUPVORM ONDERZEEER (US)
                   1957 SPOETNIK 1
               1956 HOVERCRAFT
           1954 NUCLEAIRE ONDERZEEBOOT (USS NAUTILUS)
       1947 EERSTE VLUCHT SUPERSONISCH STRAALVLIEGTUIG
   1940 AUTOMATISCHE VERSNELLINGSBAK
   1939 EERSTE SUCCESVOLLE HELIKOPTERVLUCHT
 1924 AUTOSNELWEG ITALIE
 1914 VERKEERSLICHT
 1913 ZEILPLANK
 1908 FORD PRODUCEERT AAN DE LOPENDE BAND
 1907 TRANSATLANTISCHE PAKKETBOTEN
 1903 GEBROEDERS WRIGHT VLIEGEN MET HUN VLIEGTUIG
 1900 METRO PARIJS
 1899 ZEPPELIN
 1898 DICHTE AUTO MET VERSNELLINGSBAK (RENAULT)
 1895 AUTOBAND (MICHELIN)
 1894 MOTORFIETS (HILDEBRAND & WOLFMULLER)
```

tot de Tweede Wereld-
merkt zich dan ook door
t van de (vracht)auto, een
vervoermiddel bij uitstek.
te Wereldoorlog groeit
autobezitters sterk, als
de seriefabricage van
et (tijdens WOII) bewezen
lle verplaatsingen met
o's. Vanaf de jaren vijftig
autogebruik pas echt een
t. Het resultaat is dat de
ur al snel begint te knellen.
de weginfrastructuur was
at van een evolutie over
heen. De eerste land-
Nederland werden aan-
le 'dijken' langs de rivieren,
ruggen en op de hoge
het midden en oosten
d. Met de opkomst van de
a napoleontische tijd
an de wegen zich verder.
gen werden aangelegd,

die nu nog vaak te herkennen zijn in
het landschap: lange rechten wegen
met aan weerszijden een bomenrij,
de as vaak zuiver gericht op een
kerktoren (Metzelaar). De auto vroeg
echter om meer ruimte, zowel in de
stad als op de verbindingen tussen de
steden. De inrichting van de steden
werd in de vijftiger en zestiger jaren
dan ook toegesneden op de auto.
Huizen, wijken en zelfs grachten en
singels maakten plaats voor grote
doorgangswegen en parkeerplaatsen
in de stad.
Tussen de steden werd uiteindelijk
het autosnelwegennet aangelegd.
Een netwerk dat zich kenmerkt door
ongelijkvloerse kruisingen, meerdere
rijstroken per rijbaan (rijrichting) en
keurig langs de steden geleide
wegen. Nieuwe constructietechnieken
zoals wegfundaties, asfalt en beton,
en de (stoom)wals maakten dit
mogelijk, doordat het aanleggen van

wegen minder afhankelijk werd van
de ondergrond.
De volgende beperking stond echter
al weer voor de deur in de vorm van
een te groot geworden aanslag op
het leefmilieu, verkeersveiligheid en
omgevingskwaliteit. De grootse
plannen voor de binnensteden werden
teruggedraaid, de groei van het autosnelwegennet stokte. Binnen de
steden wordt nu ruimte terug-
gewonnen op de auto. Tussen de
steden worden we geconfronteerd
met ernstige files die de roep om
bredere autosnelwegen weer doet
aanzwellen.
Na de Tweede Wereldoorlog groeit
ook de luchtvaart. Grote afstanden
kunnen veel sneller worden overbrugd,
waardoor de internationale netwerken
worden versterkt. Grote luchthavens
blijken een aanzuigende werking te
hebben op (hoofd)kantoren van
internationaal opererende bedrijven.

Er blijkt zelfs een geheel nieuw soort
stad te ontstaan, de luchthavenstad.
De evolutie zet zich door.

(Gebaseerd op: G. Abema, H.
Hartesema, L.W. van der Veen, M.
Schoor, K. Jansma, *10.000 jaar
Geschiedenis der Nederlanden*.
Uitgeverij M.A. van Sijen,
Leeuwarden. TNO Beleidsstudies,
Universiteit Twente (1993),
*Technische innovaties in het
Personenverkeer en -Vervoer, een
inventarisatie op zoek naar duurzame
mobiliteit*. Apeldoorn. Metzelaar, W.
(1976), *Nederland Deltaland*. Stam
Technische Boeken, Culemborg.)

ertragreiches wachstum.

Durch eine erstklassige technologische Aus-
stattung und die hervorragende Kundenbasis
sind wir führend im Wettbewerb. Mit unserem
umfassenden Leistungsangebot decken wir die
Wertschöpfungskette unserer Kunden ab und
bieten ihnen Komplettlösungen.

Marktvolumen aller Werbeträger
im Jahr 2012: 31,3 Mrd. €

was ist.

OI:

was wir werden wollen.

schlott sebaldus wird Europas führender
Anbieter integrierter Kommunikations-
lösungen für Verlage und die werbetreibende
Wirtschaft. Mit der Bündelung klassischer
und neuer Medien bieten wir herausragende
Lösungen für deren Kundendialog.
So schaffen wir den höchstmöglichen Wert
für unsere Kunden und Investoren.

Kennzahlen *im Überblick*

Interactive charts visualizing the change of European high volume printing market in the future and charts showing the current financial situation.
The latest future forecasts can be seen by pulling the inserts.

ヨーロッパの大量印刷市場の将来的な変化を視覚化したインタラクティブなチャートと、最近の財務状況を示すチャート。挿入された紙を引っ張ると将来の予測が現れる。

Germany 2002
CD, AD: Jochen Rädeker   D, I: Gernot Walter   CW: Norbert Hiller   DF, S: Strichpunkt GmbH   CL: Schlott Gruppe AG

2005

December 2004   January 2005

November 2004   February 2005

2003: New building for BioEquipment   2004: Opening of sales office in the USA

1978: Market launch of KLF fermenter   1998: Market launch of multi-way valves

1990: Market launch of smallest NMR fermenter   1987: Market launch of membrane fermenter

October 2004   March 2005

1979: Move to current company site

2002: Market launch of BioWeight

1992: New assembly hall

1985: First customer contacts in the USA

The beginning of Bioengineering year 2004 / 2005

Thirty years ago, on May 3, 1974, Bioengineering AG was entered in the commercial register of the canton of Zurich. The purpose of the business was described as "Construction and planning of facilities for biology and the acceptance of engineering assignments in conjunction with biological process technologies." We have been successful in doing exactly that for the past 30 years, so we can present many sophisticated projects and technological developments that today are considered state-of-the-art around the world.

September 2004   April 2005

2003: Largest contract so far, from Celltrion Inc., Korea

1994: Opening of sales office in China   1981: Hans Müller leaves the company

2000: Market launch of CupHermann

1991: Major order from Gist-brocades NV, Delft

August 2004   May 2004

July 2004   June 2004

2004

30 Years Bioengineering AG

Diagrams showing important events and technological developments in the 30 years of corporate history.

30年におよぶ企業の歴史における重要な出来事や技術的な展開を示すチャート。

Switzerland 2004
CD, AD, D: Heinz Wild   D: Dan Petter   P: Michael Rast   CW: Kurt Schori / Erich Brandenberger   DF, S: Heinz Wild Design   CL: Bioengineering AG

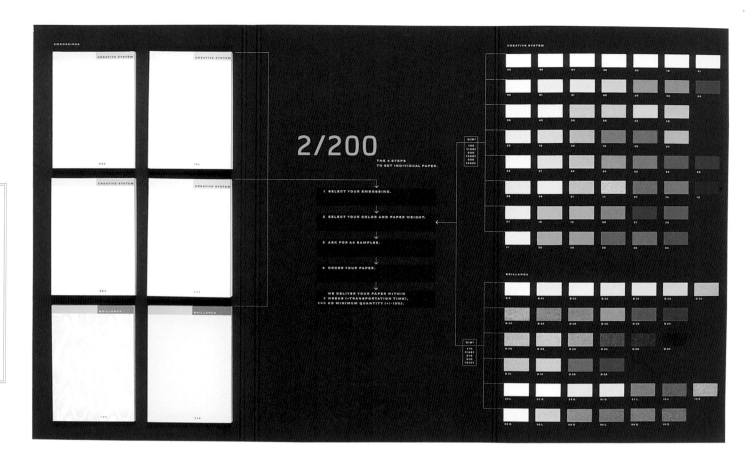

2/200 is the world's largest paper program with more than 100,000 possible combinations. Charts showing the selection process make the content easily accessible.

2/200は100,000以上もの組み合わせが可能な世界最大のペーパー・プログラム。選択プロセスを示すチャートによって簡単に利用できる。

Switzerland　2003-2004
CD, AD, D: Heinz Wild　CD: Florian Kohler　CW: Kurt Schori / Erich Brandenberger　DF, S: Heinz Wild Design　CL: Büttenpapierfabrik Gmund GmbH & Co. KG

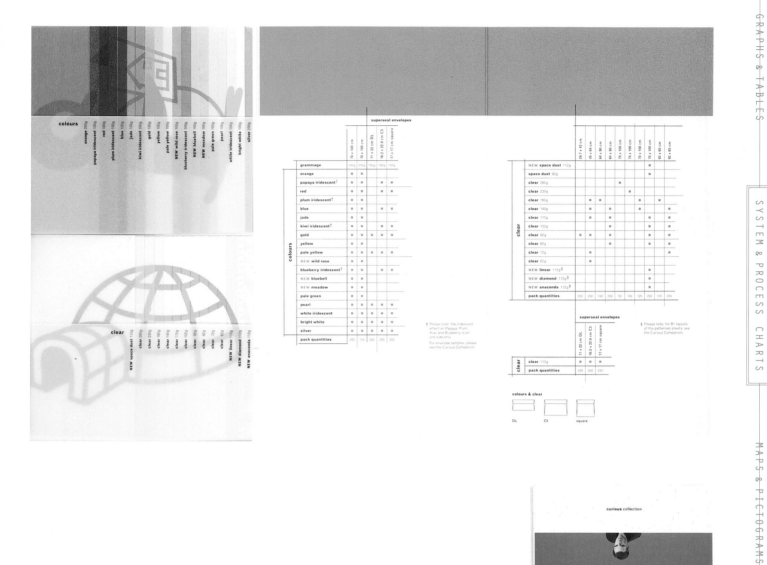

superseal envelopes

colours	70 x 100 cm	70 x 100 cm	11 x 22 cm DL	16.2 x 22.9 cm C5	17 x 17 cm square
grammage	100g	200g	100g	100g	100g
orange	■	■			
papaya iridescent†	■	■		■	■
red	■	■			
plum iridescent†	■	■			
blue	■	■			
jade	■	■			
kiwi iridescent†	■	■			
gold	■	■	■	■	
yellow	■	■			
pale yellow	■	■			
NEW wild rose	■	■			
blueberry iridescent†	■	■			
NEW bluebell	■	■			
NEW meadow	■	■			
pale green	■	■			
pearl	■	■	■	■	
white iridescent	■	■	■	■	
bright white	■	■	■	■	
silver	■	■	■	■	
pack quantities	250	125	250	250	250

clear	29.7 x 42 cm	45 x 64 cm	64 x 90 cm	64 x 90 cm	70 x 100 cm	70 x 100 cm	70 x 100 cm	70 x 100 cm	92 x 65 cm	92 x 65 cm
NEW space dust 112g							■			
space dust 90g							■			
clear 285g				■						
clear 230g			■							
clear 180g		■	■		■			■		
clear 140g		■		■		■			■	
clear 113g		■		■			■			
clear 102g		■		■				■		
clear 90g	■	■		■				■		
clear 80g					■			■		
clear 72g								■	■	
clear 62g		■								
NEW linear 112g							■			
NEW diamond 112g†							■			
NEW anaconda 112g†							■			
pack quantities	250	250	100	250	50	100	125	250	125	250

superseal envelopes

clear	11 x 22 cm DL	16.2 x 22.9 cm C5	17 x 17 cm square
clear 112g			
pack quantities	250	250	250

colours & clear

DL   C5   square

† Please note: the iridescent effect on Papaya, Plum, Kiwi and Blueberry is on one side only.
For envelope samples, please see the Curious Companion.

‡ Please note: for B1 layouts of the patterned sheets, see the Curious Companion.

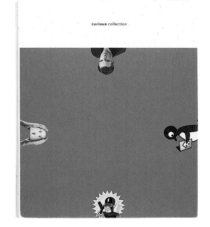

curious collection

Range charts designed to ensure that recipients could easily find and understand the availability, sheet dimension, weight, texture, and color of every paper of the "Curious" system.

"Curious"という紙のシリーズのためのチャート。入手可能かどうか、シートの寸法、斤量、テクスチャー、色を利用者が簡単に探したり理解することができる。

Canada 2004
CD, AD, D, I: Frank Viva   P: Ron Baxter Smith   I: Seth   CW: Doug Dolan   DF, S: Viva Dolan Communications & Design Inc.   CL: Arjomggins

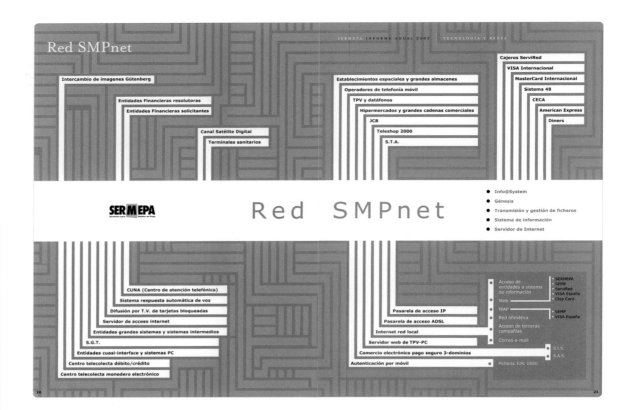

An organization chart showing affiliates of the VISA Group.

VISAグループのアニュアル・レポートから抜粋した、関連会社を示す組織図。

Spain 2003
CD: Emilio Gil   D: Ingrid Forbord   DF, S: Tau Diseño   CL: Sermepa

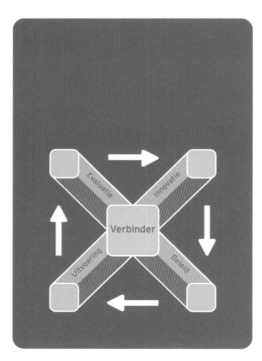
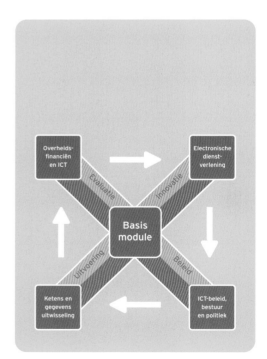

Diagrams explaining how information management works.

情報管理がどのように作用するかを説明する図。

Netherlands 2004
D: Toon Tesser   DF, S: TelDesign   CL: IMAC

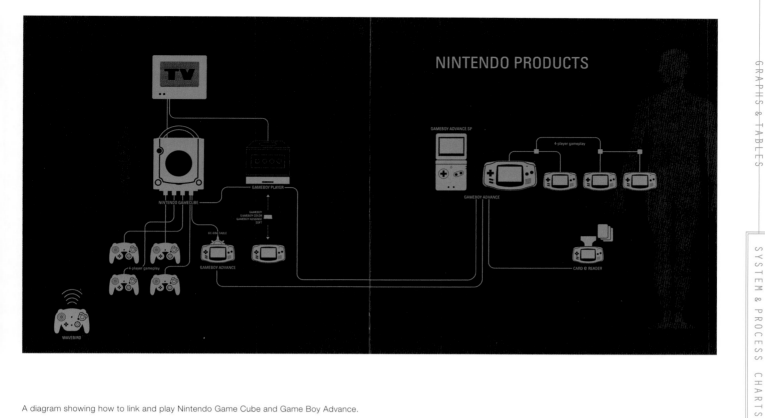

A diagram showing how to link and play Nintendo Game Cube and Game Boy Advance.

ニンテンドーゲームキューブとゲームボーイアドバンスをつなげて遊べることを表す図。

Japan 2003
CD: Shin Kojo   AD, D: Takashi Maeda   CL, S: Nintendo Co., Ltd.

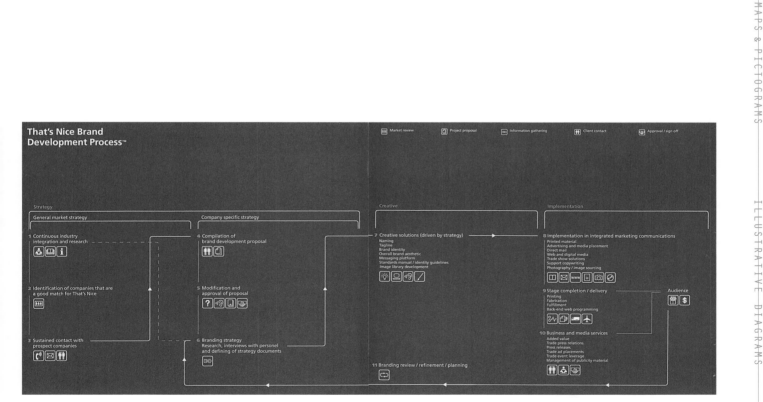

Charts showing "Brand Development Process" of That's Nice, an integrated marketing specialist.

総合的マーケティングのスペシャリスト、That's Nice社の「ブランド開発のプロセス」を示すチャート。

USA 2003
CD, CW: Mark Allen   AD: Nigel Walker   D: Beatriz Cifuentes   P: Brian Pierce   DF, CL, S: That's Nice LLC

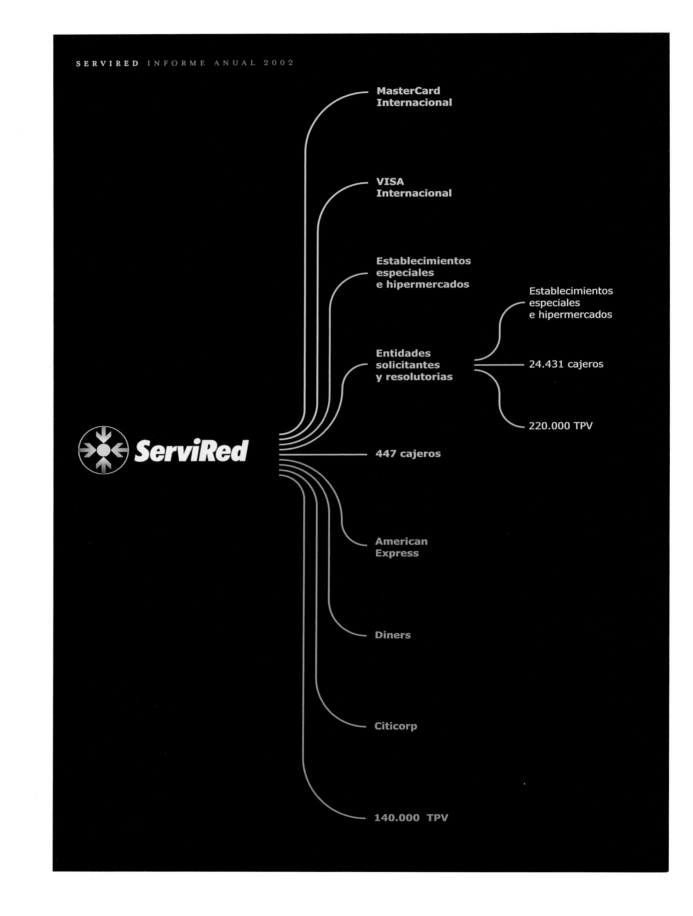

MasterCard
Internacional

VISA
Internacional

Establecimientos
especiales
e hipermercados

Establecimientos
especiales
e hipermercados

Entidades
solicitantes
y resolutorias

24.431 cajeros

220.000 TPV

447 cajeros

American
Express

Diners

Citicorp

140.000 TPV

An organization chart showing business partners of ServiRed.

ServiRedの取引先企業を示す組織図。

Spain   2003
CD: Emilio Gil   D: Ingrid Forbord   DF, S: Tau Diseño   CL: Sermepa

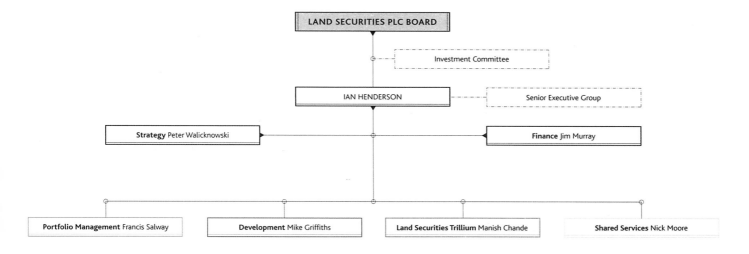

LAND SECURITIES BUSINESS MODEL

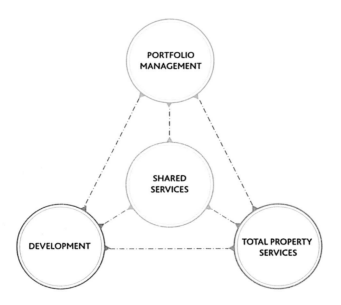

An organizational chart and business model chart for Land Securities.

Land Securities社の組織図およびビジネスモデルを説明するチャート。

UK 2001
CD: Gilmar Wendt / Nick Austin   AD, D, I: Mike Hall   P: Chris Mouse / Marcus Lyon   DF, S: SAS   CL: Land Securities

Business Software Implementation

Implementation Methodology

Implementation Project Workflow

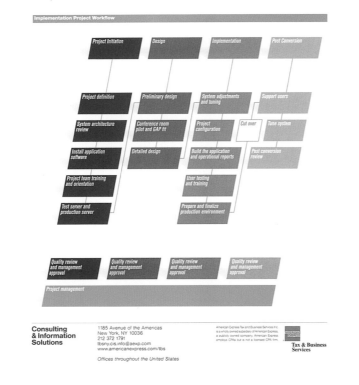

Not-for-Profit

Enterprise Resource Planning for Not-for-Profit Organizations (ERP/NFP)

Enterprise Component Model

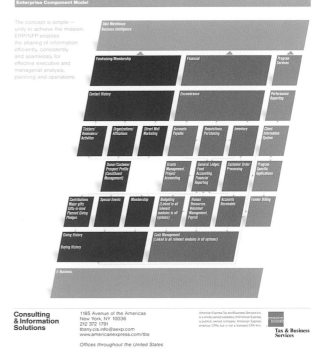

From the project sheets to support the management consulting unit of American Express. Charts outline the unit's services.

American Expressのマネジメント・コンサルタント部門をサポートするプロジェクト・シートより。部門のサービス概要を示すチャート。

USA   2003
CD, D: Graham Hanson   DF, S: Graham Hanson Design   CL: American Express

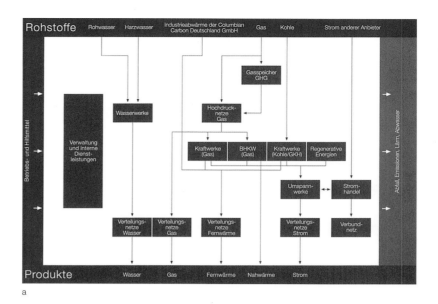

a

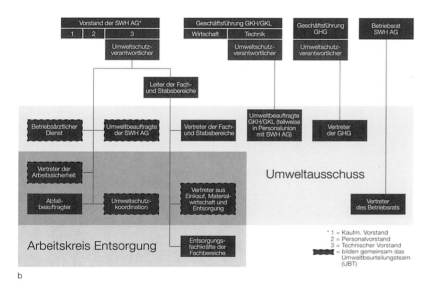

b

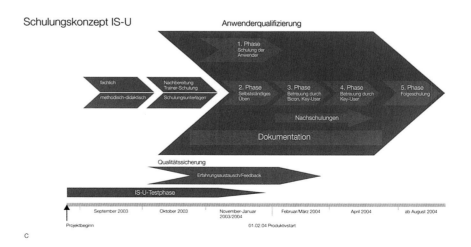

c

Diagrams showing the material flow of a power company. (a)
Diagrams explaining relationships between environmental groups and companies. (b)
Chart explaining the training concept and flow of IS-U(Industry Solutions for Utilities). (c)

電力会社の物流を示すチャート。 (a)
環境保護団体と企業の関係を説明するチャート。 (b)
IS-U（電気・ガスなどの公益企業向けの業務別料金システム・ソリューション）の研修コンセプトや流れを説明したチャート。 (c)

Germany 2003
CL, S: Stadtwerke Hannover AG

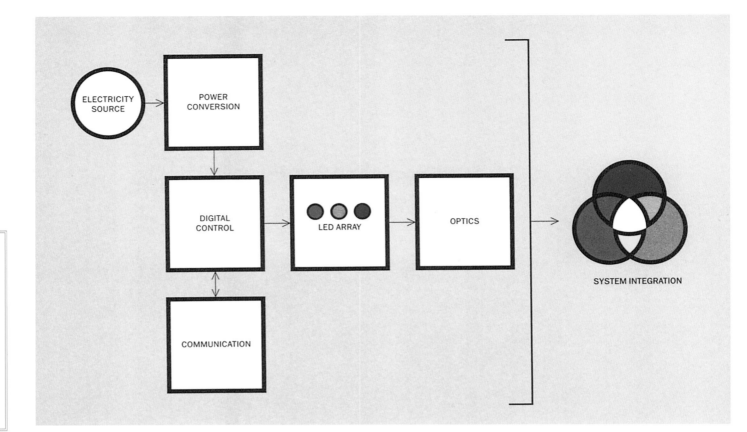

Charts explains the key technologies that are foundations of lighting systems.

照明システムの基盤である主要なテクノロジーを説明するチャート。

USA 2001
CD, AD, D: Dave Mason   AD, D: Pamela Lee   D: Nancy Willett   P: Victor John Penner   DF, S: Samata Mason   CL: TIR Systems Ltd.

(6) The layered network architecture
We are building flexible and cost-efficient
networks that make it easier for operators to
handle new services at lower cost

(8) Always best connected
We are leading the way into the new world of user-focused networks
by unifying personal, local and wide area mobile technology

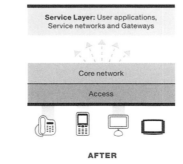

● **Personal Area Network**
Wireless connections between laptops,
phones and pda's using bluetooth.

Local Area Network
Access to high capacity networks in locations
such as airports and offices through WLAN/WiFi

○ **Wide Area Network**
Access to voice and data services using
global mobile systems

Diagram explaining the layered network architecture.

階層型ネットワーク構築を説明する図。

UK 2004
CD, AD: Gilmar Wendt   CD: David Stocks   D, I: John-Paul Sykes   P: Peter Hoelstad   CW: Tim Rich / Mats Thoren   DF, S: SAS   CL: Ericsson

1. Maatschappelijk gedreven investeerder in (woning) vastgoed

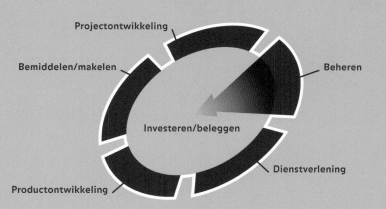

Projectontwikkeling

Bemiddelen/makelen

Beheren

Investeren/beleggen

Dienstverlening

Productontwikkeling

2. Componenten van (direct) rendement

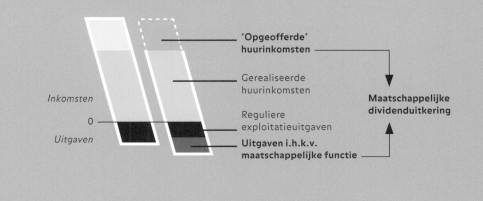

Inkomsten

0

Uitgaven

'Opgeofferde' huurinkomsten

Gerealiseerde huurinkomsten

Reguliere exploitatieuitgaven

Uitgaven i.h.k.v. maatschappelijke functie

Maatschappelijke dividenduitkering

3. 'Revolving fund': rendements-distributie

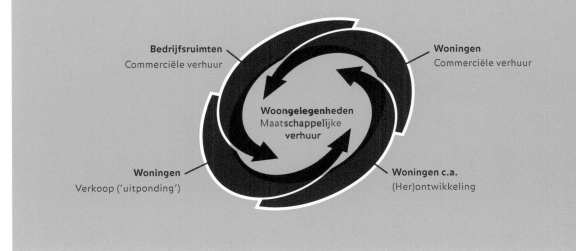

Bedrijfsruimten
Commerciële verhuur

Woningen
Commerciële verhuur

Woongelegenheden
Maatschappelijke verhuur

Woningen
Verkoop ('uitponding')

Woningen c.a.
(Her)ontwikkeling

Diagrams explaining investments, efficiency, and revolving fund of a real estate company.

不動産会社の投資、効率性、回転資金に関するダイアグラム。

Netherlands 2001
CD, D: Jaco Emmen   DF, S: TelDesign   CL: AEDEX

Technical Initiatives

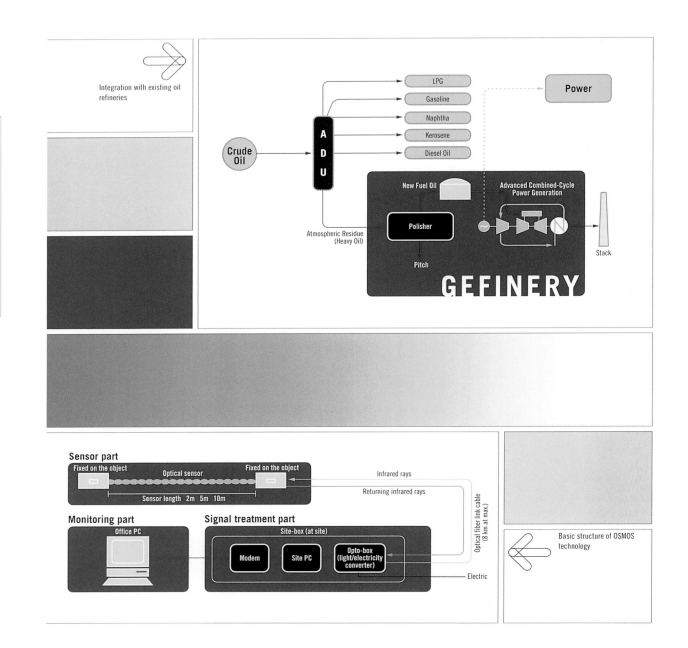

14

a

Biorek process flow chart showing the refining and combined cycle power generation of heavy crude oil and the basic composition of OSMOS. (a, d)
A chart showing the applicability and synthesis of dimethyl ether in addition to the position of an online marketing company. (b, c)

重質油の精製・複合発電、オスモスの基本構成、Biorekプロセスフローのチャート。 (a, d)
ジメチルエーテルの適用分野と合成フロー、並びに電子商取引市場運営会社の位置付けを表すチャート。 (b, c)

Japan **2000** (a, d) **/ 2001** (b, c)
D: Mayumi Noguchi (a, d) / Shinji Suzuki (b, c)   CL: JGC Corporation   S: The IR Corporation

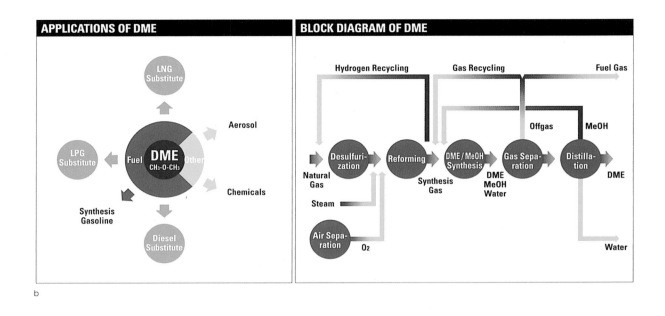

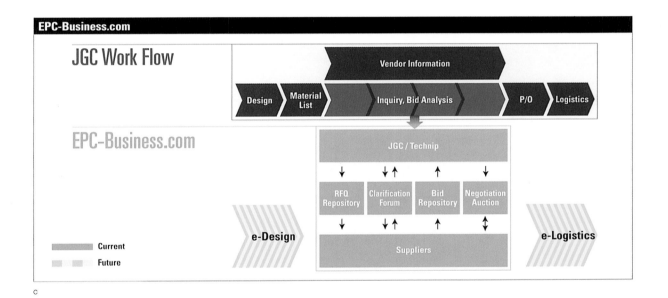

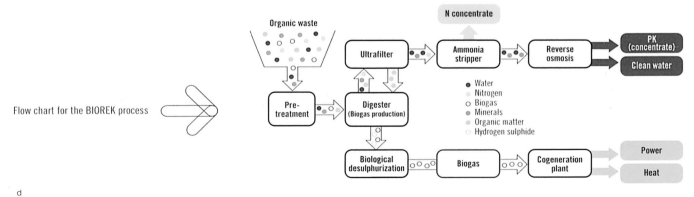

Flow chart for the BIOREK process

a

PRESENTATION DEVICE LAYER

PC With Browser	WAP Phone	ITV	Touch Tone Phone	Industry	Emulator for Performance Testing
HTML	WSP	VARIOUS	DTMF	XML	

PRESENTATION LOGIC LAYER

Web Services	WAP Service	ITV Service	Voice Service	B2B Service

BUSINESS LOGIC LAYER

Content Management services

Search Services	Personalization Membership Services	Ad Serveces	E-Commerce Services	Collavorative Services

Application Intergration services

DATA LAYER

Relational Database	Relational Database	Relational Database

AGENCY.COM Handles the Layers Above

AGENCY.COM Partners for The Layer Below

Legacy System   ERP System   E Mail System

EXTERNAL SYSTEMS LAYER

a

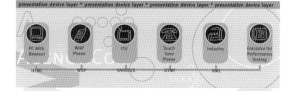

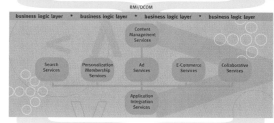

b

Diagram explaining the various layers that the agency handles, and those that the agency partners handle. (a)
Diagram illustrating the routes of communication and services between working levels of management. (b)

広告代理店やそのパートナーが扱っている様々なビジネス層を説明するチャート。 (a)
マネジメントの作業レベル間のコミュニケーションやサービスのルートを説明するチャート。 (b)

USA 2001

CD, AD, D, I: Mike Quon   D: Anna Leonard / Ole Haentzschel   DF, S: Mike Quon / designation Inc.   CL: Agency.com

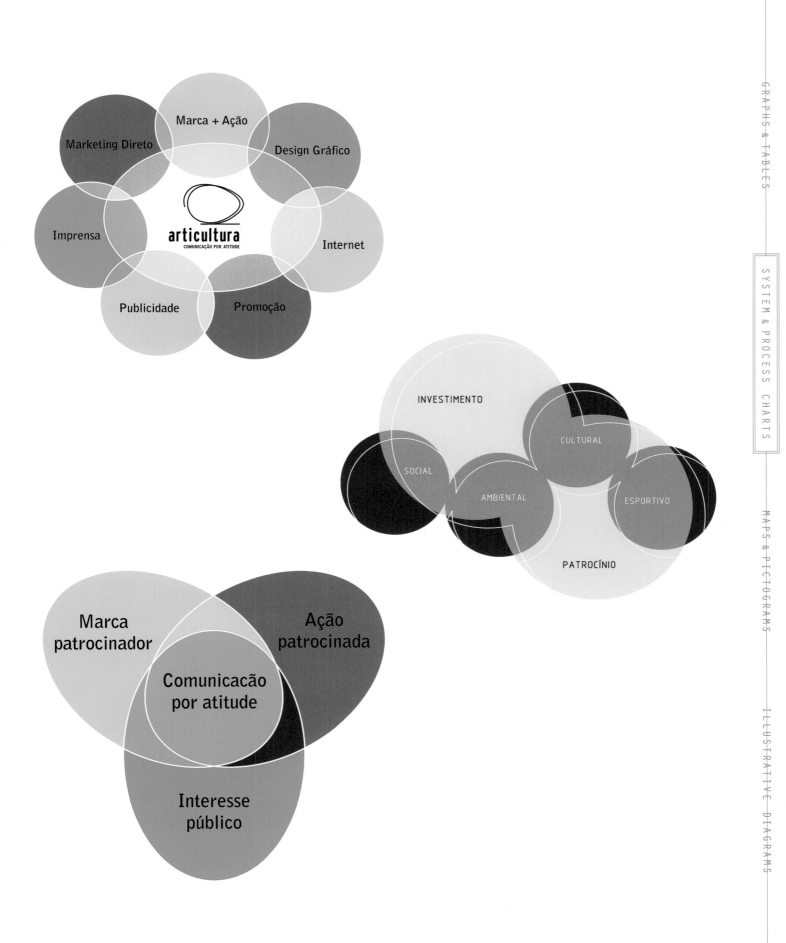

These diagrams highlight the concept of "communication by attitude," as an intersection of cultural events, sports sponsorship, social responsibility actions, and etc.

文化イベント、スポーツ・スポンサーシップ、社会的責任行動などを包括する、「態度によるコミュニケーション」というコンセプトを表すダイアグラム。

Brazil 2003
AD: Rico Lins   D: Marina Siqueira / Marina Oruê   DF, S: Rico Lins + Studio   CL: Articultura Comunicação Por Atitude

A periodic table of the elements expressed with triangles.

元素の周期表を三角形で表現。

Japan 2000

CD, AD, D, S: Tetsuya Ota   CL: Sanseido Publishing Co.,Ltd.

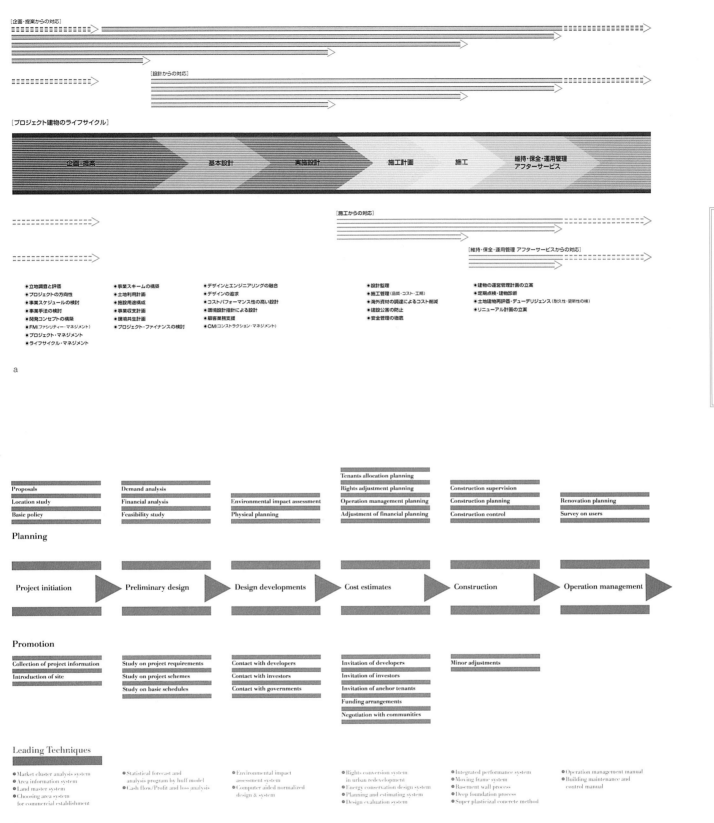

Lifecycle of a building expressed as single flow. (a)
Visualization of workflow using bars, typography and color only. (b)

プロジェクト建物のライフサイクルを一つのフローとして表現。 (a)
仕事の流れをバーとタイポグラフィと色のみで表現。 (b)

Japan 1999
CD, AD, D, S: Tetsuya Ota CL: Takenaka Corporation

近未来へのビジョン。

ビジネスチャンスとして。
2000年3月、電気事業法の改正により、
お客さまが電力の購入先を自由に選ぶことができる
「電力小売りの部分自由化」がスタートしました。
現在は、対象となるお客さまを、大規模なビルや
工場などの大口需給者に限定する部分的な自由化ですが、
将来的にはさらなる自由化が検討されています。
従来の常識からは考えられない
売買のしくみができる可能性があり、
今後ますます、熾烈な競争市場となることは必至です。
沖縄電力では、経営の効率化を推進する一方、
これを大きなビジネスチャンスと捉え、
新しいプランに乗り出しました。

総合産業企業をめざして。
今回の改正では兼業規制が廃止され、電気事業者の
事業多角化が可能となりました。沖縄電力は、
電気事業以外の新規事業を積極的に拡大していく方針です。
情報処理や情報提供サービスおよびIT関連事業、ホテルや
マリンレジャー施設などの経営に関する観光関連事業、
エネルギー利用と環境の調査・コンサルティング事業など、
その他さまざまな事業展開を図っていきます。
新規事業の展開にあたっては、株主や地域社会から
コンセンサスを得られる事業であり、かつ直接、間接的に
電気事業と県内産業の発達に寄与するとともに、
お客さまへのサービスの充実・拡大をもたらす
事業でなくてはならないと考えています。
現在は、IT関連事業と観光関連事業の計画が進行中です。
将来的には、電力事業を全事業の6〜7割で保持し、
多角化事業を3〜4割まで拡大する方向で進めています。
沖縄電力がめざしているのは、電気という
エネルギーを軸とした総合産業企業なのです。

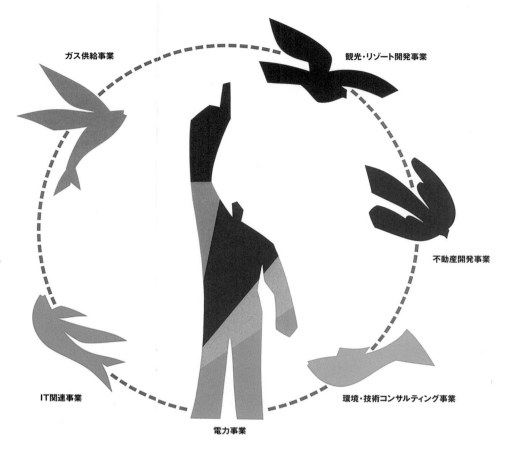

ガス供給事業

観光・リゾート開発事業

不動産開発事業

環境・技術コンサルティング事業

電力事業

IT関連事業

4

5

a

沖縄電力
The Okinawa Electric Power Company 2003

Capability charts expressing a vision of the near future. (a)
Illustration explaining the flow of electricity. (b)
Chart system explaining educational training. (c)

近未来のビジョンを表す機能チャート。 (a)
電気の流れをイラストレーションで解説。 (b)
教育研修を解説するチャート。 (c)

Japan   2003
CD, AD, D, S: Tetsuya Ota   I: Zenji Funabashi (a)   CL: Okinawa Electric Power Company

お客さまと電気をつなぐ、無限のパワーたち。

いつでもどこでもお客さまの家庭や職場などに電力を供給できるよう、沖縄電力の様々なセクションは日夜動き続けています。燃料の調達から、定期的なメンテナンス、万一のトラブルへの備え、より環境にやさしい新エネルギーの開発、窓口でのサービスなども、多種多様な業務のほんの一部です。
私たちは、安全で効率的かつ安定的に電力をお届けするために、互いに協力をおしまず、そして刺激しあって、ひとりひとりの個性と無限に広がる可能性を磨きつつ高めていきたいと考えています。
そして、より豊かな「ふるさと沖縄」を創るため、みんなの「おきでんパワー」をいかんなく発揮していきます。

電力輸送の動脈

自然災害で片方の送電がストップしても、もう一方から供給することで停電を未然に防ごうと二つの輸送ルートを確保し、送電線のループ化を図っています。

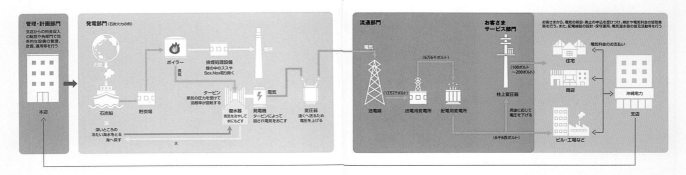

管理・計画部門
支店からの料金収入の総括や各部門で効率的な設備の管理、計画、運用等を行う

本店

発電部門（石炭火力の例）

石炭　石炭船　貯炭場

ボイラー

排煙処理設備
煙の中のススや
Sox,Noxを取り除く

煙突

蒸気

タービン
蒸気の圧力を受けて
羽根車が回転する

復水器
蒸気を冷やして
水にもどす

発電機
タービンによって
回され電気をおこす

変圧器
遠くへ送るため
電圧を上げる

電気

深いところの
冷たい海水をとる
海へ戻す　　水

流通部門

電気

送電線

（13万2千ボルト）

送電用変電所

配電用変電所

（6万6千ボルト）

**お客さま
サービス部門**

柱上変圧器

（100ボルト
〜200ボルト）

用途に応じて
電圧を下げる

（6千6百ボルト）

お客さまから、電気の新設・廃止の申込を受けつけ、検針や電気料金の受取業務を行う。また、配電線路の設計・保守運用、電気温水器の普及活動等を行う

電気料金のお支払い

住宅

商店

ビル・工場など

沖縄電力

支店

石炭運搬船

外国から輸入されてきた石炭は、揚炭機によって陸揚げされ、ベルトコンベヤで屋内貯炭場、石炭バンカへと運ばれます。最後に微粉炭機で粉末にされ、ボイラーに吹き込まれて燃やされます。

蒸気タービン発電機

ボイラーでつくられた高温、高圧の蒸気はタービンを回転させ、同軸の発電機をまわして電気を発生させます。

給電指令所

発電所の熱効率の向上と発電から配電に至る電力系統の最適経済負荷配分による効率的な運用に努めています。

b

階層別研修

管理職研修

新任特管職研修

新任係長研修

新任主任研修

新任主務II研修

新入社員研修

部門別研修

各種資格取得研修

技術系研修

事務系研修

特別教育

その他研修
語学研修・パソコン教室
通信教育・講演会
その他研修

派遣研修
県内外派遣研修
海外留学研修
海外派遣研修
社外セミナー

年代別研修（人生設計研修）

c

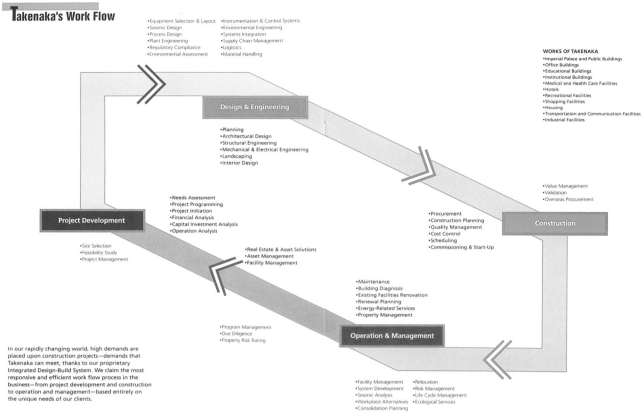

Takenaka's Work Flow

•Equipment Selection & Layout
•Seismic Design
•Process Design
•Plant Engineering
•Regulatory Compliance
•Environmental Assessment

•Instrumentation & Control Systems
•Environmental Engineering
•Systems Integration
•Supply Chain Management
•Logistics
•Material Handling

WORKS OF TAKENAKA
•Imperial Palace and Public Buildings
•Office Buildings
•Educational Buildings
•Institutional Buildings
•Medical and Health Care Facilities
•Hotels
•Recreational Facilities
•Shopping Facilities
•Housing
•Transportation and Communication Facilities
•Industrial Facilities

Design & Engineering

•Planning
•Architectural Design
•Structural Engineering
•Mechanical & Electrical Engineering
•Landscaping
•Interior Design

•Needs Assessment
•Project Programming
•Project Initiation
•Financial Analysis
•Capital Investment Analysis
•Operation Analysis

Project Development

•Site Selection
•Feasibility Study
•Project Management

•Value Management
•Validation
•Overseas Procurement

•Procurement
•Construction Planning
•Quality Management
•Cost Control
•Scheduling
•Commissioning & Start-Up

Construction

•Real Estate & Asset Solutions
•Asset Management
•Facility Management

•Maintenance
•Building Diagnosis
•Existing Facilities Renovation
•Renewal Planning
•Energy-Related Services
•Property Management

•Program Management
•Due Diligence
•Property Risk Rating

Operation & Management

In our rapidly changing world, high demands are
placed upon construction projects—demands that
Takenaka can meet, thanks to our proprietary
Integrated Design-Build System. We claim the most
responsive and efficient work flow process in the
business—from project development and construction
to operation and management—based entirely on
the unique needs of our clients.

•Facility Management
•System Development
•Seismic Analysis
•Workplace Alternatives
•Consolidation Planning

•Relocation
•Risk Management
•Life Cycle Management
•Ecological Services

10 ———   ——— 11

a

Flow chart expressing work process. (a)
Section chart representing an organization. (b)

仕事の流れを表すフローチャート。 (a)
組織を表す区分図。 (b)

Japan 2003
CD, AD, D, S: Tetsuya Ota   CL: Takenaka Corporation

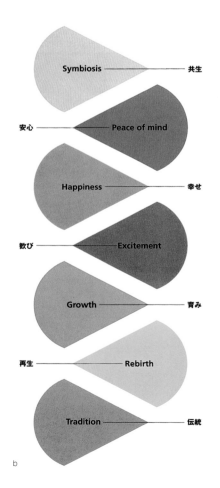

Symbiosis ——— 共生

安心 ——— Peace of mind

Happiness ——— 幸せ

歓び ——— Excitement

Growth ——— 育み

再生 ——— Rebirth

Tradition ——— 伝統

b

Opened in 1994 as Japan's first full-scale 24-hour airport, it provides direct flights to 30 countries and regions and 66 cities. One-day business trips to major Asian cities are now possible for busy businesspeople. The construction of the second 4,000-meter runway is slated for completion by 2007.

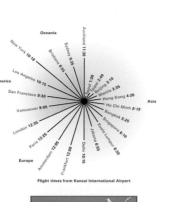

Oceania

Auckland 11:30
New York 16:18
Sydney 8:35
Brisbane 8:55
Seoul 1:30
Taipei 2:40
Beijing 3:10
Los Angeles 10:15
Manila 3:35
North America
San Francisco 9:30
Hong Kong 4:20
Ho Chi Minh 5:15
Vancouver 9:05
Bangkok 5:25
Asia
Singapore 6:10
Kuala Lumpur 6:30
London 12:35
Delhi 10:15
Jakarta 6:55
Paris 12:25
Amsterdam 12:05
Frankfurt 12:00
Europe

Flight times from Kansai International Airport

Population **8.8** million

Area **1,893** km²

OSAKA

Business establishments **533,566**

Employees **5,220,923**

Factory **34,910**

Gross Prefectural Product US$ **331,755** million

Manufacturing Output US$ **172,325** million

Foreign trade Imports US$ **39,473** million

Exports US$ **37,664** million

Reference Date
1US$= 122.07 (1997)

OSAKA is the crossing point of major transportation systems and expressways spreading in all directions. Two key airports provide air transportation to many domestic and overseas points. They form a distribution network with Osaka and Sakai-Semboku international trade ports.

1:55 Sapporo
1:00 Tokyo 2:30
Nagoya 0:52
Osaka
Hiroshima 1:14
1:05 Fukuoka 2:17
2:00 Naha
By Airplane (Time)
By JR Shinkansen (Time)

Access Time to Major Cities in Japan

大阪府

Osaka, a strategic base
for international business,
is an ideal metropolis for
corporate activities.

●SAKA

Diagrams used in a pamphlet to attract foreign business to Osaka showing the population and area of the city,
flight times from Osaka to overseas destinations and travel times to other Japanese cities.

大阪への海外企業誘致のためのパンフレットに使用されたダイアグラム。大阪の人口と平面積、大阪から各国へのフライト時間、日本国内各都市への所要時間などを示している。

Japan 2000
AD: Shinnoske Sugisaki   D: Chiaki Okuno / Reika Kusaka   DF, S: Shinnosuke Inc.   CL: Osaka Prefecture

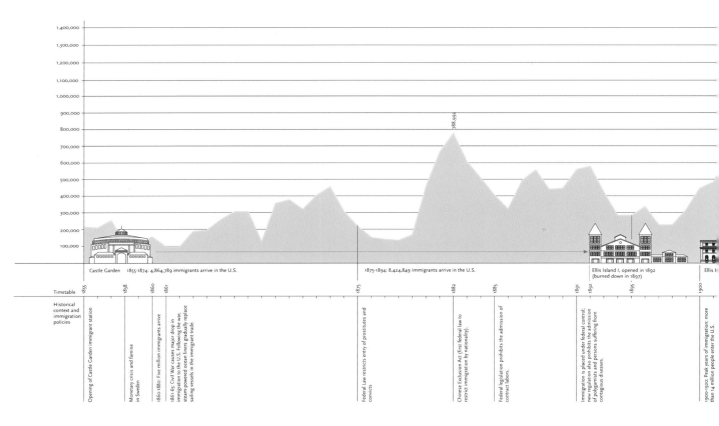

Graphic representation plotting the historical development of immigration to the U.S. (1855-1954) with peaks and troughs following political movements.

アメリカへの移民の歴史（1855年〜1954年）を、政局の動向に伴う人数の増減とともに示したグラフィック。

Germany   2002
D, I: Lisa Nieschlag   DF, S: Nieschlag + Wentrup

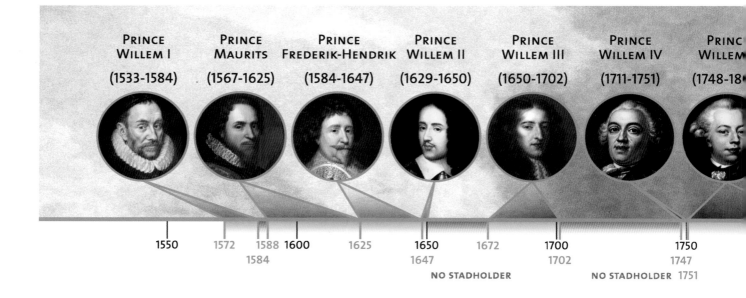

A chronological table of the sovereigns of the Netherlands.

歴代のオランダ君主を紹介する年表。

Netherlands   2004
CD: Paul Vermijs   D: Toon Tesser   DF, S: TelDesign   CL: Ministry Of Foreign Affairs

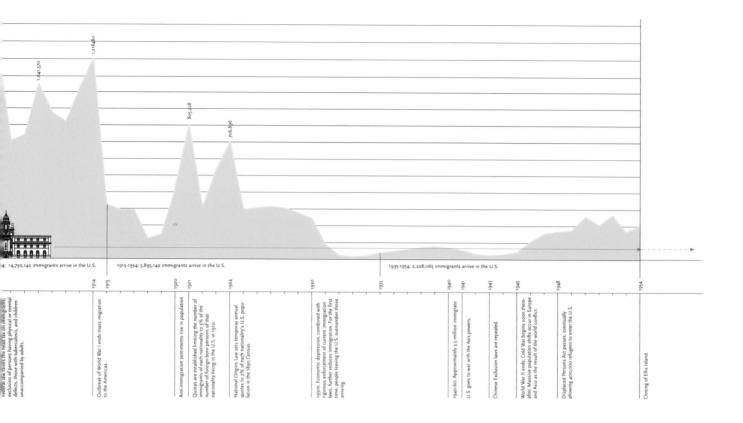

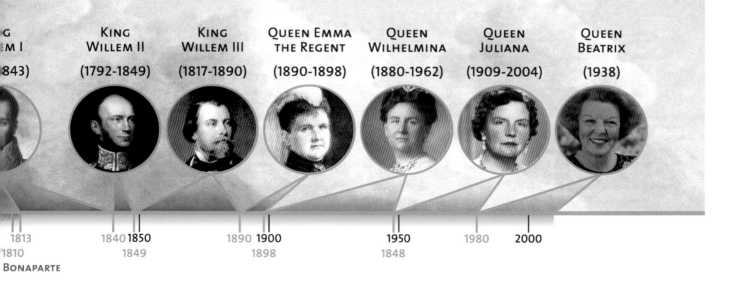

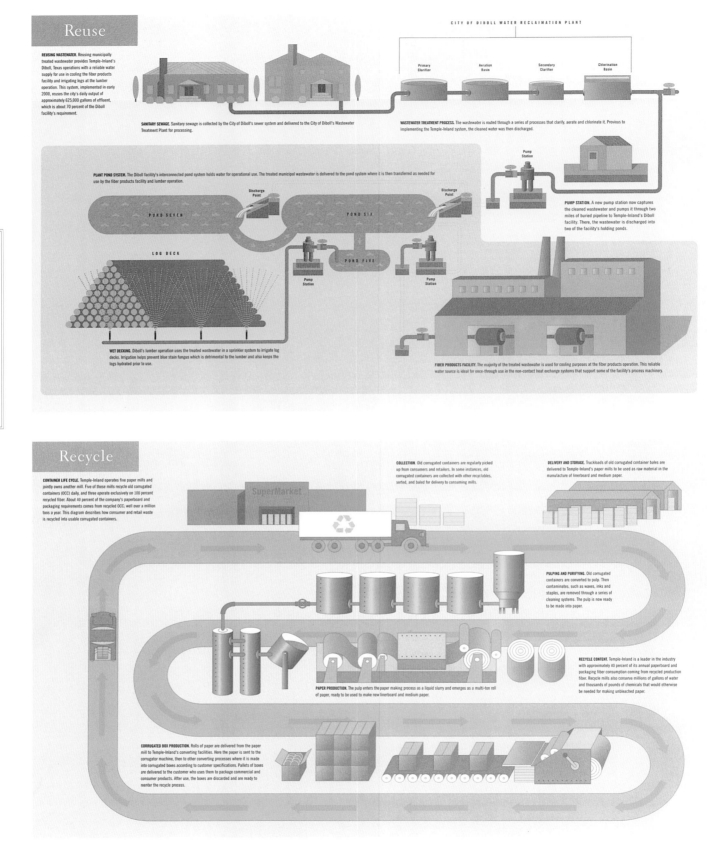

A step-by-step introduction to Temple-Inland's enviromentally friendly philosophy and process.

Temple-Inland社の環境に配慮した理念とプロセスを順を追って紹介する図。

USA 2000

AD, D, I, CW: Rex Peteet   D, I: Carrie Echo / Kristianne Kossler   P: Jay Brittain   CW: Carla Kienast   DF, S: Sibley Peteet   CL: Temple-Inland

Reclaim

HOW SYNTHETIC GYPSUM IS FORMED at the Tennessee Valley Authority's (TVA) Cumberland Fossil Power Plant. Using flue gases to make synthetic gypsum annually reclaims over one million tons of material that would have been added to the landfill.

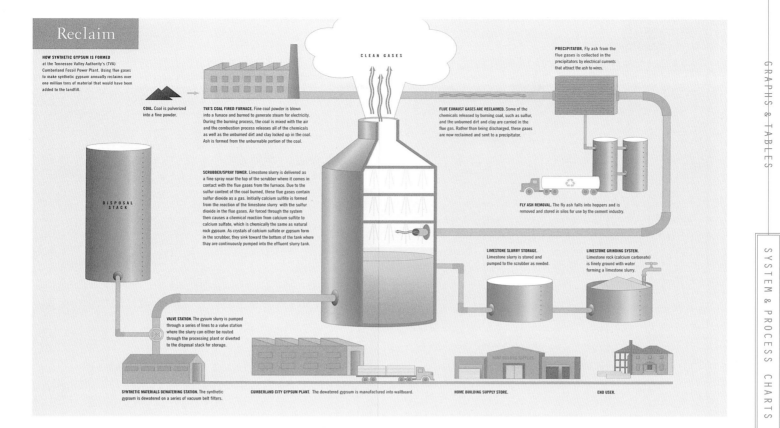

CLEAN GASES

PRECIPITATOR. Fly ash from the flue gases is collected in the precipitators by electrical currents that attract the ash to wires.

COAL. Coal is pulverized into a fine powder.

TVA'S COAL FIRED FURNACE. Fine coal powder is blown into a funace and burned to generate steam for electricity. During the burning process, the coal is mixed with the air and the combustion process releases all of the chemicals as well as the unburned dirt and clay locked up in the coal. Ash is formed from the unburnable portion of the coal.

FLUE EXHAUST GASES ARE RECLAIMED. Some of the chemicals released by burning coal, such as sulfur, and the unburned dirt and clay are carried in the flue gas. Rather than being discharged, these gases are now reclaimed and sent to a precipitator.

SCRUBBER/SPRAY TOWER. Limestone slurry is delivered as a fine spray near the top of the scrubber where it comes in contact with the flue gases from the furnace. Due to the sulfur content of the coal burned, these flue gases contain sulfur dioxide as a gas. Initially calcium sulfite is formed from the reaction of the limestone slurry with the sulfur dioxide in the flue gases. Air forced through the system then causes a chemical reaction from calcium sulfite to calcium sulfate, which is chemically the same as natural rock gypsum. As crystals of calcium sulfate or gypsum form in the scrubber, they sink toward the bottom of the tank where they are continuously pumped into the effluent slurry tank.

FLY ASH REMOVAL. The fly ash falls into hoppers and is removed and stored in silos for use by the cement industry.

DISPOSAL STACK

LIMESTONE SLURRY STORAGE. Limestone slurry is stored and pumped to the scrubber as needed.

LIMESTONE GRINDING SYSTEM. Limestone rock (calcium carbonate) is finely ground with water forming a limestone slurry.

VALVE STATION. The gysum slurry is pumped through a series of lines to a valve station where the slurry can either be routed through the processing plant or diverted to the disposal stack for storage.

SYNTHETIC MATERIALS DEWATERING STATION. The synthetic gypsum is dewatered on a series of vacuum belt filters.

CUMBERLAND CITY GYPSUM PLANT. The dewatered gypsum is manufactured into wallboard.

HOME BUILDING SUPPLY STORE.

END USER.

Renew

RENEWABLE FOREST. Temple-Inland's extensive 2.2 million acres of forest holdings are invaluable. They are an important, integral part of America's landscape and an essential, renewable fiber source. Temple-Inland has a century-old commitment to nurture, protect and renew this resource and also to conserve it by utilizing each harvested tree to its fullest potential. Through creative solutions developed over the years, Temple-Inland has implemented ways to use 98 percent of each sawlog. This not only conserves the existing resources, but also helps protect the environment by dramatically reducing the amount of waste produced.

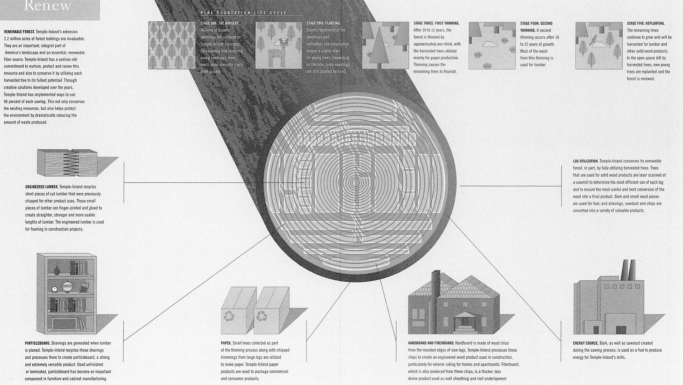

PINE PLANTATION LIFE CYCLE

STAGE ONE: THE NURSERY. Millions of superior seedlings are nurtured in Temple-Inland's nursery. By assisting and nurturing young seedlings, trees reach semi-maturity much more quickly.

STAGE TWO: PLANTING. Careful treatment of the seedlings and individual site preparation ensure a viable start for young trees. Depending on the site, some seedlings are still planted by hand.

STAGE THREE: FIRST THINNING. After 10 to 12 years, the forest is thinned by approximately one-third, with the harvested trees utilized mainly for paper production. Thinning causes the remaining trees to flourish.

STAGE FOUR: SECOND THINNING. A second thinning occurs after 18 to 22 years of growth. Most of the wood from this thinning is used for lumber.

STAGE FIVE: REPLANTING. The remaining trees continue to grow and will be harvested for lumber and other solid wood products. In the open space left by harvested trees, new young trees are replanted and the forest is renewed.

ENGINEERED LUMBER. Temple-Inland recycles short pieces of cut lumber that were previously chipped for other product uses. These small pieces of lumber are finger-jointed and glued to create straighter, stronger and more usable lengths of lumber. The engineered lumber is used for framing in construction projects.

LOG UTILIZATION. Temple-Inland conserves its renewable forest, in part, by fully utilizing harvested trees. Trees that are used for solid wood products are laser scanned at a sawmill to determine the most efficient use of each log and to ensure the most useful and best conversion of the wood into a final product. Bark and small wood pieces are used for fuel, and shavings, sawdust and chips are converted into a variety of valuable products.

PARTICLEBOARD. Shavings are generated when lumber is planed. Temple-Inland recycles these shavings and processes them to create particleboard, a strong and extremely versatile product. Used unfinished or laminated, particleboard has become an important component in furniture and cabinet manufacturing.

PAPER. Small trees collected as part of the thinning process along with chipped trimmings from large logs are utilized to make paper. Temple-Inland paper products are used to package commercial and consumer products.

HARDBOARD AND FIBERBOARD. Hardboard is made of wood chips from the rounded edges of saw logs. Temple-Inland processes these chips to create an engineered wood product used in construction, particularly for exterior siding for homes and apartments. Fiberboard, which is also produced from these chips, is a thicker, less dense product used as wall sheathing and roof underlayment.

ENERGY SOURCE. Bark, as well as sawdust created during the sawing process, is used as a fuel to produce energy for Temple-Inland's mills.

Productive Presentation

Our primary operation is food, which consists of divisions for flour milling, vegetable oils, cornstarch and corn sweeteners, household foods and frozen foods. The food operations involve producing and selling a wide range of products for commercial and household use. The products, made from grains such as wheat, soybeans and corn, are a part of people's diet in a variety of forms.

We also makes good use of the by-products generated in the processing of these grains by producing and selling mixed animal feed. The animal feed operation also includes producing and selling eggs.

Other operations include warehousing business for grains and real-estate leasing business for effective use of real estates.

BUSINESS DEVELOPMENT

Showa Sangyo Group　　Others

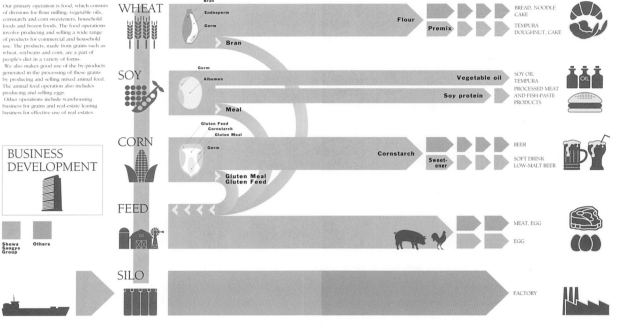

WHEAT

Bran
Endosperm
Germ

Bran

Flour

Premix

BREAD, NOODLE CAKE

TEMPURA DOUGHNUT, CAKE

SOY

Germ
Albumen

Meal

Vegetable oil

Soy protein

SOY OIL
TEMPURA
PROCESSED MEAT AND FISH-PASTE PRODUCTS

CORN

Gluten Feed
Cornstarch
Gluten Meal
Germ

Gluten Meal
Gluten Feed

Cornstarch

Sweet-ener

BEER

SOFT DRINK
LOW-MALT BEER

FEED

MEAT, EGG

EGG

SILO

FACTORY

6

7

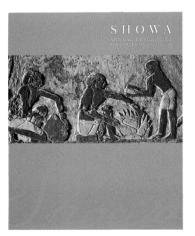

Easy to understand charting of the process from whole grains to products.

穀物から最終的なプロダクツに至るまでのプロセスを分かりやすくチャート化。

Japan　2002

DF: Interlux, Inc.　　CL: Showa Sangyo Co., Ltd.　　S: Nomura Investor Relations Co., Ltd.

Market strategy Ericsson is a business-to-business telecommunications supplier. We sell systems, services and technology to operators and service providers in 140 countries. We also create revenue through our licensed solutions and intellectual property rights. And we sell handsets to operators and retailers through Sony Ericsson.

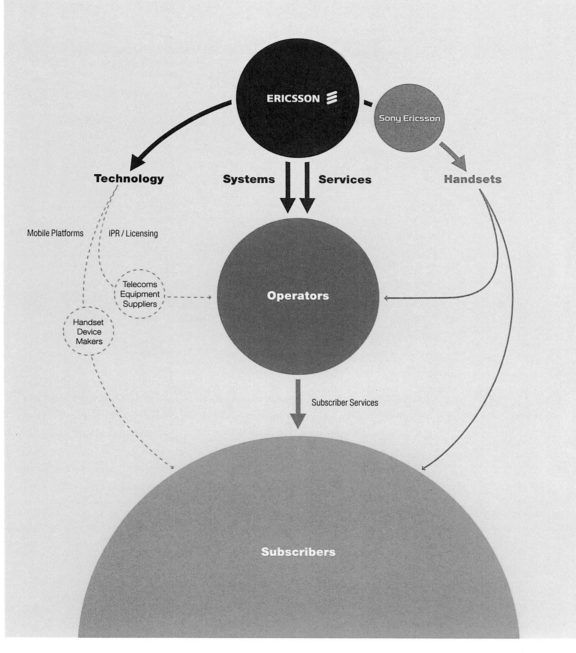

10 Ericsson 2002 Our Strategy

Diagrams Illustrating Ericsson's market strategy and customer service.

Ericsson社のマーケット戦略や顧客サービスを表すダイアグラム。

UK 2002
CD, AD, D, I: Gilmar Wendt   CD: David Stocks   P: Stefan Almers / Alexander farnsworth / Lee Mawdsley
CW: Tim Rich / Leonard Rau   DF, S: SAS   CL: Ericsson

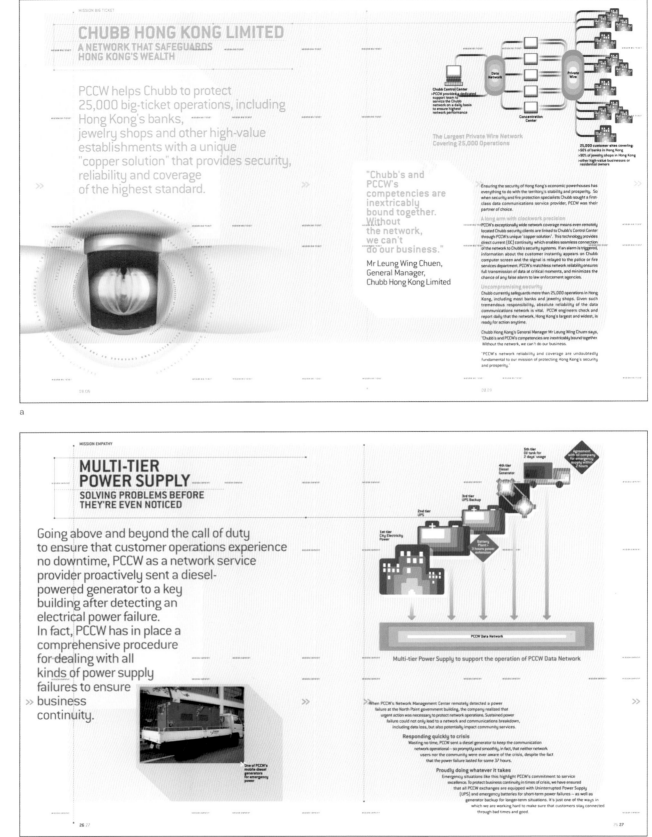

Illustrations indicate seamless network connections to security systems. (a)
Illustrations showing a comprehensive procedure for dealing with power supply failures to ensure network connections. (b)

セキュリティ・システムへの途切れのないネットワーク接続を示す図。(a)
電力供給が遮断されてもネットワーク接続を保証する包括的な手順を説明する図。(b)

China 2004
CD: Eric Chan   AD, D: Francis Lee   DF, S: Eric Chan Design Co., Ltd.   CL: PCCW

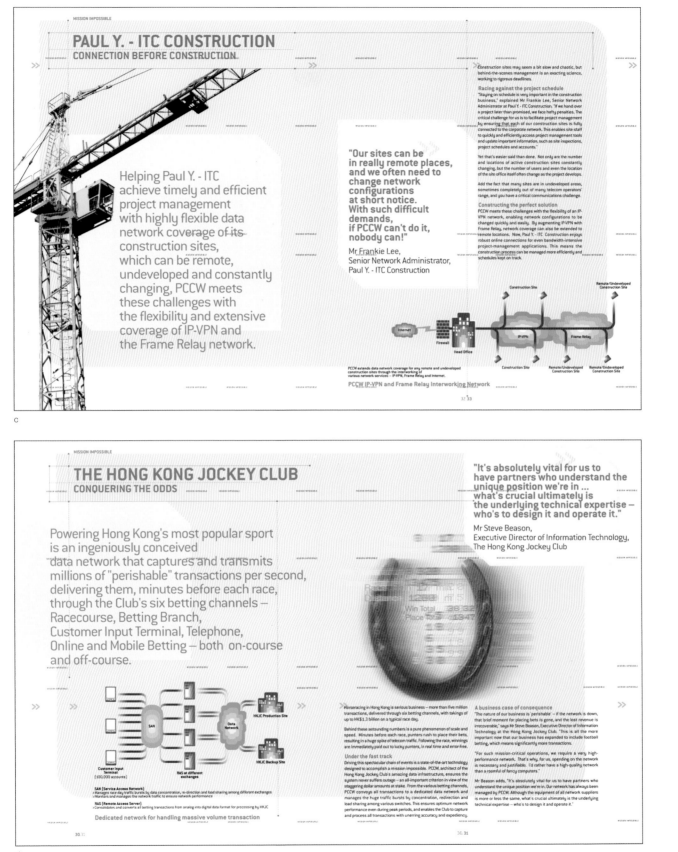

Illustrations explain the construction company's computer network extended to remote locations. (c)
Horseracing is an important business transaction in Hong Kong. Illustrations showing the Hong Kong Jockey Club's data infrastructure. (d)

遠隔地にまでおよぶ建設会社のコンピュータ・ネットワークを説明する図。(c)
競馬は香港で重要なビジネスである。図は香港ジョッキー・クラブのデータ・インフラストラクチャを表している。 (d)

図05 | 自動車に使われている高張力鋼板・高強度部材

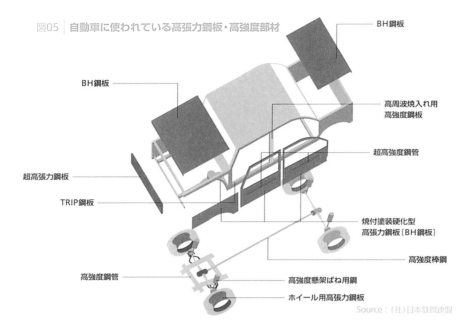

BH鋼板

BH鋼板

高周波焼入れ用
高強度鋼板

超高強度鋼管

超高張力鋼板

TRIP鋼板

焼付塗装硬化型
高張力鋼板［BH鋼板］

高強度棒鋼

高強度鋼管

高強度懸架ばね用鋼

ホイール用高張力鋼板

Source：（社）日本鉄鋼連盟

図06 | 燃料電池の発電原理
Source：日本ガス協会

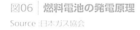
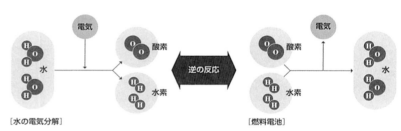

電気

水

酸素

水素

逆の反応

酸素

水素

電気

水

［水の電気分解］

［燃料電池］

図07 | 廃プラスチック再資源化

プラスチックの主成分は石炭と同じ炭素と水素です。そのために石炭の替わりに廃プラスチックを使うことができます。これによって、廃プラスチックは燃料ガスとして活用されたり、新しいプラスチックの原料に生まれ変わります。また、工程の途中で発生する水素ガスは未来のエネルギーとして期待されています。

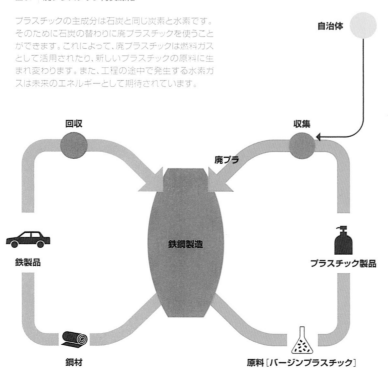

自治体

回収

収集

廃プラ

鉄鋼製造

鉄製品

プラスチック製品

鋼材

原料［バージンプラスチック］

From a pamphlet on global warming.
38 key words defined using easy-to-understand comments
and illustrations.

地球温暖化に関するパンフレットより。
38のキーワードを分かりやすい解説と図で説明。

Japan   2004
CD: Reiji Oshima   AD: Kenzo Nakagawa
D: Satoshi Morikami / Infogram   I: Kumiko Nagasaki
CW: Yasuko Seki   DF, S: NDC Graphics Inc.
CL: The Japan Iron and Steel Federation

DocGenerator's automated process

1. 2. 3. 4. 5. 6. 7.

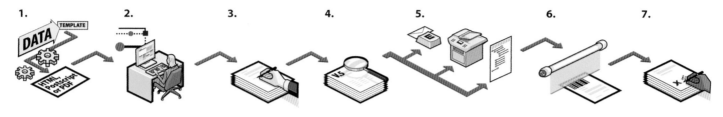

Illustrations showing the process of the web-based solution for automated document management.
自動書類管理のためのウェブ基盤のソリューション・プロセスを説明する図表。

USA 2004
CD: Mark Allen   AD: Nigel Walker   D: Erica Heitman   I: Elan Harris   CW: Tamera Adams   DF, S: That's Nice Llc   CL: Scrittura

Sony style PlayStation, introduced more than a decade ago, has become Sony's
all-time bestseller. Airboard, a wireless TV, will roll out in the U.S. this year.

*Purchased for $2 billion. **Purchased for $5 billion. Sources: Bloomberg, Sony

Timeline of Sony's achievements.
ソニーの業績を示す年表。

USA 2004
AD: Carol Macrini   D, I, S: Eliot Bergman   CL: Bloomberg Markets Magazine

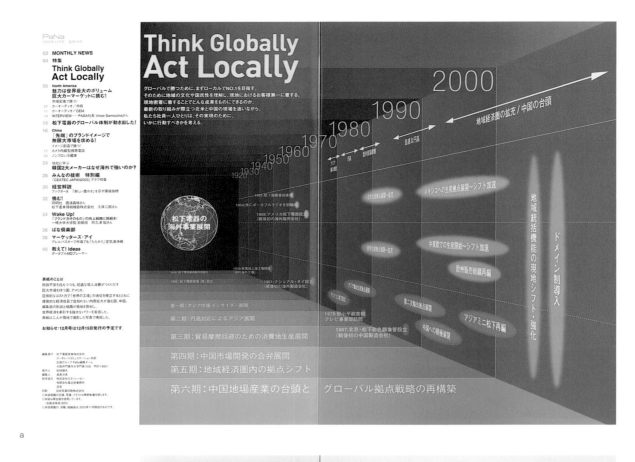

a

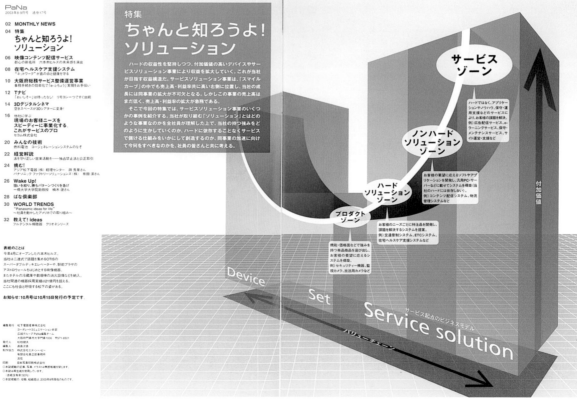

b

A chart showing foreign-operations deployment of Matsushita Electric Industrial Co., Ltd. (a)
A chart showing position of the service solution business. (b)

松下電器産業の海外事業展開を表すチャート。 (a)
サービスソリューション事業の位置を表すチャート。 (b)

Japan 2003
AD: Shinnoske Sugisaki   D: Jun Itadani / Shinsuke Suzuki   DF, S: Shinnoske Inc.   CL: Matsushita Electric Industrial Co., Ltd.

A diagram showing the drug discovery process of
BioNumerik Pharmaceuticals, Inc.

製薬会社、BioNumerik Pharmaceuticals社の創薬プロセスを表す図。

USA   2000
CD, AD, D: Wing Chan   I: Jared Schneidman (JSD)
DF, S: Wing Chan Design, Inc.   CL: BioNumgrik Pharmacauticats, Inc.

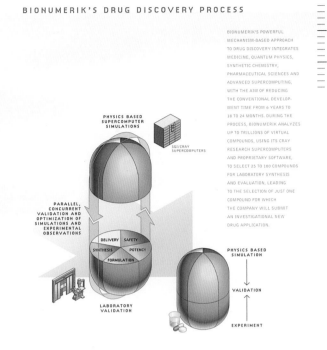

BIONUMERIK'S DRUG DISCOVERY PROCESS

BIONUMERIK'S POWERFUL MECHANISM-BASED APPROACH TO DRUG DISCOVERY INTEGRATES MEDICINE, QUANTUM PHYSICS, SYNTHETIC CHEMISTRY, PHARMACEUTICAL SCIENCES AND ADVANCED SUPERCOMPUTING, WITH THE AIM OF REDUCING THE CONVENTIONAL DEVELOPMENT TIME FROM 6 YEARS TO 18 TO 24 MONTHS. DURING THE PROCESS, BIONUMERIK ANALYZES UP TO TRILLIONS OF VIRTUAL COMPOUNDS, USING ITS CRAY RESEARCH SUPERCOMPUTERS AND PROPRIETARY SOFTWARE, TO SELECT 25 TO 100 COMPOUNDS FOR LABORATORY SYNTHESIS AND EVALUATION, LEADING TO THE SELECTION OF JUST ONE COMPOUND FOR WHICH THE COMPANY WILL SUBMIT AN INVESTIGATIONAL NEW DRUG APPLICATION.

integrating disciplines

お客さまの満足度向上と裾野拡大

日立ソフトウェア エンジニアリング   日本IBM   SAPジャパン
マイクロソフト   日本ヒューレット・パッカード
ビジネス領域の拡大   信頼性・生産性の向上   競争力の強化

豊富な実績と業務への精通
信頼性
経済性   発展性
強力なパートナーとのアライアンス
WebRings
メインフレームからオープンシステムへ

a   b

Projected effects of partnerships and alliances with INES. (a)
Three feautures of a software product reflecting the strengths of INES. (b)

アイネス社の提携先とアライアンスによって期待できる効果。 (a)
アイネス社の強みが凝縮されたソフトウェア製品の3つの特長。 (b)

Japan   2003
Producer: Akiyo Yamamoto   AD: Yukichi Asahara (Asahara Design Company)   D: Yuka suzuki (Asahara Design Company)
DF: Asahara Design Company   CL: INES Corporation   S: Alex-Net Corporation

‹Backup›

GRAPHIC SANDWICH I BY NIGEL HOLMES

Four Flavors of Fast

Cable, DSL, satellite, or wireless. Take your pick of broadband options.

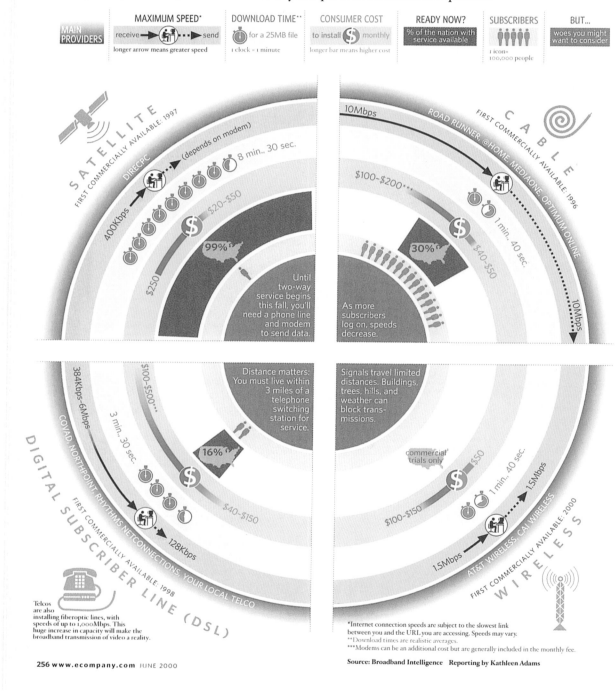

MAIN PROVIDERS

MAXIMUM SPEED*
receive ➜ ➜ send
longer arrow means greater speed

DOWNLOAD TIME**
for a 25MB file
1 clock = 1 minute

CONSUMER COST
to install $ monthly
longer bar means higher cost

READY NOW?
% of the nation with service available

SUBSCRIBERS
1 icon = 100,000 people

BUT...
woes you might want to consider

*Internet connection speeds are subject to the slowest link between you and the URL you are accessing. Speeds may vary.
**Download times are realistic averages.
***Modems can be an additional cost but are generally included in the monthly fee.

Source: Broadband Intelligence   Reporting by Kathleen Adams

Diagrams explaining 4 broad band options: cable, DSL, Satellite, and wireless.

ケーブル、DSL、衛星、ワイヤレスという、4つのブロードバンドの選択肢を説明する図。

USA 2000
CD: Susan Casey   AD: Susan Scandrett   D, I, CW, S: Nigel Holmes   DF: Explanation Graphics   CL: E-Company

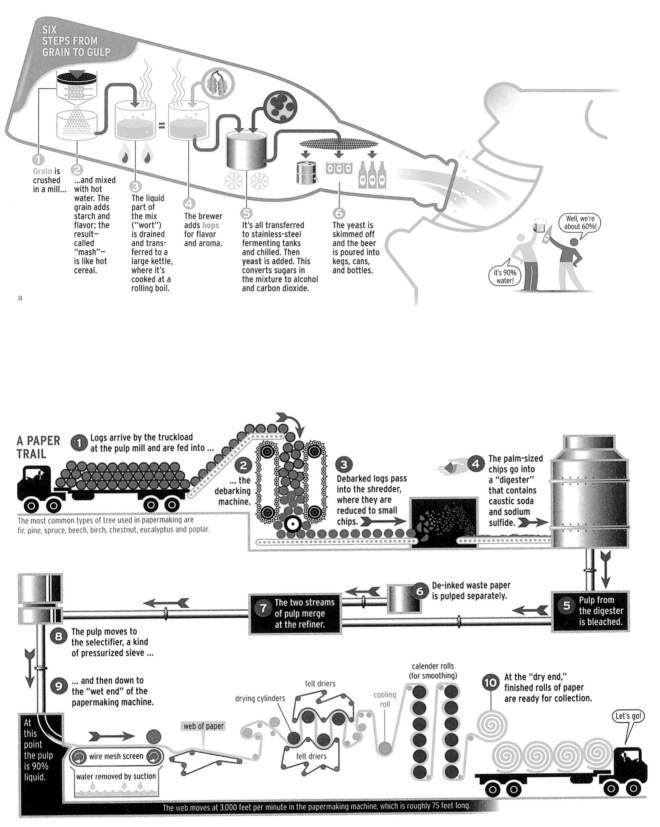

SIX STEPS FROM GRAIN TO GULP

① **Grain** is crushed in a mill...

② ...and mixed with hot water. The grain adds starch and flavor; the result—called "mash"—is like hot cereal.

③ The liquid part of the mix ("wort") is drained and transferred to a large kettle, where it's cooked at a rolling boil.

④ The brewer adds **hops** for flavor and aroma.

⑤ It's all transferred to stainless-steel fermenting tanks and chilled. Then **yeast** is added. This converts sugars in the mixture to alcohol and carbon dioxide.

⑥ The yeast is skimmed off and the beer is poured into kegs, cans, and bottles.

It's 90% water!

Well, we're about 60%!

a

A PAPER TRAIL

① Logs arrive by the truckload at the pulp mill and are fed into ...

The most common types of tree used in papermaking are fir, pine, spruce, beech, birch, chestnut, eucalyptus and poplar.

② ... the debarking machine.

③ Debarked logs pass into the shredder, where they are reduced to small chips.

④ The palm-sized chips go into a "digester" that contains caustic soda and sodium sulfide.

⑤ Pulp from the digester is bleached.

⑥ De-inked waste paper is pulped separately.

⑦ The two streams of pulp merge at the refiner.

⑧ The pulp moves to the selectifier, a kind of pressurized sieve ...

⑨ ... and then down to the "wet end" of the papermaking machine.

At this point the pulp is 90% liquid.

wire mesh screen

water removed by suction

web of paper

drying cylinders

felt driers

felt driers

cooling roll

calender rolls (for smoothing)

⑩ At the "dry end," finished rolls of paper are ready for collection.

Let's go!

The web moves at 3,000 feet per minute in the papermaking machine, which is roughly 75 feet long.

b

Diagram showing the process of beer making. (a)
The process of paper manufacturing. (b)

ビールの製造過程を図解。 (a)
紙ができるまでの過程を図解。 (b)

USA 2001
AD: Holly Holliday   D, I, S: Nigel Holmes   DF: Explanation Graphics   CL: Attaché Magazine

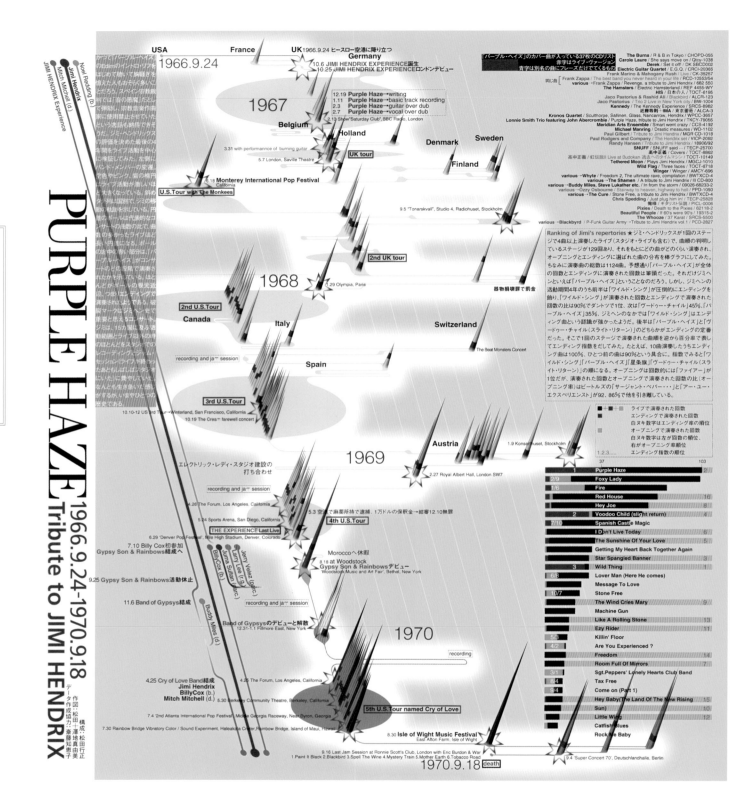

Jimi Hendrix concert history: a tour of Jimi Hendrix concerts centered on the position occupied by "Purple Haze."

ジミ・ヘンドリックス・ライブ史──「パープル・ヘイズ」の占める位置を軸としたジミヘン・コンサートめぐり。

Japan   2000

CD, AD, D, CW, S: Yukimasa Matsuda   I: Mayumi Sawachi   CL: INAX Publishing Co., Ltd.

The BEATLES:GET BACK (回帰点) 1957-1970

ビートルズの結成から解散までの約10年の軌跡——メディア露出、ライブ＆ツアーでの疲弊、ニヒリズムの蔓延と迷走、ソロワーク……

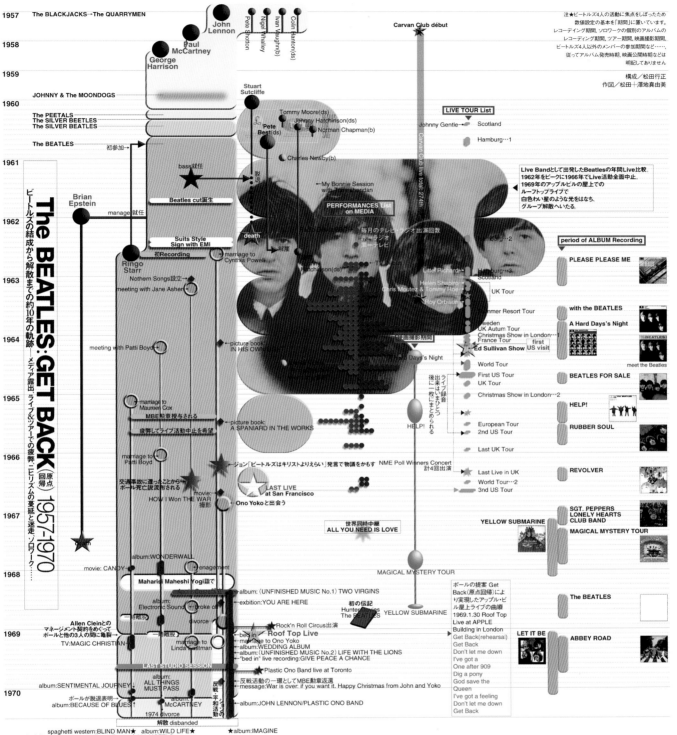

1957	The BLACKJACKS→The QUARRYMEN　　John Lennon　　Pete Shotton　Nigel Whalley　Ivan Vaughn(b)　Colin Hanton(ds)
1958	Paul McCartney
1959	George Harrison
1960	JOHNNY & The MOONDOGS　　Stuart Sutcliffe
	The PEETALS / The SILVER BEETLES / The SILVER BEATLES
	The BEATLES
1961	Brian Epstein
1962	
1963	Ringo Starr
1964	
1965	
1966	
1967	
1968	
1969	
1970	

注★ビートルズ4人の活動に焦点をしぼったため
数値設定の基本を「期間」に置いています。
レコーディング期間、ソロワークの個別のアルバムの
レコーディング期間、ツアー期間、映画撮影期間、
ビートルズ4人以外のメンバーの参加期間など……、
従ってアルバム発売時期、映画公開時期などは
明記してありません

構成／松田行正
作図／松田＋澤地真由美

Carvan Club début

LIVE TOUR List

Johnny Gentle　　Scotland

Hamburg…1

Tommy Moore(ds)　Johnny Hatchinson(ds)
Pete Best(ds)　　Norman Chapman(b)

Charles Newby(b)

bass就任

Beatles cut誕生

manage就任

Suits Style
Sign with EMI

初Recording

Nothern Songs設立→
meeting with Jane Asher→

meeting with Patti Boyd→

marriage to Cynthia Powell

death

→My Bonnie Session
with Tony Sheridan

PERFORMANCES List on MEDIA

毎月のテレビ・ラジオ出演回数
赤＝ラジオ
黒＝テレビ

Johnny Hatchinson(ds)

Littel Richard→
Helen Shapiro→
Chris Moutez & Tommy Roe→
Roy Orbison→

→picture book:
IN HIS OWN...
映画撮影期間
A Hard Days's Night

marriage to Maureen Cox

MBE勲章授与される

疲弊してライブ活動中止を希望

→picture book:
A SPANIARD IN THE WORKS

marriage to Patti Boyd

ジョン「ビートルズはキリストよりえらい」発言で物議をかもす

交通事故に遭ったことから
ポール死亡説流布される

movie:→
HOW I Won THE WAR
撮影

LAST LIVE
at San Francisco

Ono Yokoと出会う

世界同時中継
ALL YOU NEED IS LOVE

album:WONDERWALL

movie: CANDY→

engagement

Maharishi Maheshi Yogi詣で

Apple Corps設立→
album:
Electronic Sound →broke off

→album: (UNFINISHED MUSIC No.1) TWO VIRGINS

別離脱

divorce

→exibition:YOU ARE HERE

→Rock'n Roll Circus出演

Allen Cleinとの
マネージメント契約をめぐって
ポールと他の3人の間に亀裂→

TV:MAGIC CHRISTIAN→

bed in→ Roof Top Live
marriage to Ono Yoko
album:WEDDING ALBUM
album: (UNFINISHED MUSIC No.2) LIFE WITH THE LIONS
"bed in" live recording:GIVE PEACE A CHANCE

marriage to Linda Eastman

LAST STUDIO SESSION

Plastic Ono Band live at Toronto

album:SENTIMENTAL JOURNEY

album:
ALL THINGS
MUST PASS

反戦活動の一環としてMBE勲章返還
message:War is over, if you want it. Happy Christmas from John and Yoko

ポールが脱退表明→
album:BECAUSE OF BLUES！

album:
McCARTNEY

album:JOHN LENNON/PLASTIC ONO BAND

1974 divorce

解散 disbanded

spaghetti western:BLIND MAN★　album:WILD LIFE★　　★album:IMAGINE
psychedelic collage movie by Frank Zappa:★200 MOTELS

Carvan Club live total 274th

Live Bandとして出発したBeatlesの年間Live比較。
1962年をピークに1966年でLive活動全面中止。
1969年のアップルビルの屋上での
ルーフトップライブで
白色わい星のような光をはなち、
グループ解散へいたる。

Hamburg…2

period of ALBUM Recording

Hamburg…3
Scotland

UK Tour

Summer Resort Tour

Sweden
UK Autum Tour
France Tour

Christmas Show in London…1

first US visit
Ed Sullivan Show

World Tour

First US Tour
UK Tour

Christmas Show in London…2

European Tour
2nd US Tour

Last UK Tour

NME Poll Winners Concert
計4回出演

Last Live in UK
World Tour…2
3nd US Tour

ライブ録音
後に1枚にまとめられる

HELP！

MAGICAL MYSTERY TOUR

YELLOW SUBMARINE

period of ALBUM Recording	
PLEASE PLEASE ME	
with the BEATLES	
A Hard Days's Night	meet the Beatles
BEATLES FOR SALE	
HELP!	
RUBBER SOUL	
REVOLVER	
SGT. PEPPERS LONELY HEARTS CLUB BAND	
MAGICAL MYSTERY TOUR	
The BEATLES	
LET IT BE	ABBEY ROAD

初の伝記
Hunter Davies
The BEATLES

ポールの提案 Get
Back(原点回帰)によ
り実現したアップル・ビ
ル屋上ライブの曲順
1969.1.30 Roof Top
Live at APPLE
Building in London
Get Back(rehearsal)
Get Back
Don't let me down
I've got a
One after 909
Dig a pony
God save the
Queen
I've got a feeling
Don't let me down
Get Back

Beatles history: a roughly ten-year history of The Beatles' live concerts comparing number of concerts per year.

ビートルズ史——年間のライブ数比較を軸に展開するライブバンド・ビートルズの約10年の歴史。

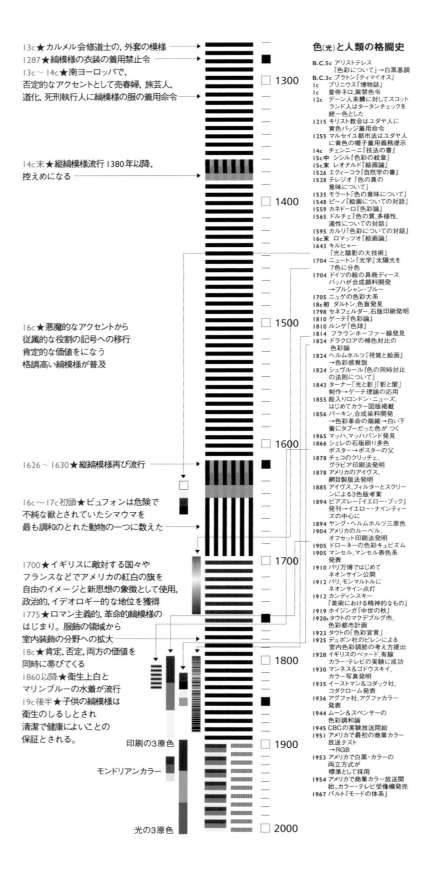

色(光)と人類の格闘史

13c★カルメル会修道士の, 外套の模様

1287★縞模様の衣装の着用禁止令

13c〜14c★南ヨーロッパで,
否定的なアクセントとして売春婦, 旅芸人,
道化, 死刑執行人に縞模様の服の着用命令

14c末★縦縞模様流行 1380年以降,
控えめになる

16c★悪魔的なアクセントから
従属的な役割の記号への移行
肯定的な価値をになう
格調高い縞模様が普及

1626〜1630★縦縞模様再び流行

16c〜17c初頭★ビュフォンは危険で
不純な獣とされていたシマウマを
最も調和のとれた動物の一つに数えた

1700★イギリスに敵対する国々や
フランスなどでアメリカの紅白の旗を
自由のイメージと新思想の象徴として使用,
政治的, イデオロギー的な地位を獲得

1775★ロマン主義的, 革命的縞模様の
はじまり。服飾の領域から
室内装飾の分野への拡大

18c★肯定, 否定, 両方の価値を
同時に帯びてくる

1860以降★衛生上白と
マリンブルーの水着が流行

19c後半★子供の縞模様は
衛生のしるしとされ
清潔で健康によいことの
保証とされる。

印刷の3原色

モンドリアンカラー

光の3原色

B.C.5c アリストテレス
『色彩について』→白黒基調
B.C.3c プラトン『ティマイオス』
1c プリニウス『博物誌』
1c 皇帝ネロ, 紫禁色令
12c デーン人来襲に対してスコット
ランド人はタータンチェックを
統一色とした
1215 キリスト教会はユダヤ人に
黄色バッジ着用命令
1255 マルセイユ都市法はユダヤ人
に黄色の帽子着用義務提示
14c チェンニーニ『技法の書』
15c中 シシル『色彩の紋章』
15c末 レオナルド『絵論』
1526 エクィーコラ『自然学の書』
1528 テレジオ『色の真の
意味について』
1535 モラート『色の意味について』
1548 ピーノ『絵画についての対話』
1559 カネードロ『色彩論』
1565 ドルチェ『色の質, 多様性,
適性についての対話』
1595 カルリ『色彩についての対話』
16c末 ロマッツオ『絵画論』
1643 キルヒャー
『光と陰影の大技術』
1704 ニュートン『光学』太陽光を
7色に分色
1704 ドイツの絵の具商ディース
バッハが合成顔料開発
→プルシャン・ブルー
1705 ニュゲの色彩大系
18c初 ダルトン, 色盲発見
1798 セネフェルダー, 石版印刷発明
1810 ゲーテ『色彩論』
1810 ルンゲ『色球』
1814 フラウンホーファー線発見
1824 ドラクロアの補色対比の
色彩論
1824 ヘルムホルツ『視覚と絵画』
→色彩感覚説
1824 シュヴルール『色の同時対比
の法則について』
1843 ターナー「光と影」「影と闇」
制作→ゲーテ理論の応用
1855 絵入りロンドン・ニューズ,
はじめてカラー図版掲載
1856 パーキン, 合成染料開発
→色彩革命の端緒→白い下
着にタブーだった色がつく
1965 マッハ, マッハバンド発見
1866 シェレの石版刷り多色
ポスター→ポスターの父
1878 チェコのクリッチェ,
グラビア印刷法発明
1878 アメリカのアイヴス,
網目製版法発明
1885 アイヴス, フィルターとスクリー
ンによる3色版考案
1894 ビアズレー『イエロー・ブック』
発刊→イエロー・ナインティー
ズの中心に
1894 ヤング・ヘルムホルツ三原色
1904 アメリカのルーベル,
オフセット印刷法発明
1905 ドローネーの色彩キュビズム
1905 マンセル, マンセル表色系
発表
1910 パリ万博ではじめて
ネオンサイン公開
1912 パリ, モンマルトルに
ネオンサイン点灯
1912 カンディンスキー
『美術における精神的なもの』
1919 ホイジンガ『中世の秋』
1920s タウトのマクデブルグ市,
色彩都市計画
1923 タウトの「色彩宣言」
1925 デュポン社のビレンによる
室内色彩調節の考え方提出
1928 イギリスのベアード, 有線
カラー・テレビの実験に成功
1930 マンネス&ゴドウスキイ,
カラー写真発明
1935 イーストマン&コダック社,
コダクローム発表
1936 アグファ社, アグファカラー
発表
1944 ムーン&スペンサーの
色彩調和論
1945 CBCの実験放送開始
1951 アメリカで最初の商業カラー
放送テスト
→RGB
1953 アメリカで白黒・カラーの
両立方式が
標準として採用
1954 アメリカで商業カラー放送開
始。カラー・テレビ受像機開発
1967 バルト『モードの体系』

1300
1400
1500
1600
1700
1800
1900
2000

The history of stripes, from their role as pattern of discrimination to their counteractive role as a symbol of revolution.

差別のための模様から, その反作用としての革命の模様という両極端の使われ方をしたストライプの歴史。

Japan 1999
CD, AD, D, CW, S: Yukimasa Matsuda   I: Mayumi Sawachi   CL: JT Biohistory Research Hall

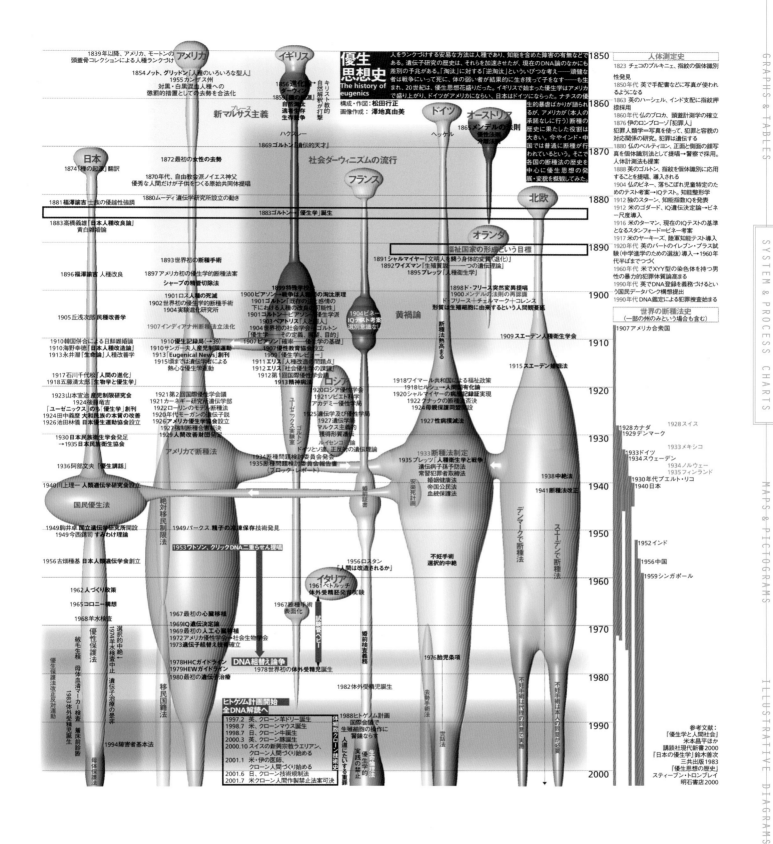

Tracing the history of eugenic thought, the most discriminatory ideology of the 20th century, which seeks identity through race and breed.

優生思想史——20世紀最大の差別思想は人種と血にアイデンティティを求めた優生思想。その断種の歴史を追う。

Japan　2001

CD, AD, D, CW, S: Yukimasa Matsuda　I: Mayumi Sawachi　CL: INAX Publishing Co., Ltd.

Tracing the lives and deaths of the characters appearing in Ridley Scott's "Alien" centering around Ripley and the aliens.

リドリー・スコット監督の映画『エイリアン』のリプリーとエイリアンを中心とした登場人物の生死の軌跡。

Japan 2002
CD, AD, D, CW, S: Yukimasa Matsuda   I: Mayumi Sawachi   CL: INAX Publishing Co., Ltd.

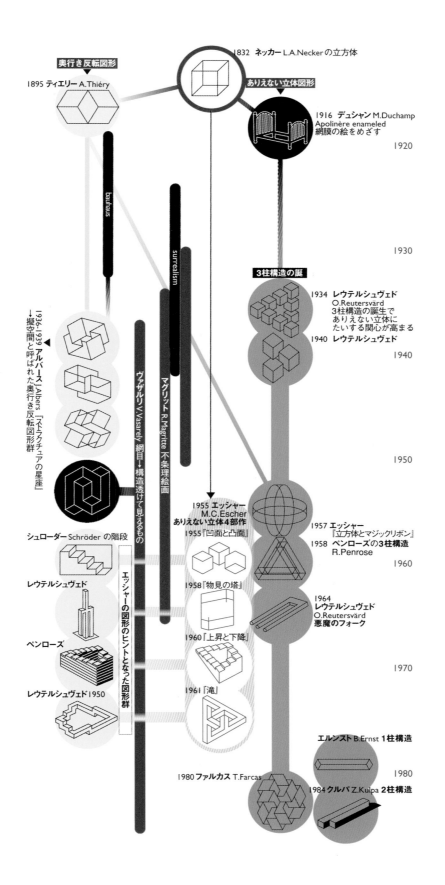

1832 ネッカー L.A.Necker の立方体

奥行き反転図形

1895 ティエリー A.Thiéry

ありえない立体図形

1916 デュシャン M.Duchamp
Apolinère enameled
網膜の絵をめざす

1920

bauhaus

surrealism

1930

3柱構造の誕

1934 レウテルシュヴェド
O.Reutersvärd
3柱構造の誕生で
ありえない立体に
たいする関心が高まる

1940 レウテルシュヴェド

1940

1936-1939 アルバース J.Albers
→擬空間と呼ばれた奥行き反転図形群

『ストラクチュアの星座』

ヴァザルリ V.Vasarely 網目→構造透けて見えるもの

マグリット R.Magritte 不条理絵画

1950

1955 エッシャー
M.C.Escher
ありえない立体4部作

1957 エッシャー
『立方体とマジックリボン』

シュローダー Schröder の階段

1955『凹面と凸面』

1958 ペンローズの3柱構造
R.Penrose

1960

レウテルシュヴェド

1958『物見の塔』

1964 レウテルシュヴェド
O.Reutersvärd
悪魔のフォーク

ペンローズ

1960『上昇と下降』

エッシャーの図形のヒントとなった図形群

1970

レウテルシュヴェド1950

1961『滝』

エルンスト B.Ernst 1柱構造

1980

1980 ファルカス T.Farcas

1984 クルパ Z.Kulpa 2柱構造

The history of two-dimensional expression of "preposterous 3-D form."

平面図形で表された「ありえない立体」の表現の歴史。

Japan   2000
CD, AD, D, CW, S: Yukimasa Matsuda   I: Mayumi Sawachi   CL: JT Biohistory Research Hall

ORIENTE-SE
UMA COPA EM TRÊS TEMPOS

UMA QUESTÃO

A vitória do Rubinho na F-1 é um sinal de que a época é boa para o Brasil levantar troféus ou é a prova de que até Coréia e Turquia podem vencer a Copa do Mundo?

DEPOIS DE

"I KISS YOU"

Mahir Cagri, o turco mais conhecido da internet (www.ikissyou.org), manda sua mensagem aos amigos da seleção

Confira a tabela da primeira fase no site da Folha Online

AMANHÃ
KING KAHN
PODERÁ O VINGADOR MASCARADO SAIR DESTA?

8h30

AMANHÃ

ESTE É O HOMEM

Já que os árbitros também são os grandes destaques (negativos) deste Mundial, é bom saber: quem apita Brasil x Turquia é o Kim. Mas não o Kim coreano, do jogo de estréia na Copa. Dessa vez o apito é do dinamarquês Kim Milton Nielsen, considerado um dos três melhores do mundo. Esse será o seu terceiro jogo neste Mundial. Antes, apitou Alemanha 1 x 1 Irlanda e Bélgica 3 x 2 Rússia. Foi econômico nos cartões: nos dois jogos somados, distribuiu apenas cinco amarelos. O suíço Urs Meier encara a pedreira de apitar Alemanha x Coréia do Sul e terá de enfrentar a desconfiança que ronda os jogos da Coréia, sobretudo depois das vitórias contra Itália e Espanha.

NÃO CONFUNDA: ESTE KIM É O DO "PÉNALTI" NO LUIZÃO

LADRÓN! Jornais espanhóis expressam indignação com a atuação do árbitro Gandhour, que acabou tirando a seleção da Copa; ao lado, os primeiros-ministros Aznar (Espanha) e Berlusconi (Itália) "comentam", no encerramento da reunião da cúpula européia, o desempenho da arbitragem neste Mundial

AMANHÃ
ALEMANHA X CORÉIA DO SUL

O veloz time coreano do mascarado Kim Tae-young vai precisar de todo o apoio da sua fanática torcida para vencer o pragmático time alemão do goleiro Oliver Kahn, conhecido em seu país como "King Kahn" e melhor goleiro da Copa segundo o Júri Folha. Além da total ocupação do estádio de Seul, 7 milhões (3 milhões apenas na capital) de pessoas devem tingir as ruas e praças de vermelho para acompanhar o jogo nos 400 telões espalhados pelo país.

AAAAAHHHHHHHHH

VAI, ALEMANHA! A partir da esq., Clara Bierhoff, Coony Lehmann, Pia Ziege e Claudia Rehmer, que estarão em Seul torcendo pelos respectivos maridos

TABELA

OITAVAS-DE-FINAL		QUARTAS		SEMI		SEMI		QUARTAS		OITAVAS-DE-FINAL	
DINAMARCA	0									ALEMANHA	1
Niigata 15.jun 8h30	X	INGLATERRA						ALEMANHA		Seogwipo 15.jun 8h30	X
INGLATERRA	0	Shizuoka 21.jun 8h30	1	BRASIL		ALEMANHA		Ulsan 21.jun 8h30	1	PARAGUAI	1
BRASIL	2		2							MÉXICO	0
Kobe 17.jun 8h30	X	BRASIL		DOMINGO FINAL Yokohama 8h						Jeonju 17.jun 3h30	X
BÉLGICA	0							EUA		EUA	2
SUÉCIA	1	QUARTA 8h30				AMANHÃ 8h30		ESPANHA		ESPANHA	1*
Oita 16.jun 3h30	X	SENEGAL								Suwon 16.jun 8h30	X
SENEGAL	2*	Osaka 22.jun 8h30		SÁBADO TERCEIRO LUGAR Daegu 8h				ESPANHA	0	IRLANDA	1
JAPÃO	0		X	TURQUIA		CORÉIA		Gwangju 22.jun 3h30	X	CORÉIA	2*
Miyagi 18.jun 3h30	X	TURQUIA	**1						O*	Daejeon 18.jun 8h30	X
TURQUIA	1							CORÉIA		ITÁLIA	1

REGULAMENTO Oitavas-de-final, quartas-de-final, semifinal e final: jogos eliminatórios, empate no tempo normal provoca prorrogação, com morte súbita (quem marcar vence), empate na prorrogação provoca a disputa por pênaltis

* Decidido por pênaltis ** Decidido na morte súbita

DUELO DAS GRIFES

As semifinais marcam dois confrontos entre Nike (Brasil e Coréia) e Adidas (Turquia e Alemanha). As duas fornecedoras vestiram mais da metade das seleções da Copa (dez times para a Adidas e oito para a Nike). A final também pode ser entre as marcas, como foi no Mundial de 1998 entre França e Brasil.

NIKE X ADIDAS

A SELEÇÃO SÓ FOI CAMPEÃ COM A MARCA INGLESA

Brasil | Coréia do Sul | Alemanha | Turquia

1958 Umbro | 1962 Umbro | 1966 Umbro | 1970 Umbro | 1974 Adidas | 1978 Adidas | 1982 Topper | 1986 Topper | 1990 Topper | 1994 Umbro | 1998 Nike | 2002 Nike

VEJA QUEM VESTIU O BRASIL NAS COPAS

OH! DÚVIDA CRUEL... QUEM ENTRA NO LUGAR DO RONALDINHO?

HOJE

Denilson

Ricardinho

Juninho

Kaká

VOU APROVEITAR A FOLGA. ALGUÉM AÍ TEM O TELEFONE DO CABELEIREIRO DO BECKHAM?

5 GOLS: Klose (Alemanha), Ronaldo e Rivaldo (Brasil)
4 GOLS: Tomasson (Dinamarca) e Vieri (Itália)
3 GOLS: Wilmots (Bélgica), Raúl, Morientes (Espanha), Keane (Irlanda), Pauleta (Portugal), Diop (Senegal) e Larsson (Suécia)
2 GOLS: Ballack (Alemanha), Ronaldinho (Brasil), Gómez (Costa Rica), Ahn (Coréia), Hierro (Espanha),

ESTE VAI SER ARTILHEIRO

The task was to inform readers about the past, present and future of the world cup, as well as to entertain them.
The red marks and the handwritten letters assumed the role of the readers.

ワールドカップの過去、現在、未来について読者に伝えると同時に、読者を楽しませることが目的。赤いマークや手書きの文字は読者が書いたという想定。

Brazil 2002
CD, S: Eduardo Asta   CW: José Mariante / Luiz Rivoiro / Lúcio Ribeiro / Rodrigo Bertolotto   CL: Folha de São Paulo

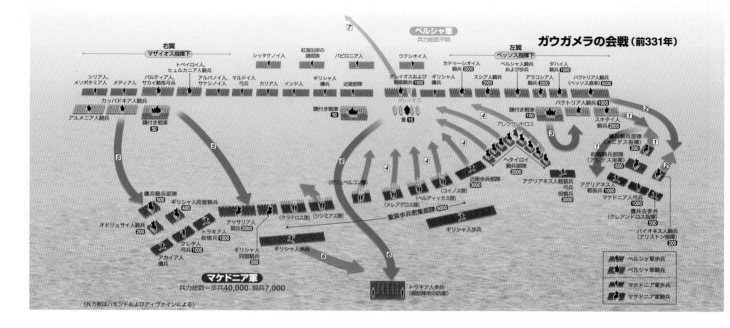

Diagram illustrating the Macedonian victory of over the Persian army in the Battle of Gaugamela.

ガウガメラの会戦におけるペルシャ軍とマケドニア軍の戦いの様子を図解した。

Japan   2003

CD: Hiroyuki Kimura   D: Sachiko Hagiwara   DF, S: Tube Graphics   CL: Japan Broadcast Publishing Co., Ltd.

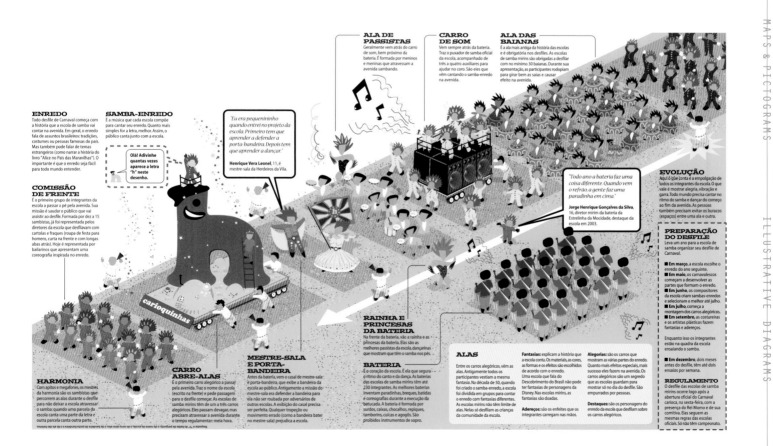

Illustration explains children how a parade of Samba's school is organized. The character "h" on the first car is the mascot of this children's supplement.

サンバのパレードがどのように編成されているのかを子どもに説明するためのイラスト。先頭の車に乗っている「h」の形をしたキャラクターは、この子ども向けの付録のマスコット。

Brazil   2001

CD, S: Eduardo Asta   CL: Folha de São Paulo

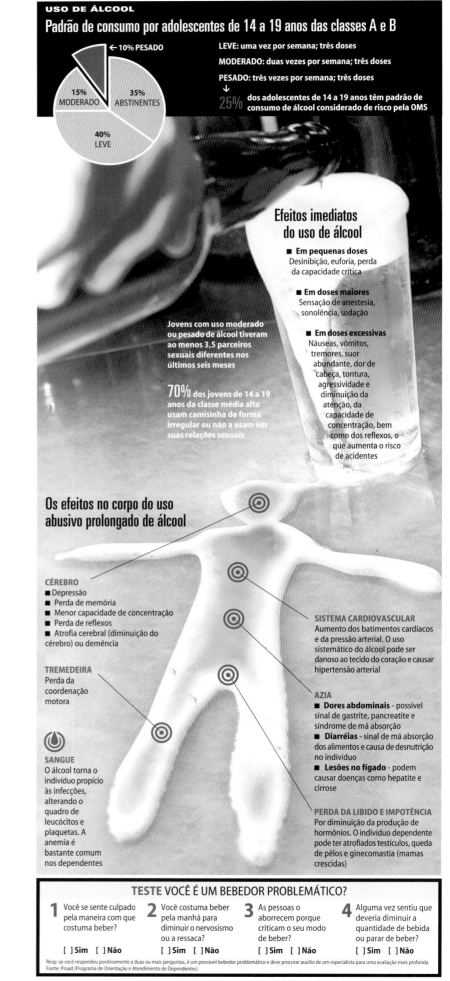

USO DE ÁLCOOL

Padrão de consumo por adolescentes de 14 a 19 anos das classes A e B

← 10% PESADO

15% MODERADO

35% ABSTINENTES

40% LEVE

LEVE: uma vez por semana; três doses

MODERADO: duas vezes por semana; três doses

PESADO: três vezes por semana; três doses
↓

25% dos adolescentes de 14 a 19 anos têm padrão de consumo de álcool considerado de risco pela OMS

Efeitos imediatos do uso de álcool

■ **Em pequenas doses**
Desinibição, euforia, perda da capacidade crítica

■ **Em doses maiores**
Sensação de anestesia, sonolência, sedação

■ **Em doses excessivas**
Náuseas, vômitos, tremores, suor abundante, dor de cabeça, tontura, agressividade e diminuição da atenção, da capacidade de concentração, bem como dos reflexos, o que aumenta o risco de acidentes

Jovens com uso moderado ou pesado de álcool tiveram ao menos 3,5 parceiros sexuais diferentes nos últimos seis meses

70% dos jovens de 14 a 19 anos da classe média alta usam camisinha de forma irregular ou não a usam em suas relações sexuais

Os efeitos no corpo do uso abusivo prolongado de álcool

CÉREBRO
■ Depressão
■ Perda de memória
■ Menor capacidade de concentração
■ Perda de reflexos
■ Atrofia cerebral (diminuição do cérebro) ou demência

TREMEDEIRA
Perda da coordenação motora

SANGUE
O álcool torna o indivíduo propício às infecções, alterando o quadro de leucócitos e plaquetas. A anemia é bastante comum nos dependentes

SISTEMA CARDIOVASCULAR
Aumento dos batimentos cardíacos e da pressão arterial. O uso sistemático do álcool pode ser danoso ao tecido do coração e causar hipertensão arterial

AZIA
■ **Dores abdominais** - possível sinal de gastrite, pancreatite e síndrome de má absorção
■ **Diarréias** - sinal de má absorção dos alimentos e causa de desnutrição no indivíduo
■ **Lesões no fígado** - podem causar doenças como hepatite e cirrose

PERDA DA LIBIDO E IMPOTÊNCIA
Por diminuição da produção de hormônios. O indivíduo dependente pode ter atrofiados testículos, queda de pêlos e ginecomastia (mamas crescidas)

TESTE VOCÊ É UM BEBEDOR PROBLEMÁTICO?

1 Você se sente culpado pela maneira com que costuma beber?
[ ] **Sim** [ ] **Não**

2 Você costuma beber pela manhã para diminuir o nervosismo ou a ressaca?
[ ] **Sim** [ ] **Não**

3 As pessoas o aborrecem porque criticam o seu modo de beber?
[ ] **Sim** [ ] **Não**

4 Alguma vez sentiu que deveria diminuir a quantidade de bebida ou parar de beber?
[ ] **Sim** [ ] **Não**

Resp: se você respondeu positivamente a duas ou mais perguntas, é um provável bebedor problemático e deve procurar auxílio de um especialista para uma avaliação mais profunda
Fonte: Proad (Programa de Orientação e Atendimento de Dependentes)

The graph brings information about the increasing number of teenagers addicted to alcohol and the consequences of the addiction on the body.

増加しつつあるアルコール中毒のティーンエイジャーの人数と、中毒が身体へ及ぼす影響に関する情報を伝える図。

Brazil 2001

CD, S: Eduardo Asta   I: Sandro Falsetti   CL: Folha de São Paulo

A calendar showing all summer events in Salvador, Brazil.

ブラジルのサルバドルで行われる夏のイベントを紹介するカレンダー。

Brazil　2003
D, S: Douglas Okasaki　P: Antônio Saturnino　CW: Roberto Albergaria　CL: A Tarde Newspaper

A chart explains the history of Christmas tree including the origin of its rite and its ornaments.

クリスマス・ツリーを飾る習慣やツリーの飾りなどに関する歴史を説明するチャート。

Germany　2000
CD, D: Jlka Eiche　DF, CL, S: Eiche, Oehjne Design

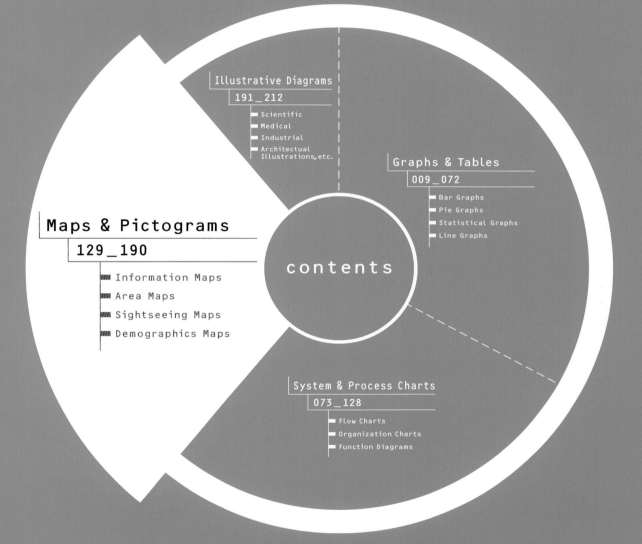

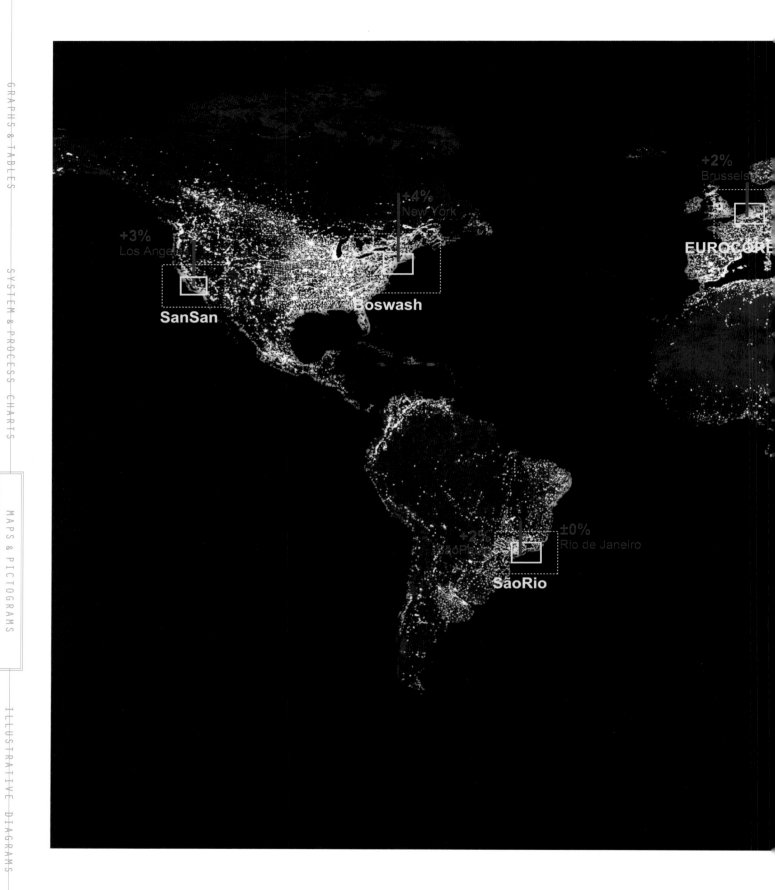

+4%
New York

+3%
Los Angeles

Boswash

SanSan

+2%
Brussels

EUROCORE

+2%
São Paulo

±0%
Rio de Janeiro

SãoRio

A map indicating the world's ten most populous urban cores with annual GDP growth and population density.

世界で最も人口の多い10大都心部を、年間のGDP成長率や人口密度とともに示したマップ。

Netherlands 2002-2003
Material, S: AMO

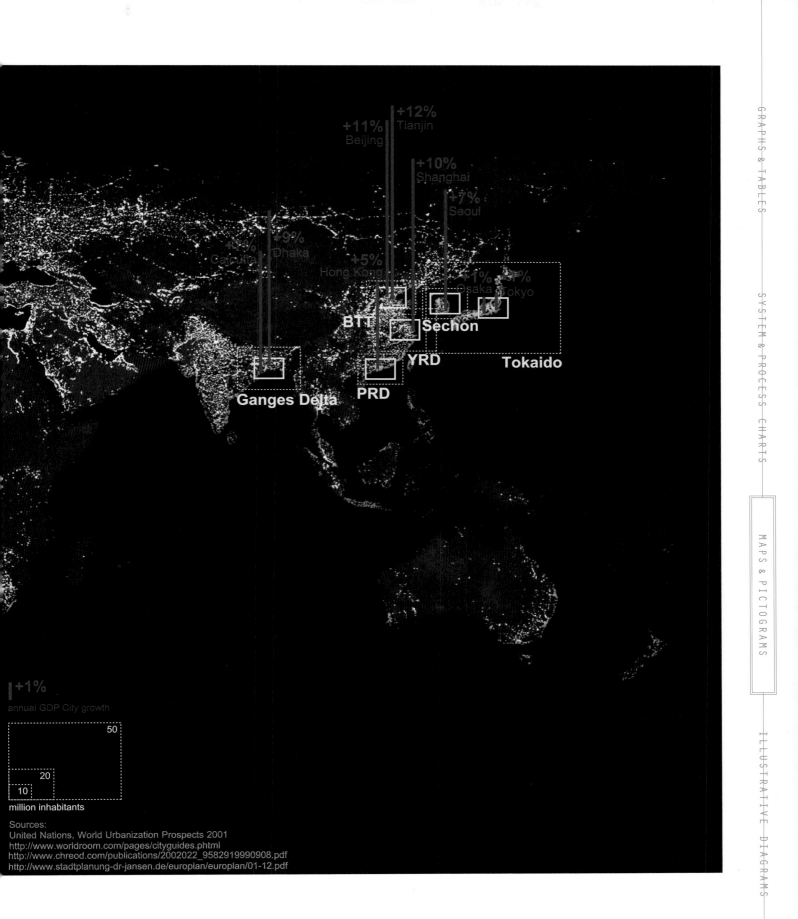

+12%
Tianjin

+11%
Beijing

+10%
Shanghai

+7%
Seoul

+9%
Dhaka

+5%
Hong Kong

Calcutta

+1%
Osaka Tokyo

BTT

Sechon

YRD

Ganges Delta

PRD

Tokaido

+1%
annual GDP City growth

50

20

10

million inhabitants

Sources:
United Nations, World Urbanization Prospects 2001
http://www.worldroom.com/pages/cityguides.phtml
http://www.chreod.com/publications/2002022_9582919990908.pdf
http://www.stadtplanung-dr-jansen.de/europlan/europlan/01-12.pdf

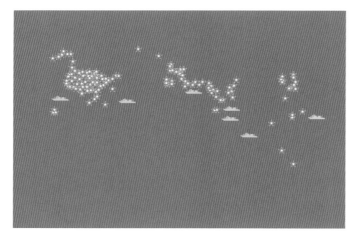

6,702 US military bases located in 41 countries.
41ヵ国に6,702の米軍基地が置かれている。

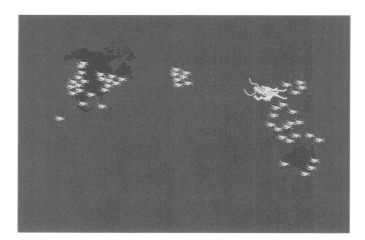

37 Chinatowns in 13 countries.
チャイナタウンは13ヵ国に37ある。

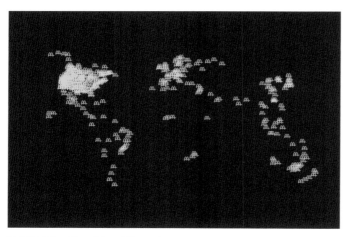

31,295 McDonalds outlets in 119 coutries.
マクドナルドは119ヵ国に31,295店舗ある。

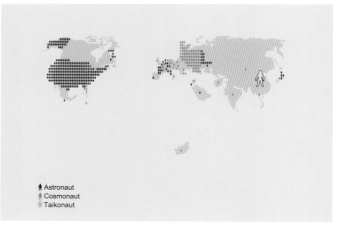

306 astronauts, 124 cosmonauts, and 1 taikonauts in 41 countries.
41ヵ国に、米国の宇宙飛行士は306人、旧ソ連・ロシアの宇宙飛行士は124人、
中国の宇宙飛行士が1人いる。

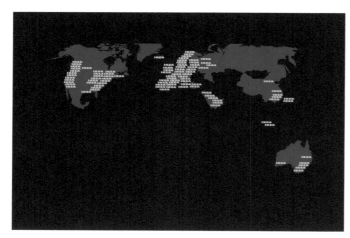

184 IKEA warehouses in 34 countries.
イケアは34ヵ国に184店舗ある。

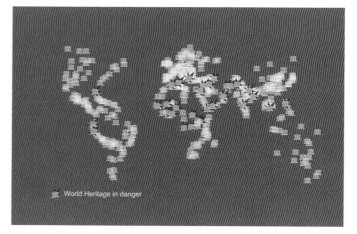

730 World Heritage Sites in 129 countries.
世界遺産に指定された地域は129ヵ国に730カ所ある。

A series of maps illustrating the various forms of globalism.
様々なグローバリズムの形態を示したマップのシリーズ。

Netherlands 2002-2003
Material, S: AMO

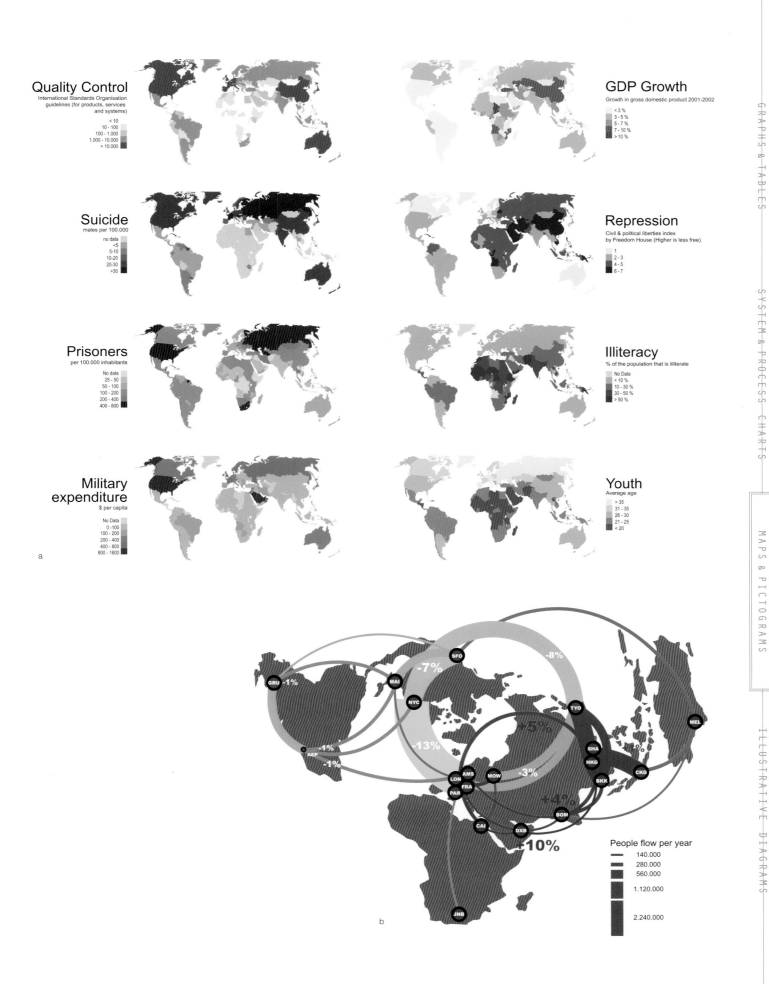

Quality Control

International Standards Organisation guidelines (for products, services and systems)

< 10
10 - 100
100 - 1.000
1.000 - 10.000
> 10.000

Suicide

males per 100.000

no data
<5
5-10
10-20
20-30
>30

Prisoners

per 100.000 inhabitants

No data
25 - 50
50 - 100
100 - 200
200 - 400
400 - 800

Military expenditure

$ per capita

No Data
0 - 100
100 - 200
200 - 400
400 - 800
800 - 1600

a

GDP Growth

Growth in gross domestic product 2001-2002

< 3 %
3 - 5 %
5 - 7 %
7 - 10 %
> 10 %

Repression

Civil & political liberties index by Freedom House (Higher is less free)

1
2 - 3
4 - 5
6 - 7

Illiteracy

% of the population that is illiterate

No Data
< 10 %
10 - 30 %
30 - 50 %
> 50 %

Youth

Average age

> 35
31 - 35
26 - 30
21 - 25
< 20

GRU -1%   SFO   -8%
MAI   -7%
NYC   TYO   MEL
AEP -1%   -13%   +5%   SHA
-1%   LON AMS MOW   HKG
FRA   -3%   CKG
PAR   BKK
+4%
CAI   BOM
DXB
+10%
JNB

People flow per year

140.000
280.000
560.000
1.120.000
2.240.000

b

Color-coded maps illustrating statistics of quality control, suicide, prisoners, military expenditure, GDP growth, repression, illiteracy, and youth. (a)
A map showing changes of passenger air traffic in the world. (b)

品質管理、自殺、囚人、軍事費、GDP成長率、弾圧、非識字率、若者の人口といった統計を示す、色分けされたマップ。 (a)
飛行機の航路別乗客数の増減を示すマップ。 (b)

M16
May 16 1998
Geneva WTO Meeting
~ 10.000 people

Geneva

N30
November 30 1999
Seattle WTO Meeting
~ 40.000 people

Seattle

A16
April 16 2000
IMF & World Bank
Meeting Washington DC
~ 50.000 people

Washington DC

J20
July 20-22 2001
G8 Summit,
Genoa, Italy
~ 280.000 people

Genoa

D20
December 20/21 2002
Global Day of Action
for Argentina
~ 500.000 people

Buenos Aires

F15

Global Action Day for Peace
February 15 2003
~ 14.000.000 people

Showing an increasing number of left-wing activists: on May 16, 1988, 10,000 people demonstrated against WTO (M16),
and on February 15, 2003, several groups orchestrated F15, the first-ever global protest against war in Iraq.

増加する左派の活動家の人数を示す。1988年5月16日、WTOに反対するデモに1万人が参加した (M16)。2003年2月15日、いくつかの団体がF15を組織した。
これはイラク戦争に反対する初の世界規模のデモである。

Netherlands   2002-2003
Material, S: AMO

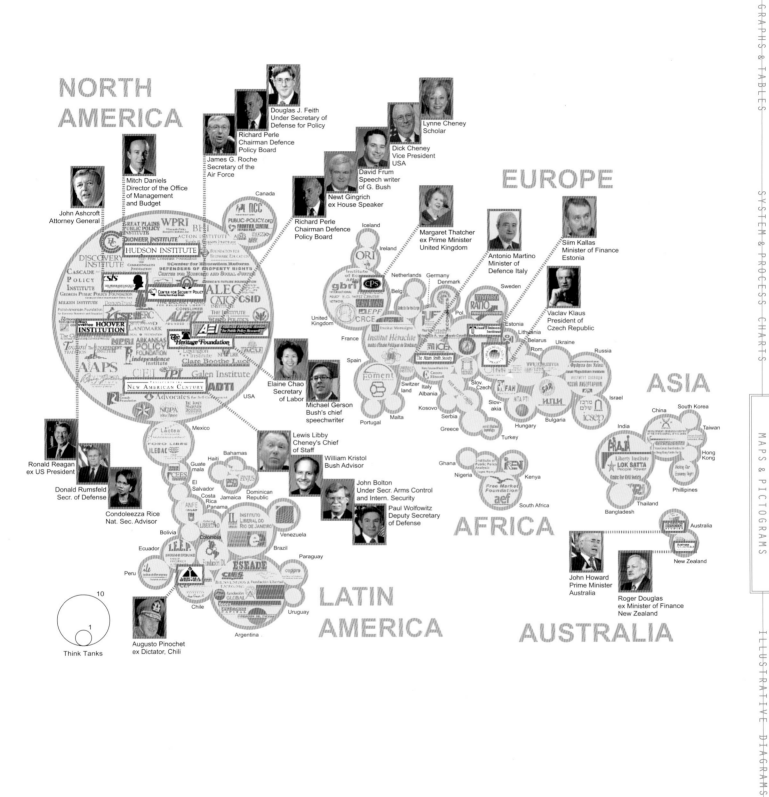

NORTH
AMERICA

Douglas J. Feith
Under Secretary of
Defense for Policy

Richard Perle
Chairman Defence
Policy Board

James G. Roche
Secretary of the
Air Force

Mitch Daniels
Director of the Office
of Management
and Budget

John Ashcroft
Attorney General

Newt Gingrich
ex House Speaker

Richard Perle
Chairman Defence
Policy Board

David Frum
Speech writer
of G. Bush

Dick Cheney
Vice President
USA

Lynne Cheney
Scholar

EUROPE

Margaret Thatcher
ex Prime Minister
United Kingdom

Antonio Martino
Minister of
Defence Italy

Siim Kallas
Minister of Finance
Estonia

Vaclav Klaus
President of
Czech Republic

ASIA

Elaine Chao
Secretary
of Labor

Michael Gerson
Bush's chief
speechwriter

Ronald Reagan
ex US President

Donald Rumsfeld
Secr. of Defense

Condoleezza Rice
Nat. Sec. Advisor

Lewis Libby
Cheney's Chief
of Staff

William Kristol
Bush Advisor

John Bolton
Under Secr. Arms Control
and Intern. Security

Paul Wolfowitz
Deputy Secretary
of Defense

AFRICA

John Howard
Prime Minister
Australia

Roger Douglas
ex Minister of Finance
New Zealand

10
1

Think Tanks

Augusto Pinochet
ex Dictator, Chili

LATIN
AMERICA

AUSTRALIA

Diagrams explaining a network of right-wing think tanks. The neoconservatives are influencing governments in America, Europe, and Asia.
右派のシンクタンクのネットワークを解説するマップ。新保守派はアメリカ大陸、ヨーロッパ、アジアの政府に影響を及ぼしている。

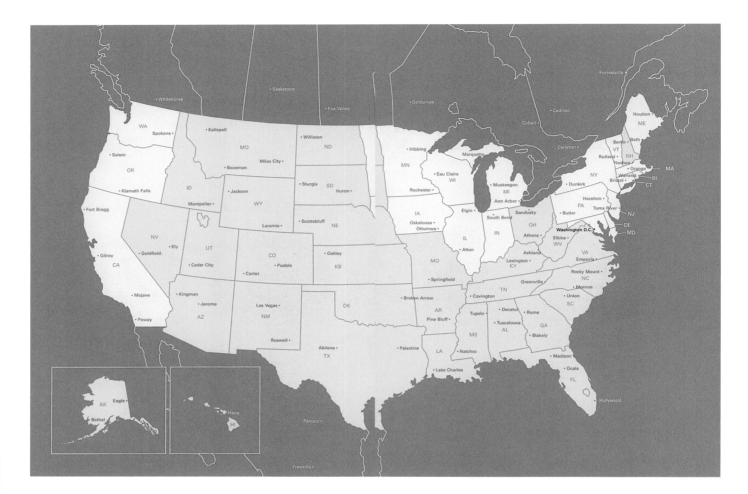

A series of maps from AIGA brochure including a guide showing landmarks in Washington D.C.

AIGAのブローシャーより。ワシントンD.C.のランドマークを示す案内図を含むマップのシリーズ。

USA 2001
CD, AD: Bill Cahan   AD, D: Michael Braley   AD, D, P: Sharrie Brooks   AD, D, P, I, CW: Bob Dinetz   AD, D, P, CW: Kevin Roberson   D, I, CW: Gary William
CW, CL: AIGA   DF, S: Cahan & Associates

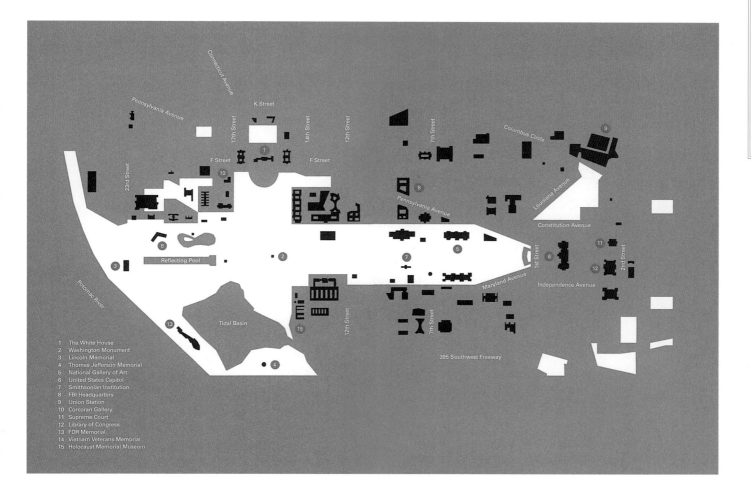

1   The White House
2   Washington Monument
3   Lincoln Memorial
4   Thomas Jefferson Memorial
5   National Gallery of Art
6   United States Capitol
7   Smithsonian Institution
8   FBI Headquarters
9   Union Station
10 Corcoran Gallery
11 Supreme Court
12 Library of Congress
13 FDR Memorial
14 Vietnam Veterans Memorial
15 Holocaust Memorial Museum

Improved customer service To create efficiencies and enhance our support for customers, we have reorganized the way we do business. Our measures include a rationalization of our companies in 140 countries into 31 market units, each responsible for providing world-class expertise to operators in that area.

We have the same global capability we had before, but it is now delivered through a more efficient and effective network. Our new organization has enabled us to create efficiencies, removing duplication and cutting costs in areas such as offices, human resources and

administration. Our market units also enhance the support we can give to our customers. The local expertise we have built up over many years remains in place, and we are continuing to help our internationalizing customers develop their activities in new areas.

Europe

World

◎ Market Unit

Market Units

Europe, Middle East & Africa

Benelux
Belgium, Netherlands and Luxemburg

Central Europe
Bosnia-Herzegovina, Croatia, Czech Republic, Hungary, Poland, Republika Srpska (Serbia), Slovakia and Slovenia

3. Eastern Europe & Central Asia
Belarus, Georgia, Kazakhstan, Russia and Ukraine

4. France

5. Germany, Austria, Switzerland & Liechtenstein (DACH)
Austria, Germany, Liechtenstein and Switzerland

6. Iberia
Portugal and Spain

7. Italy

8. Middle East
Bahrain, Iran, Jordan, Kuwait, Lebanon, Oman, Qatar, Saudi Arabia, Syria and United Arab Emirates

9. Nordic & Baltic (NOBA)
Denmark, Estonia, Finland, Iceland, Latvia, Lithuania, Norway and Sweden

10. Northern Africa
Algeria, Egypt, Eritrea, Ethiopia, Gambia, Kenya, Libya, Morocco, Sudan and Tunisia

11. North West Europe
Ireland and UK

12. South East Europe
Bulgaria, Cyprus, Greece, Moldova, and Romania

13. Southern Africa
Angola, Botswana, Ghana, Nigeria, South Africa and Zambia

Asia/Pacific

14. Australia & New Zealand
Australia, New Zealand and Pacific Islands

15. China

16. India & Sri Lanka

17. Indonesia

18. Israel & Turkey

19. Japan

20. Malaysia, Bangladesh, Pakistan and the Philippines
Bangladesh, Malaysia, Pakistan, Philippines

21. Singapore

22. South Korea

23. Taiwan

24. Thailand

25. Vietnam

Americas

26. Brazil

27. Central America
Costa Rica, Cuba, El Salvador, Guatemala, Honduras, Jamaica, Nicaragua, Panama

28. Latin America – North
Colombia, Dominican Republic, Netherlands Antilles, Puerto Rico, Trinidad & Tobago and Venezuela

29. Latin America – South
Argentina, Bolivia, Chile, Paraguay, Peru and Uruguay

30. Mexico

31. North America
Canada and US

18　Ericsson 2002　Our Market

Our Market　Ericsson 2002　19

Ericsson 2002

**2002 was tough.
Our customers bought less
equipment, competition
increased, the roll-out
of 3G was slow, and the
market was hard to predict.
Some observers see no
end to these difficulties.**

We take a very different view.

ERICSSON ⋛

A map illustrating Ericsson's customer services. Their measures include a rationalization of companies in 140 countries into 31 market units, each responsible for providing world-class expertise to operators in that area.

Ericsson社の顧客サービス拠点を表すマップ。企業の合理化を図るため、140カ国にある企業を31の市場ごとに分割し、各地域で国際的レベルの専門知識をオペレーターに提供している。

UK　2002

CD, AD, D, I: Gilmar Wendt　CD: David Stocks　P: Stefan Almers / Alexander Farnsworth / Lee Mawdsley　CW: Tim Rich / Leonard Rau　DF, S: SAS　CL: Ericsson

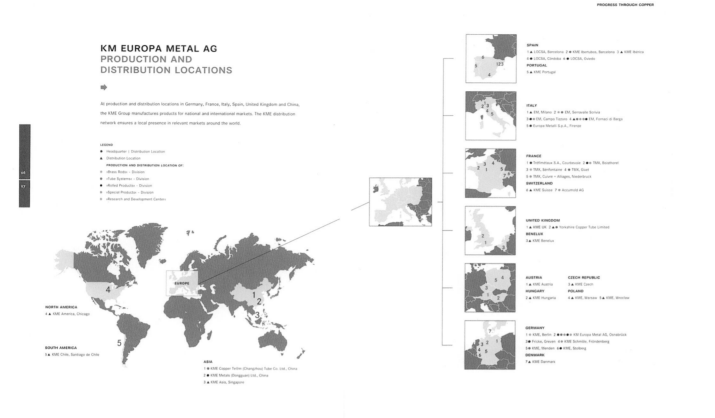

From a corporate brochure of KME Group, a world's largest manufacturers of copper and copper alloy products. Maps showing their production and distribution locations.

世界最大の銅や銅合金製品のメーカーであるKMEグループの会社案内より。同社の製造や販売部門の場所を示すマップ。

Germany　2003
AD, D: Bernd Vollmöller　CW: Franziska Schlingmann　DF, S: Simon & Goetz Design　CL: KM Europa Metal AG

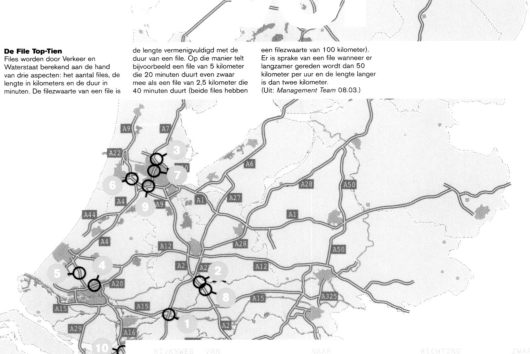

De File Top-Tien
Files worden door Verkeer en
Waterstaat berekend aan de hand
van drie aspecten: het aantal files, de
lengte in kilometers en de duur in
minuten. De filezwaarte van een file is

de lengte vermenigvuldigd met de
duur van een file. Op die manier telt
bijvoorbeeld een file van 5 kilometer
die 20 minuten duurt even zwaar
mee als een file van 2,5 kilometer die
40 minuten duurt (beide files hebben

een filezwaarte van 100 kilometer).
Er is sprake van een file wanneer er
langzamer gereden wordt dan 50
kilometer per uur en de lengte langer
is dan twee kilometer.
(Uit: *Management Team* 08.03.)

	RIJKSWEG	VAN	NAAR	RICHTING	ZWAARTE	AANTAL
1	A27	AVELINGEN	MERWEDEBRUG	BREDA	78591	124
2	A2	KP EVERDINGEN	EVERDINGEN	'S-HERTOGENBOSCH	74526	120
3	A8	OOSTZAAN	KP COENPLEIN	AMSTERDAM	72167	124
4	A20	KP KLEINPOLDERPLEIN	ROTTERDAM-CENTRUM	GOUDA	72165	191
5	A13	DELFT-ZUID	BERKEL EN RODENRIJS	ROTTERDAM	69701	191
6	A9	KP ROTTEPOLDERPLEIN	HAARLEM-ZUID	AMSTELVEEN	67865	145
7	A10	HEMHAVENS S101	COENTUNNEL	KP COENTUNNEL	64656	187
8	A2	CULEMBORG	EVERDINGEN	UTRECHT	60527	119
9	A4	SLOTEN	KP DE NIEUWE MEER	AMSTERDAM	52196	211
10	A16	KP KLAVERPOLDER	MOERDIJK	BREDA	48872	61

Map showing the top ten traffic jams in the Netherlands.

オランダ国内の交通渋滞のベストテンを示すマップ。

Netherlands   2003
CD, AD: André Toet   CD: Jan Sevenster   D: Bas Meulendijks   CW: Paul Van Koningsbruggen   DF, S: Samenwerkende Ontwerpers   CL: Grafische Cultuurstichting

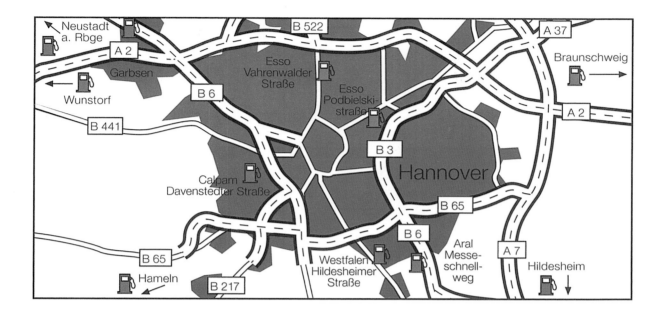

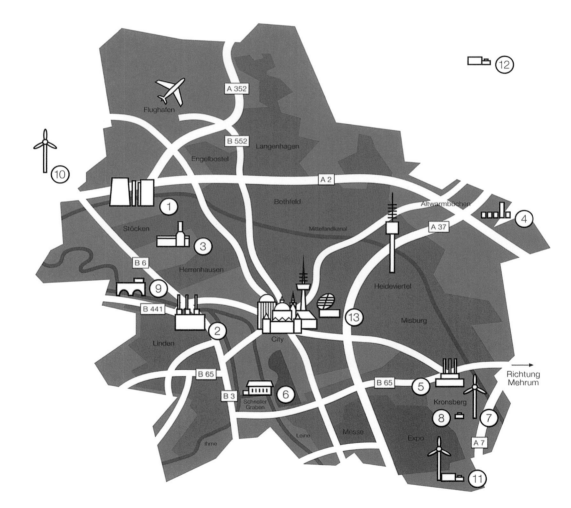

From a corporate brochure of a power company. Maps showing the locations of power plants, manufacturing plants, gas stations, and so on.

電力会社の会社案内より。発電所や製造工場、ガソリンスタンドなどの位置を示すマップ。

Germany 2003
CL, S: Stadtwerke Hannover AG

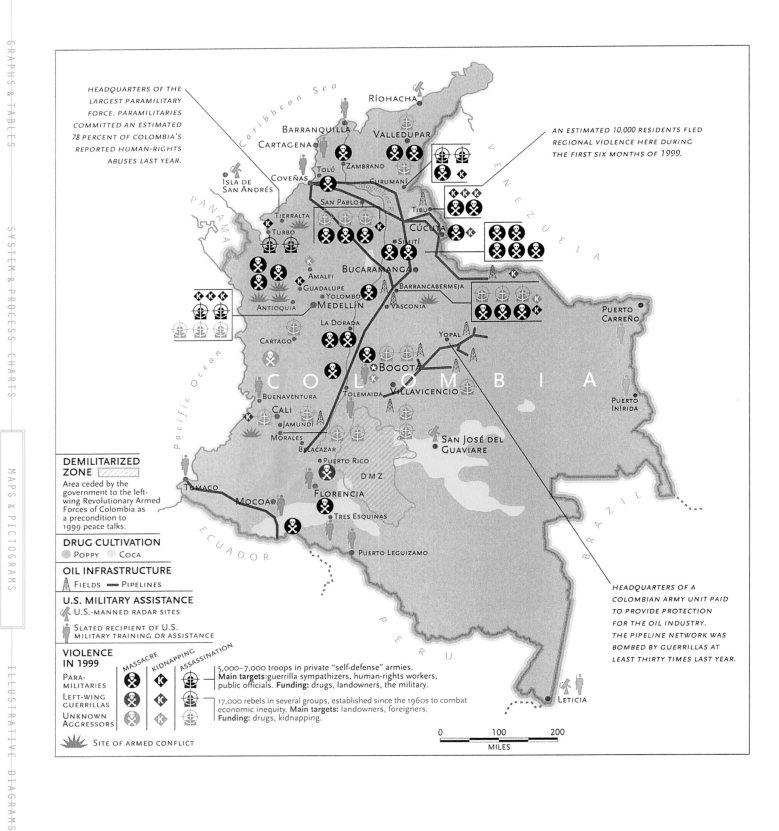

HEADQUARTERS OF THE LARGEST PARAMILITARY FORCE. PARAMILITARIES COMMITTED AN ESTIMATED 78 PERCENT OF COLOMBIA'S REPORTED HUMAN-RIGHTS ABUSES LAST YEAR.

AN ESTIMATED 10,000 RESIDENTS FLED REGIONAL VIOLENCE HERE DURING THE FIRST SIX MONTHS OF 1999.

HEADQUARTERS OF A COLOMBIAN ARMY UNIT PAID TO PROVIDE PROTECTION FOR THE OIL INDUSTRY. THE PIPELINE NETWORK WAS BOMBED BY GUERRILLAS AT LEAST THIRTY TIMES LAST YEAR.

DEMILITARIZED ZONE
Area ceded by the government to the left-wing Revolutionary Armed Forces of Colombia as a precondition to 1999 peace talks.

DRUG CULTIVATION Poppy Coca

OIL INFRASTRUCTURE Fields — Pipelines

U.S. MILITARY ASSISTANCE U.S.-manned radar sites. Slated recipient of U.S. military training or assistance

VIOLENCE IN 1999 MASSACRE KIDNAPPING ASSASSINATION
PARAMILITARIES · LEFT-WING GUERRILLAS · UNKNOWN AGGRESSORS

5,000–7,000 troops in private "self-defense" armies. **Main targets:** guerrilla sympathizers, human-rights workers, public officials. **Funding:** drugs, landowners, the military.

17,000 rebels in several groups, established since the 1960s to combat economic inequity. **Main targets:** landowners, foreigners. **Funding:** drugs, kidnapping.

Site of armed conflict

0 100 200 MILES

A map of Colombia showing drug-related activity.

麻薬関連の活動を示すコロンビアのマップ。

USA 2000
AD: Angela Riechers D, I, S: Nigel Holmes DF: Explanation Graphics CL: Harper's

WHICH CAME FIRST, THE CHICKEN OR THE TOWN?

Some people liked animals so much, they named their whole town after them. Here are some beastly examples.

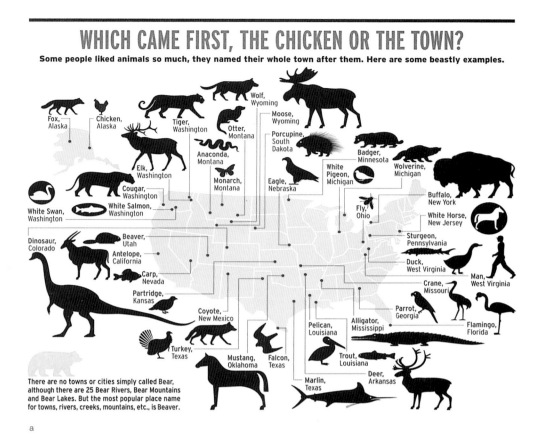

Fox, Alaska
Chicken, Alaska
Tiger, Washington
Otter, Montana
Wolf, Wyoming
Moose, Wyoming
Porcupine, South Dakota
Badger, Minnesota
Wolverine, Michigan
Elk, Washington
Anaconda, Montana
Monarch, Montana
White Pigeon, Michigan
Buffalo, New York
Cougar, Washington
Eagle, Nebraska
Fly, Ohio
White Horse, New Jersey
White Swan, Washington
White Salmon, Washington
Sturgeon, Pennsylvania
Dinosaur, Colorado
Beaver, Utah
Duck, West Virginia
Man, West Virginia
Antelope, California
Carp, Nevada
Crane, Missouri
Partridge, Kansas
Parrot, Georgia
Coyote, New Mexico
Alligator, Mississippi
Flamingo, Florida
Pelican, Louisiana
Turkey, Texas
Mustang, Oklahoma
Falcon, Texas
Trout, Louisiana
Marlin, Texas
Deer, Arkansas

There are no towns or cities simply called Bear, although there are 25 Bear Rivers, Bear Mountains and Bear Lakes. But the most popular place name for towns, rivers, creeks, mountains, etc., is Beaver.

a

HEY! WHAT PLANET ARE YOU FROM?

These days you can hop in your car and drive to the next planet. Oh, OK, it *is* just the next town, but we bet you never thought the United States had so many places named for otherworldly locales. We sure didn't.

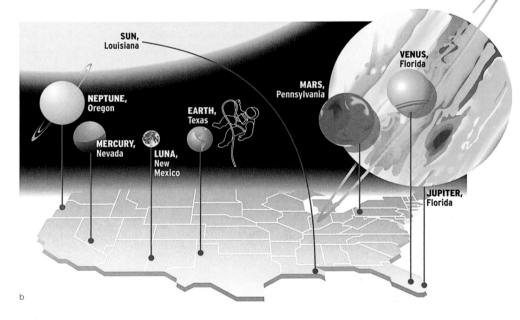

SUN, Louisiana
VENUS, Florida
MARS, Pennsylvania
NEPTUNE, Oregon
EARTH, Texas
MERCURY, Nevada
LUNA, New Mexico
JUPITER, Florida

b

A map of America with cities that are named after animals. (a)
A map of America with cities that are named after planets. (b)

動物にちなんで名付けられたアメリカの町を示すマップ。 (a)
惑星にちなんで名付けられたアメリカの町を示すマップ。 (b)

USA 2000 (a) / 2001 (b)
AD: Kevin De Miranda   D, I, S: Nigel Holmes   DF: Explanation Graphics   CL: Navigator Magazine

BEYOND COLUMBINE

espite the outcry over the multiple killings at schools in Kentucky, Arkansas, Oregon, and Colorado in the last two years, these incidents represent less than half of all violent school deaths during that period. Although the annual number of fatalities—on campus, at off-campus school events, and in transit to and from school—has dropped since the early Nineties, the portion involving guns has remained fairly steady. At the same time, the incidence of suicide has increased by a third. Girls, who once accounted for 5 percent of murder victims, now account for 27 percent. In the 1992–93 school year, nearly one in two of all school deaths took place in California, Texas, or New York; last year one in six did.

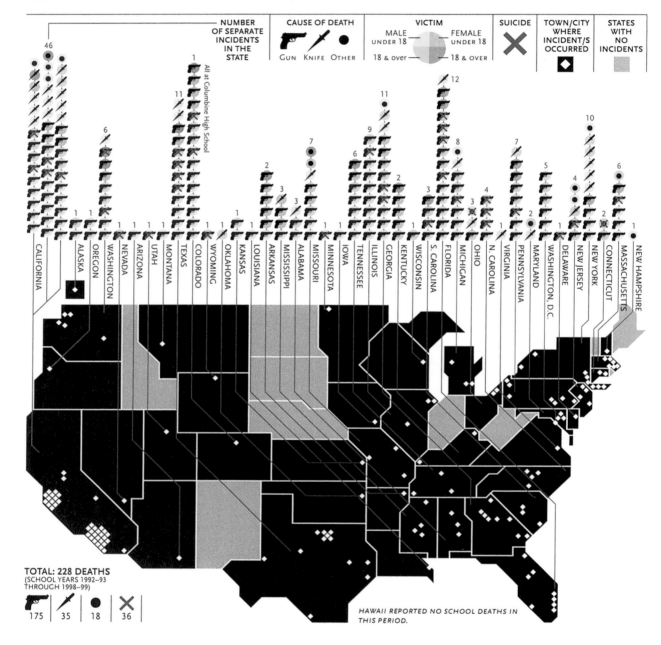

TOTAL: 228 DEATHS
(SCHOOL YEARS 1992–93
THROUGH 1998–99)

| 175 | 35 | 18 | 36 |

HAWAII REPORTED NO SCHOOL DEATHS IN THIS PERIOD.

Map by Nigel Holmes, based on information from the National School Safety Center

A map of America showing killings at schools around the country.

アメリカ国内の学校で起きた殺人についての様々なデータを示すマップ。

USA 1999
AD: Angela Riechers   D, I, S: Nigel Holmes   DF: Explanation Graphics   CL: Harper's

A SLICE OF AMERICA (OR FIVE)

The continental United States is a diverse place. One interesting perspective is to slice it horizontally and highlight some of the flora and elevations. Sort of makes you wish you hadn't skipped geography class, doesn't it?

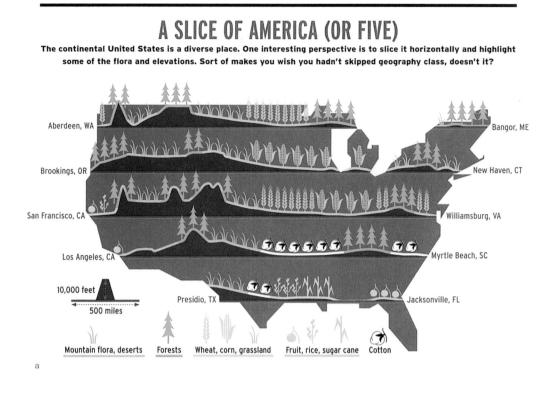

Aberdeen, WA
Bangor, ME
Brookings, OR
New Haven, CT
San Francisco, CA
Williamsburg, VA
Los Angeles, CA
Myrtle Beach, SC
10,000 feet
500 miles
Presidio, TX
Jacksonville, FL

Mountain flora, deserts | Forests | Wheat, corn, grassland | Fruit, rice, sugar cane | Cotton

a

FOODLAND

It's hard to imagine living in Sandwich, Massachusetts, without feeling hungry a lot. What if you lived in Mango, Florida, or Peanut, California, or (slurp) Napoleon, North Dakota? The USA is stuffed with towns that have mouth-watering names.

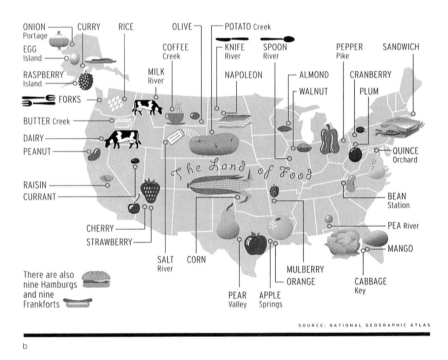

ONION Portage | CURRY | RICE | OLIVE | POTATO Creek
EGG Island | COFFEE Creek | KNIFE River | SPOON River | PEPPER Pike | SANDWICH
RASPBERRY Island | MILK River | NAPOLEON | ALMOND | CRANBERRY
FORKS | WALNUT | PLUM
BUTTER Creek
DAIRY
PEANUT | QUINCE Orchard
RAISIN | BEAN Station
CURRANT | PEA River
CHERRY | MANGO
STRAWBERRY
SALT River | CORN | MULBERRY | CABBAGE Key
PEAR Valley | APPLE Springs | ORANGE

The Land of Food

There are also nine Hamburgs and nine Frankforts

SOURCE: NATIONAL GEOGRAPHIC ATLAS

b

A map of America showing slices of across the nation with elevations and flora. (a)
A map of America with cities named after food items. (b)

アメリカ全土の標高と植物層を示す断面図。 (a)
食物の名前にちなんで名付けられたアメリカの町を示すマップ。 (b)

USA 2002 (a) / 1999 (b)
AD: Kevin De Miranda   D, I, S: Nigel Holmes   DF: Explanation Graphics   CL: Navigator Magazine

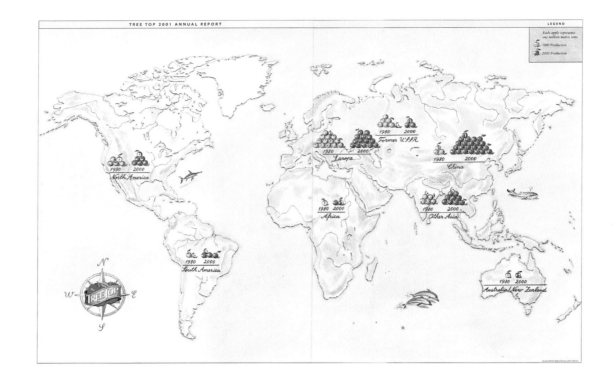

A map illustrating the production of apples both in 1980 and 2000.

1980年および2000年のリンゴの生産量を示すマップ。

USA　2001
AD, D: Katha Dalton　D: Jana Nishi / Michael Brugman　I: Rodica Prato　CW: Evelyne Rozner
DF, S: Hornall Anderson Design Works, Inc.　CL: Tree Top

A world map formed by 'cells' inside a petri dish illustrates the growing importance of genomics
in animal health and breeding programmes globally.

ペトリ皿の中の細胞が形づくる世界地図は、動物の健康や世界的な繁殖プログラムにおけるゲノミクスの重要性を表している。

UK　2001
CD: Tor Pettersen　AD: David Brown　D, CW: Jim Allsopp　DF, S: Tor Pettersen & Partners　CL: Sygen International

Dat Bavaria ontzettend populair is in Brabant,
dat wist u waarschijnlijk wel. Maar dat deze familie-
brouwerij uit Lieshout net zo succesvol wil worden
in de rest van Nederland, dat wist u waarschijnlijk
nog niet. Samen met een team van Brabantse
ambassadeurs, starten we vandaag een belangrijke
missie: Bavaria gaat Nederland veroveren. Het bier
is namelijk veel te lekker om voor ons zelf te houden.
We rekenen op uw medewerking!

**Zo Nederland,
nu eerst een Bavaria.**

Graphic showing the success of Dutch beer named Bavaria.

オランダ国内におけるBavariaというオランダ・ビールの成功を示すマップ。

Neterlands   2004
CD, AD: Erik Kessels   D: Design Politie   DF, S: Kesselskramer   CL: Bavaria

6217 B.C.

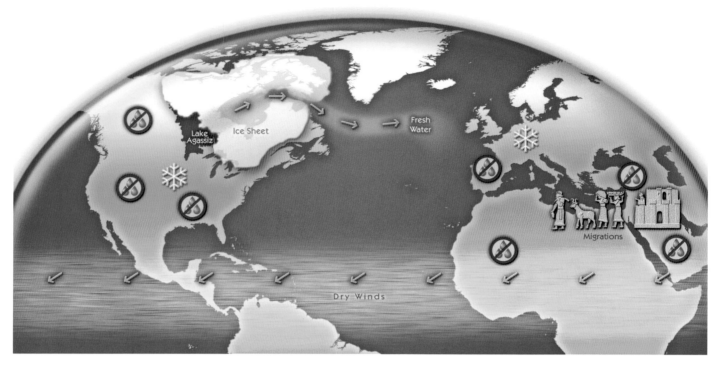

Illustration showing the impact of a global warming event in 6217 B.C. on climate, wind direction, and human migration.

紀元前6217年の地球規模の温暖化が気候や風向き、人間の移動などに与えた影響を示すイラスト。

USA   2004
CD: Blaize Mekinna   AD: Blaize Mekinna   D, I: Tracy Sabin   DF, S: Sabingrafik, Incorporated   CL: Scripps Institute of Oceanography

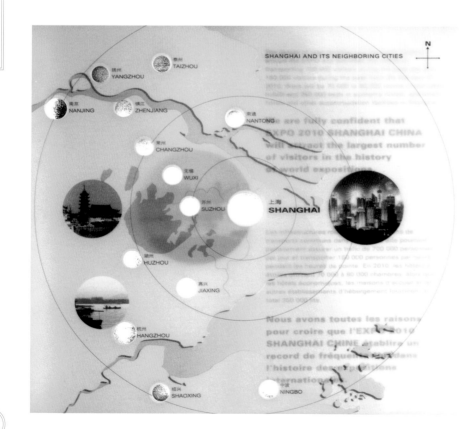

Map showing the distance between Shanghai and
its neighboring cities, with die-cutting and
silver stamping spots printed on double-folded tracing paper.
From an information brochure of Expo 2010.

上海と周辺都市との距離を示すマップ。
型抜きを使用し、トレーシングペーパーに印刷した
銀の箔押しの点が見えるようにした。
2010年のエキスポのインフォメーション・ブローシャーより。

China   2002
CD, AD, D: Hon Bing-Wah   DF, S: HS Art & Design
CL: EXPO 2010 Shanghai Bidding China Office

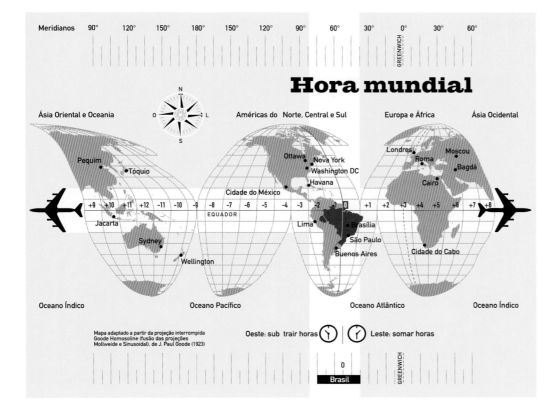

A map designed for Brazilian travellers. The task was to create a time zone chart with Brazil in the center.

ブラジル人の旅行者のためにデザインされたマップ。ブラジルを中央に配置した標準時間図を作成することが目的。

Brazil　2003
AD: Vincenzo Scarpelini　D, S: Eduardo Asta　CL: Infraero

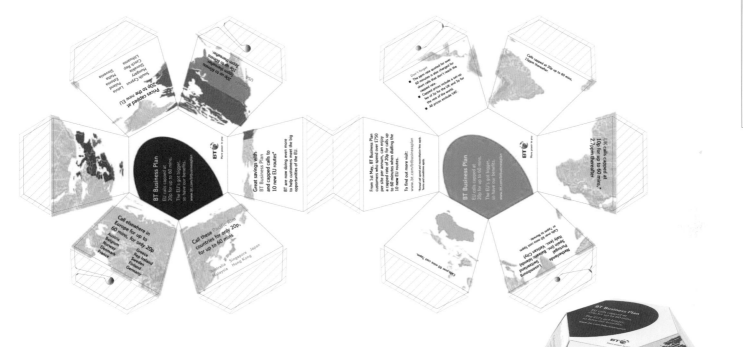

A three-dimensional piece of collateral illustrating telephone rate for around the world.

世界各国への国際電話料金を示した立体的な販促グッズ。

UK　2004
CD: Geoff Aldridge　D: Sarah Mckewan　DF, S: Communication by Design　CL: BT

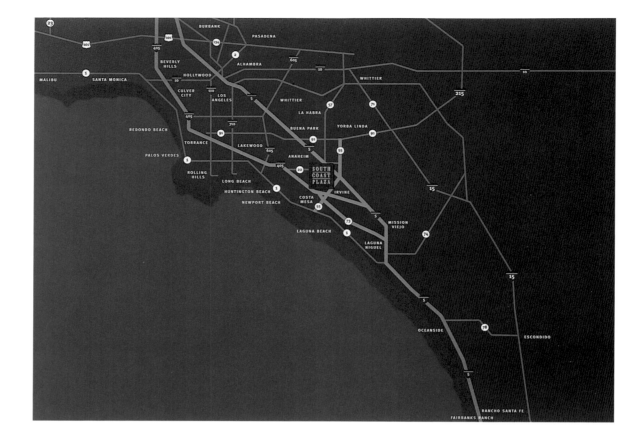

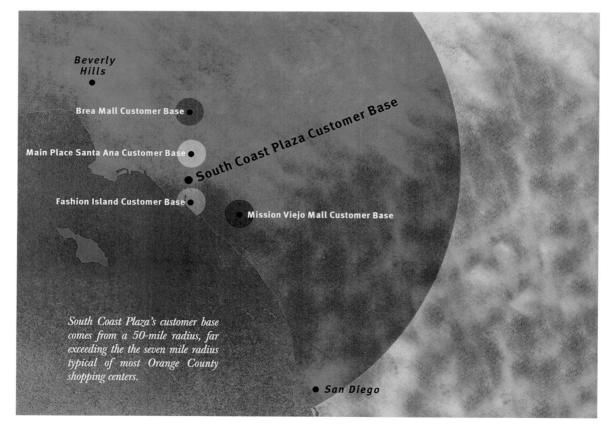

South Coast Plaza's customer base comes from a 50-mile radius, far exceeding the the seven mile radius typical of most Orange County shopping centers.

Maps of South Coast Plaza, a newly developed shopping center.

新しく開発されたショッピング・センター、South Coast Plazaのマップ。

USA 2003
AD: Mike Salisbury   DF, S: Mike Salisbury LLC.   CL: South Coast Plaza

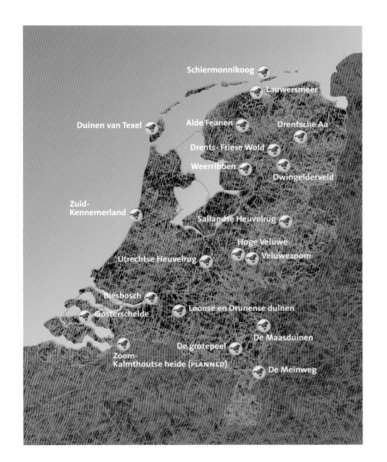

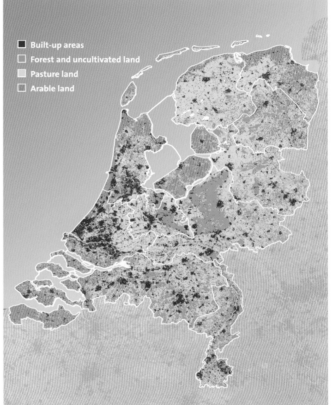

- Built-up areas
- Forest and uncultivated land
- Pasture land
- Arable land

Map from a book on the Netherlands providing various data.

オランダを紹介する本から抜粋された、様々なデータを示すマップ。

Netherlands 2004
CD: Paul Vermijs   D: Toon Tesser   DF, S: TelDesign   CL: Ministry of Foreign Affairs

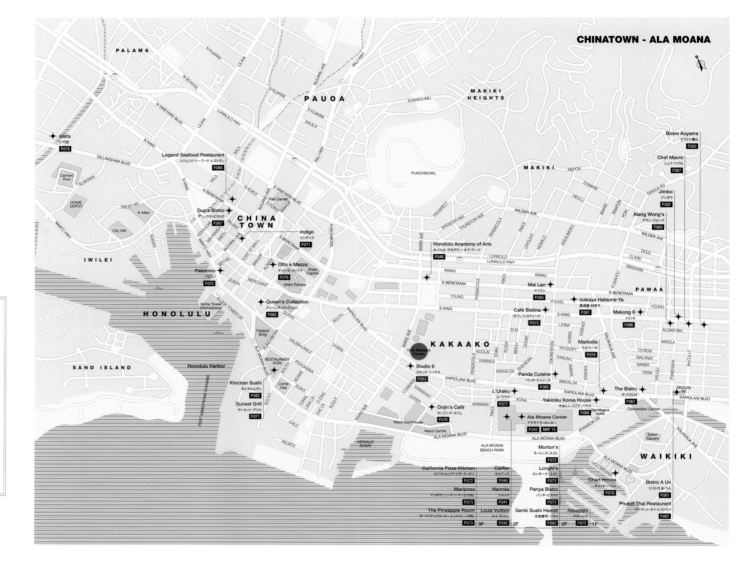

A guide map of Oahu from the magazine "Priority Hawaii."

雑誌『プライオリティーハワイ』より。オアフ島のガイドマップ。

Japan　2004
AD: Takahito Noguchi　D: Takahiro Imai　I: Tokuma　DF: Dynamite Brothers Syndicate Co., Ltd.　CL: Access Publishing Co., Ltd.　S: Bowlgraphics

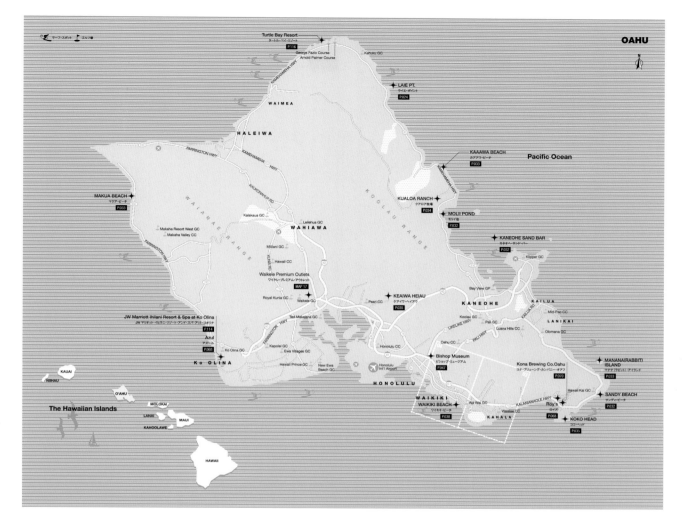

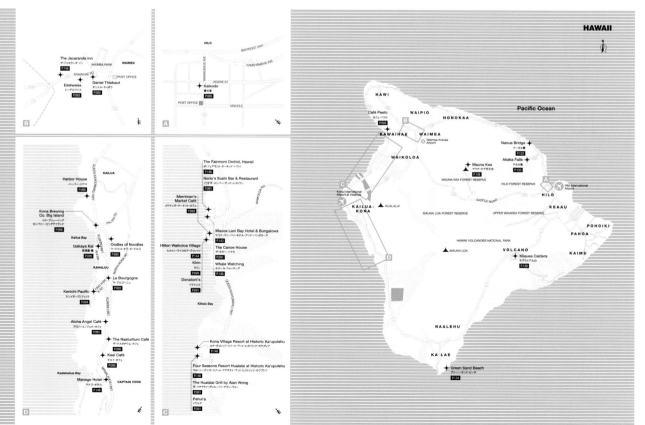

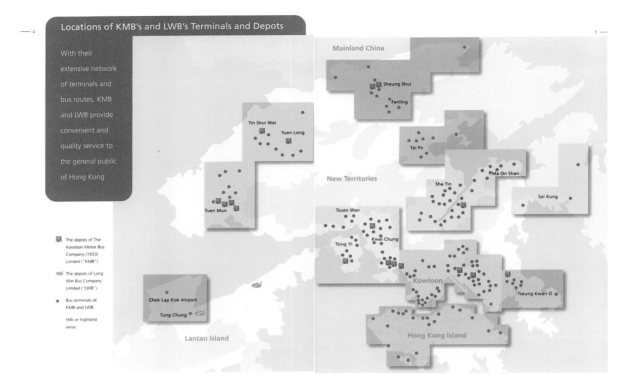

Locations of KMB's and LWB's Terminals and Depots

With their extensive network of terminals and bus routes, KMB and LWB provide convenient and quality service to the general public of Hong Kong

Mainland China

Sheung Shui
Fanling

Tin Shui Wai
Yuen Long

Tai Po

New Territories

Ma On Shan

Sha Tin

Sai Kung

Tsuen Wan

Tsing Yi   Kwai Chung

Kowloon

Tseung Kwan O

Hong Kong Island

The depots of The Kowloon Motor Bus Company (1933) Limited ("KMB")

The depots of Long Win Bus Company Limited ("LWB")

Bus terminals of KMB and LWB

Hills or highland areas

Chek Lap Kok Airport
Tung Chung

Lantau Island

A map showing the locations of terminals and depots of the Kowloon Mortor Bus Company and Long Win Bus Company.

バス会社、Kowloon Motor Bus CompanyおよびLong Win Bus Companyのターミナルと発着場の場所を示すマップ。

Hong Kong   2000
CD, AD, D: Freeman Lau Sin Hong   AD, D: Eddy Yu   DF, S: Kan & Lau Design Consultants   CL: the Kowloon Motor Bus Holdings Ltd.

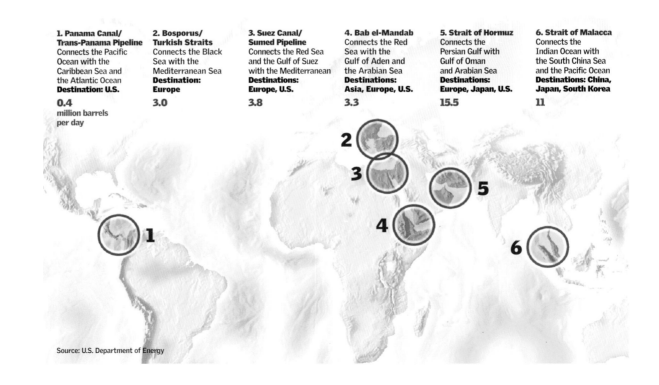

1. Panama Canal/ Trans-Panama Pipeline
Connects the Pacific Ocean with the Caribbean Sea and the Atlantic Ocean
Destination: U.S.
0.4 million barrels per day

2. Bosporus/ Turkish Straits
Connects the Black Sea with the Mediterranean Sea
Destination: Europe
3.0

3. Suez Canal/ Sumed Pipeline
Connects the Red Sea and the Gulf of Suez with the Mediterranean
Destinations: Europe, U.S.
3.8

4. Bab el-Mandab
Connects the Red Sea with the Gulf of Aden and the Arabian Sea
Destinations: Asia, Europe, U.S.
3.3

5. Strait of Hormuz
Connects the Persian Gulf with Gulf of Oman and Arabian Sea
Destinations: Europe, Japan, U.S.
15.5

6. Strait of Malacca
Connects the Indian Ocean with the South China Sea and the Pacific Ocean
Destinations: China, Japan, South Korea
11

Source: U.S. Department of Energy

Map illustrating oil-distribution choke points.

石油の流通における重要な航路を表すマップ。

USA   2004
AD: Carol Macrini   D, I, S: Eliot Bergman   CL: Bloomberg Markets Magazine

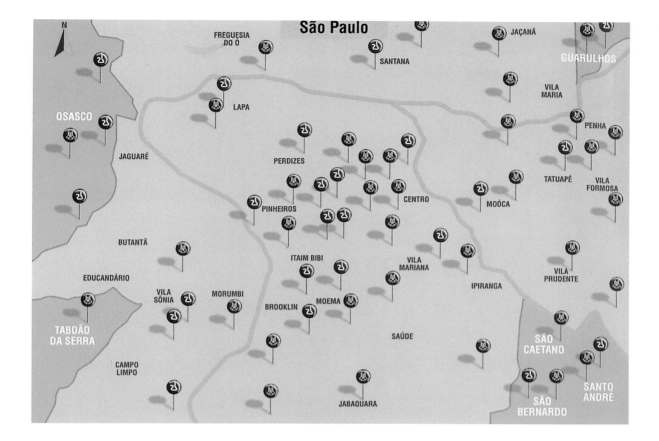

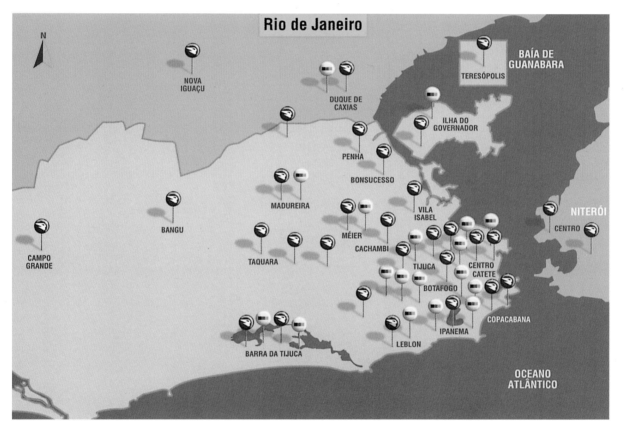

Maps indicating the locations of clinical laboratories in 3 states in Brazil.

ブラジルの3つの州にある臨床検査室の場所を示すマップ。

Brazil   2003
CD: Ronaldo da Silva Rego   AD: Celia Emy Ushizawa   D: Hamilton B. Furtado   P: Daniel Dayan / Eduardo Barcellos / Lucio Cunha / Roberto Rosa
I: Gil de Godoy   CW: Sylvia Muller   DF, S: Graphic Designers S. C. Ltda   CL: Diagnosticos da America S/A

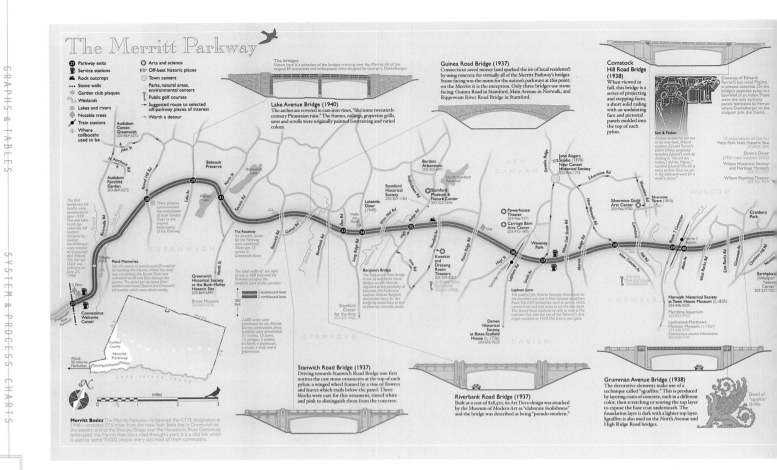

A NEW guide to the Merritt Parkway

FAMOUS BRIDGES

MAN-MADE & NATURAL FEATURES

PLACES NEARBY
THAT ARE WORTH A VISIT

Merritt Parkway Conservancy
© 2004

A map of a road in Connecticut in USA showing bridges, points of interest, and history.

橋や名所、歴史を紹介する、アメリカのコネチカット州のロードマップ。

USA 2004

CD, AD, D, I, S: Nigel Holmes   CW: Peter Szabo   DF: Explanation Graphics   CL: Merritt Parkway Conservancy

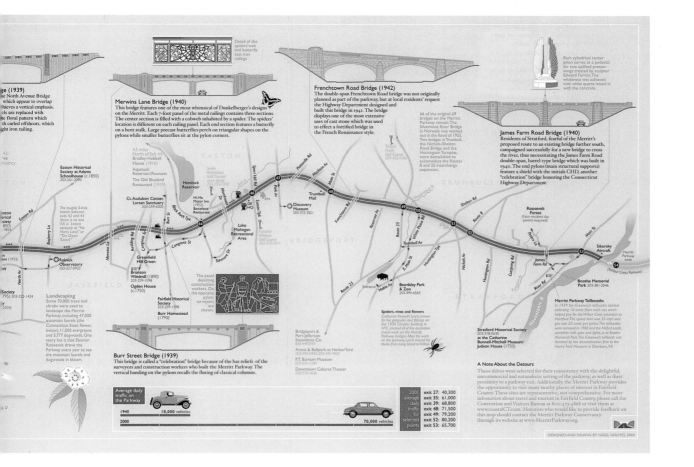

Merwins Lane Bridge (1940)
This bridge features one of the most whimsical of Dunkelberger's designs on the Merritt. Each 7-foot panel of the metal railings contains three sections. The center section is filled with a cobweb inhabited by a spider. The spiders' location is different on each railing panel. Each end section features a butterfly on a bent stalk. Large precast butterflies perch on triangular shapes on the pylons while smaller butterflies sit at the pylon corners.

Frenchtown Road Bridge (1942)
The double-span Frenchtown Road bridge was not originally planned as part of the parkway, but at local residents' request the Highway Department designed and built this bridge in 1941. The bridge displays one of the most extensive uses of cast stone which was used to effect a fortified bridge in the French Renaissance style.

James Farm Road Bridge (1940)
Residents of Stratford, fearful of the Merritt's proposed route to an existing bridge further south, campaigned successfully for a new bridge to cross the river, thus necessitating the James Farm Road double-span, barrel-type bridge which was built in 1940. The end pylons (main structural supports) feature a shield with the initials CHD, another "celebration" bridge honoring the Connecticut Highway Department.

Burr Street Bridge (1939)
This bridge is called a "celebration" bridge because of the bas reliefs of the surveyors and construction workers who built the Merritt Parkway. The vertical banding on the pylons recalls the fluting of classical columns.

Landscaping
Some 70,000 trees and shrubs were used to landscape the Merritt Parkway, including 47,000 mountain laurels (the Connecticut State flower, below), 11,000 evergreens and 3,777 dogwoods. One story has it that Eleanor Roosevelt drove the Parkway every year to see the mountain laurels and dogwoods in bloom.

A Note About the Detours
These drives were selected for their consistency with the delightful, uncommercial and naturalistic setting of the parkway, as well as their proximity to a parkway exit. Additionally, the Merritt Parkway provides the opportunity to visit many nearby places of interest in Fairfield County. These sites are representative, not comprehensive. For more information about travel and tourism in Fairfield County, please call the Convention and Visitors Bureau at 800-473-4868 or visit them at www.coastalCT.com. Motorists who would like to provide feedback on this map should contact the Merritt Parkway Conservancy through its website at www.MerrittParkway.org.

Average daily traffic on the Parkway
1940 — 18,000 vehicles
2000 — 70,000 vehicles

2001 average daily traffic for selected points	
exit 27	40,300
exit 35	61,000
exit 39	68,800
exit 48	71,500
exit 49	79,200
exit 52	80,200
exit 53	65,700

DESIGNED AND DRAWN BY NIGEL HOLMES, 2004

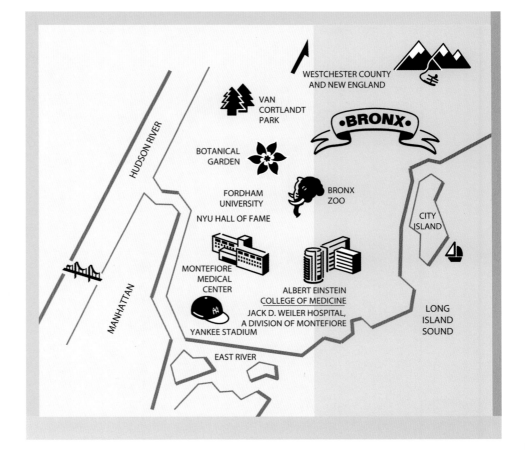

A map showing the relationship of
Montefiore Medical Center to
the New York City area, and beyond.
It also shows the relationship to its other facility of
the Albert Einstein College of Medicine,
as well as other local learning institutions.

Montefiore医療センターとニューヨーク周辺の位置関係を
示したマップ。また、薬科大学やそのほかの教育施設などの
位置も紹介している。

USA 1999
CD, AD: Diane Bennett   CD, AD, D, I: Mike Quon
DF, S: Mike Quon / Designation Inc.
CL: Montefiore Medical Center

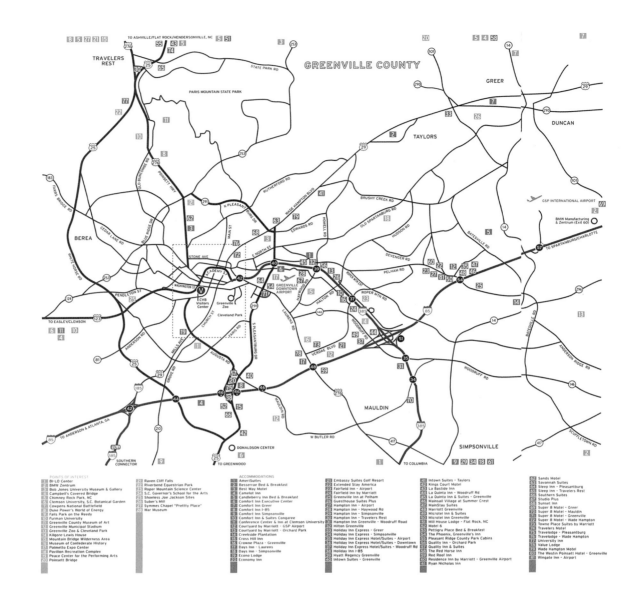

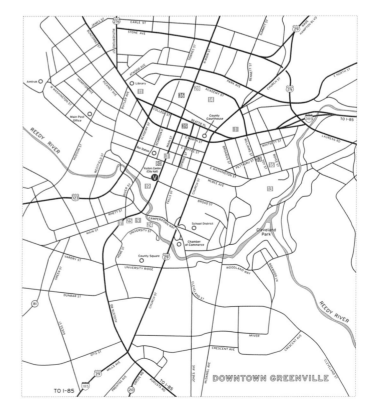

Maps for visitors to Greenville, South Carolina.

サウスカロライナ州グリーンビルを訪れる人々のためのマップ。

Canada 2004
CD, AD: Frank Viva   D, I: Todd Temporale   P: Frances Juriansz
CW: Doug Dolan   DF, S: Viva Dolan Communications & Design Inc.
CL: Greenville Convention & Visitors Bureay

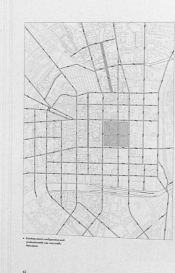

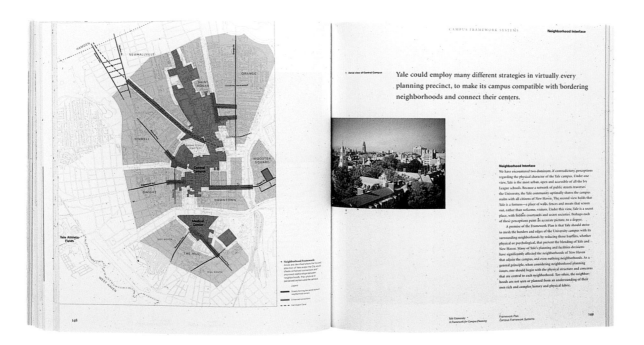

Maps and diagrams from design guidelines that provides a comprehensive plan for the future growth of the Yale University campus.
Not only did the University seek to develop its campus, but also the University's physical and aesthetic relationship to the city of New Haven.

イェール大学キャンパス拡張基本計画のデザイン・ガイドラインから抜粋したマップやダイアグラム。大学はキャンパスの拡大だけではなく、ニューヘブン市との物理的・美的な関係を模索していた。

USA 2003
D: L. Richard Poulin / Amy Kwon   DF, S: Poulin + Morris Inc.   CL: Yale University

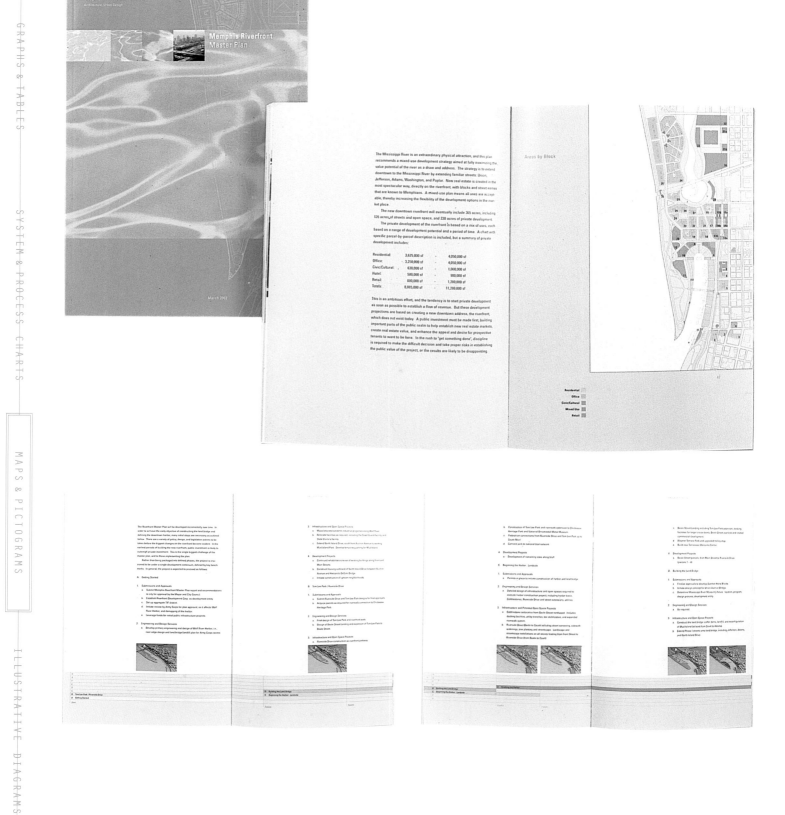

From the master plan for Memphis' riverfront incorporating over twelve miles of Mississippi River frontage with a system of connected parks leading to a new commercial harbor at the foot of downtown. Maps illustrating the site, and other diagrams showing technical data, planning and architectural criteria.

ダウンタウンにある新しい商業港へと公園が続く、メンフィスのリバーフロントのためのマスタープランより。現場を紹介するマップや、建築プランなどを示す図。

USA   2003
D: L. Richard Poulin / Rosemary Markowski   DF, S: Poulin + Morris Inc.   CL: Memphis Riverfront Redevelopment

A series of maps illustrating the site and facilities plan for Monticello.
It establishes an appropriate and achievable framework for the foundation's mission goals over the next ten years.

モンティチェッロのためのサイトプランおよび施設案を紹介するマップ。今後10年間におよぶ財団の目標の適切かつ達成可能な枠組を構築している。

USA   2003
D: L. Richard Poulin / Amy Kwon   DF, S: Poulin + Morris Inc.   CL: The Thomas Jefferson Memorial Foundation

今後20年間にわたる大学キャンパスの開発マスタープラン・ガイドラインを紹介する本から抜粋。図版は拡大・改良されたキャンパスの可能性を表現している。

The Next Step

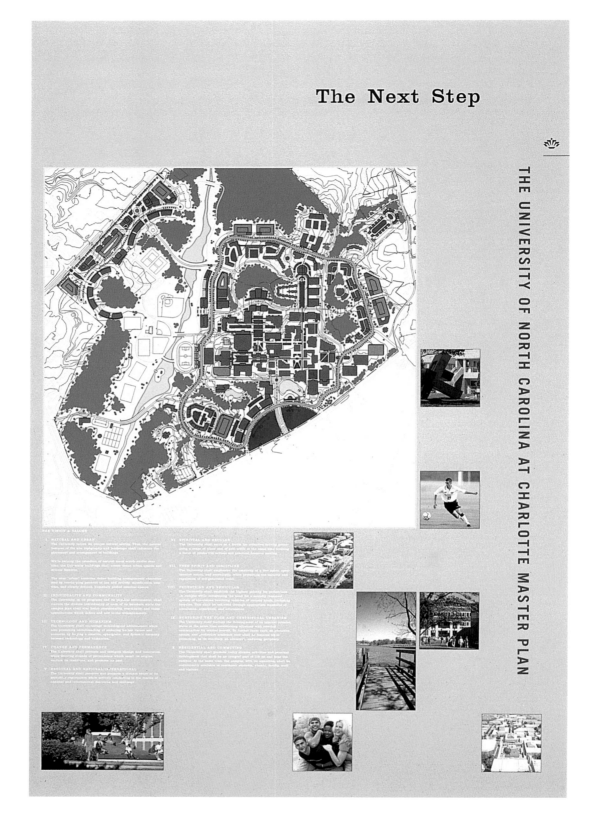

THE UNIVERSITY OF NORTH CAROLINA AT CHARLOTTE MASTER PLAN

From the publication that outlines the University's master plan guidelines for the development of their campus over the next twenty years. Drawings illustrating the potential for an improved and expanded campus.

今後20年間にわたる大学キャンパスの開発マスタープラン・ガイドラインを紹介する本から抜粋。図版は拡大・改良されたキャンパスの可能性を表現している。

USA 2003
D: L. Richard Poulin / Brian Brindisi   DF, S: Poulin + Morris Inc.   CL: University of North Carolina

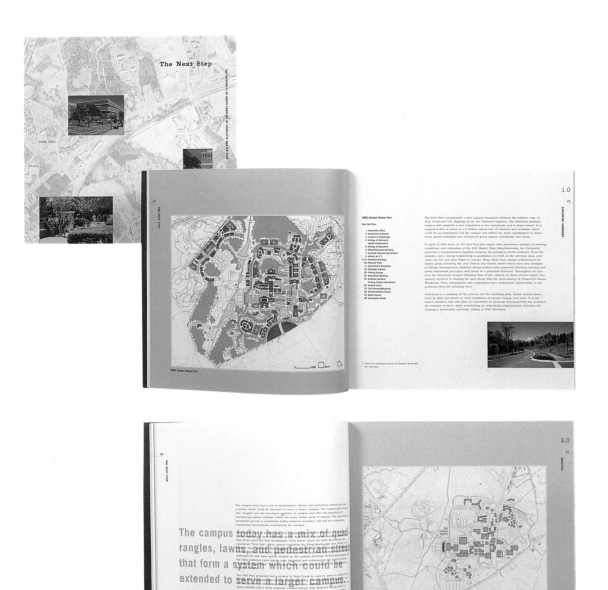

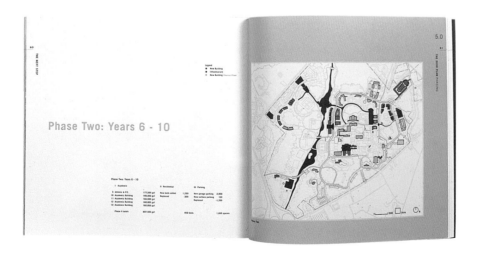

A series of illustrations from the University's master plan guidelines.
大学のマスタープラン・ガイドラインから抜粋した一連の図版。

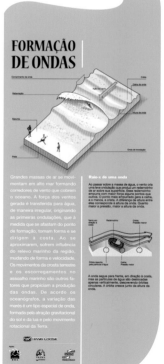

From a signage system developed for the important ecological sanctuaries.
Providing information on geography, biology, and wave of the island and the rules to protect its nature.

重要な環境保護区のために作成されたサイン・システムより。島の地理や生態系、波に関する情報や、自然保護のルールを紹介。

Brazil   2003
CD, S: Eduardo Asta   I: Daniel Lopes (Noronha Ondas. Ai)   CW: Janaina Gava   CL: Surf CO

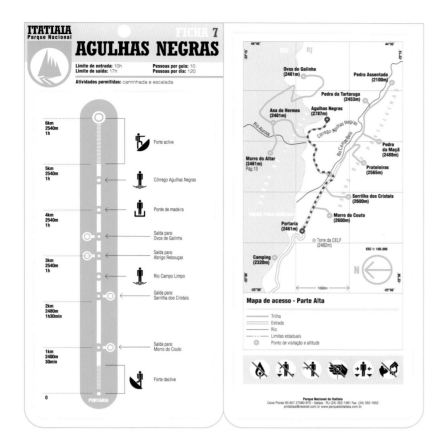

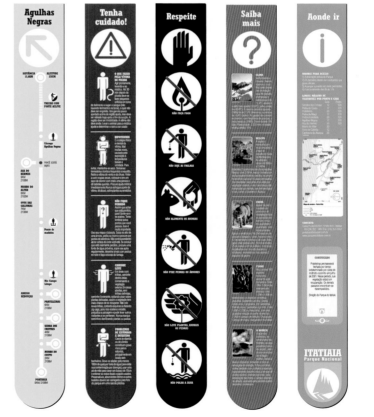

A prototype of signage system and informational diagrams designed for Itatiaia Natural Park.
There are two tasks envolved to protect visitors from dangerous situations and to protect the park from the visitors.

イタチアイア国立公園のためにデザインされた、サインのシステムとダイアグラムのプロトタイプ。危険なシチュエーションから観光客を守ること、観光客から公園を守ること、という2つの課題のもとに制作された。

Brazil   2001
CD, S: Eduardo Asta   CL: PNI Office / Ibama-RJ

Maps Illustrated in the style of 1920-30 railway posters showing commuter rail lines from London.
1920〜30年代の鉄道ポスターを思わせるマップ。ロンドンからの通勤鉄道路線を示す。

UK 2004
Graphic Editor, I, S: Phillip Green   CL: The Sunday Telegraph

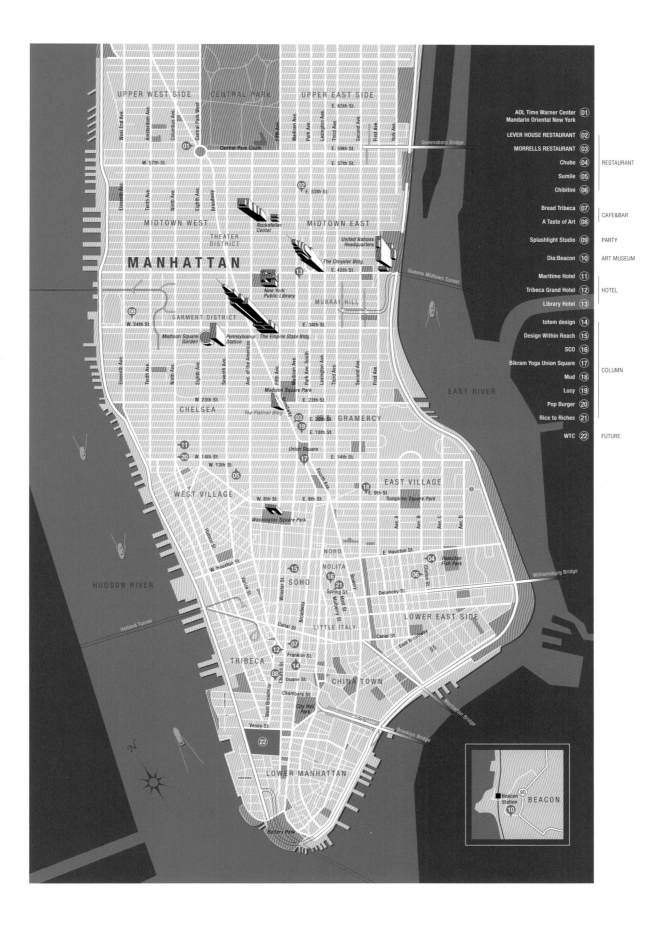

AOL Time Warner Center Mandarin Oriental New York	(01)
LEVER HOUSE RESTAURANT	(02)
MORRELLS RESTAURANT	(03)
Chubo	(04)
Sumile	(05)
Chibitini	(06)
Bread Tribeca	(07)
A Taste of Art	(08)
Splashlight Studio	(09)
Dia:Beacon	(10)
Maritime Hotel	(11)
Tribeca Grand Hotel	(12)
Library Hotel	(13)
totem design	(14)
Design Within Reach	(15)
SCO	(16)
Bikram Yoga Union Square	(17)
Mud	(18)
Lucy	(19)
Pop Burger	(20)
Rice to Riches	(21)
WTC	(22)

RESTAURANT

CAFE&BAR

PARTY

ART MUSEUM

HOTEL

COLUMN

FUTURE

A map from a feature article on New York in the magazine "Tokyo Calendar."

雑誌『東京カレンダー』より。ニューヨークの特集内で使用したマップ。

Japan 2003
AD: Mayuko Horikawa I: Tokuma DF: Dynamite Brothers Syndicate Co., Ltd. CL: Access Publishing Co., Ltd. S: Bowlgraphics

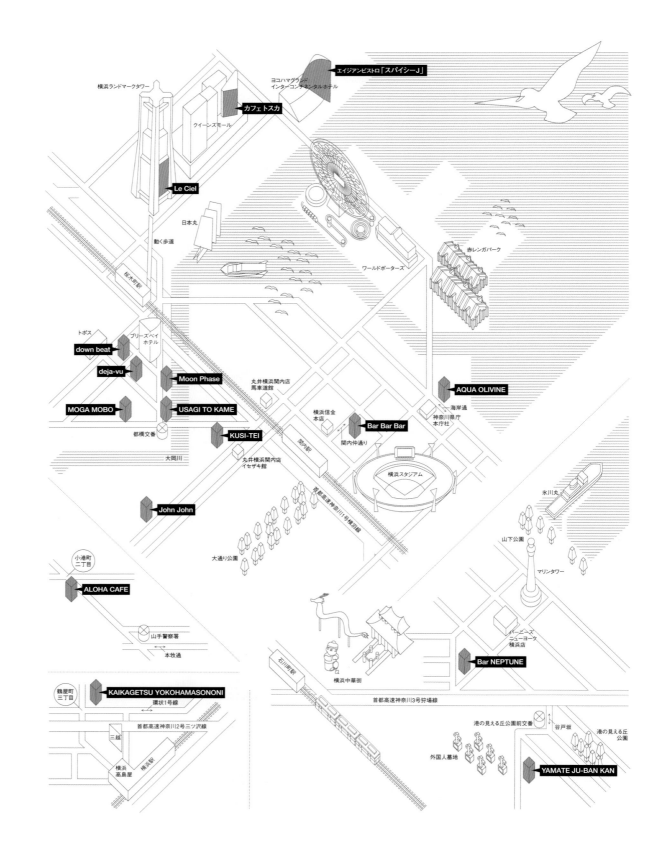

横浜ランドマークタワー

クイーンズモール

Le Ciel

日本丸

動く歩道

桜木町駅

トポス

down beat

deja-vu

Moon Phase

MOGA MOBO

USAGI TO KAME

KUSI-TEI

都橋交番

大岡川

John John

小港町
二丁目

ALOHA CAFE

山手警察署

本牧通

鶴屋町
三丁目

KAIKAGETSU YOKOHAMASONONI

環状1号線

首都高速神奈川2号三ツ沢線

三越

横浜駅

横浜
高島屋

ブリーズベイ
ホテル

丸井横浜関内店
馬車道館

横浜信金
本店

丸井横浜関内店
イセザキ館

カフェトスカ

ヨコハマグランド
インターコンチネンタルホテル

エイジアンビストロ「スパイシーJ」

ワールドポーターズ

赤レンガパーク

海岸通

AQUA OLIVINE

神奈川県庁
本庁社

Bar Bar Bar

関内仲通り

関内駅

首都高速神奈川1号横羽線

横浜スタジアム

大通り公園

石川町駅

横浜中華街

首都高速神奈川3号狩場線

氷川丸

山下公園

マリンタワー

バーニーズ
ニューヨーク
横浜店

Bar NEPTUNE

港の見える丘公園前交番

谷戸坂

港の見える丘
公園

外国人墓地

YAMATE JU-BAN KAN

A map of the Yokohama area from a feature article on Yokohama in the magazine "Monthly M."

雑誌『マンスリー・エム』より。横浜特集内で使用した横浜地区のマップ。

Japan   2002
AD: Takeshi Hamada   I: Tokuma   DF: Dynamite Brothers Syndicate Co., Ltd.   CL: Bell System 24   S: Bowlgraphics

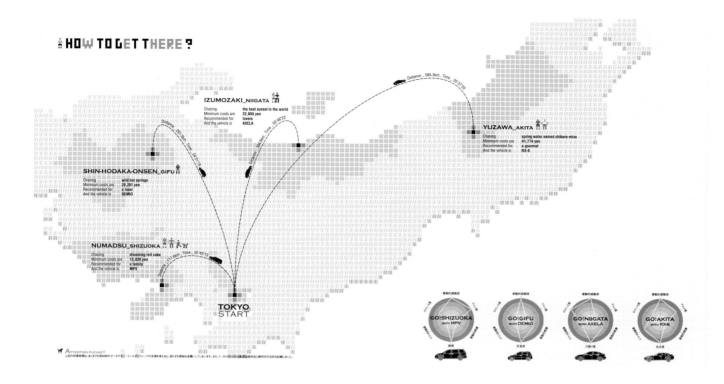

Information to aid in maximizing the pleasure of spur of the moment day trips by car from Tokyo from the magazine "Metro Minutes."

雑誌『メトロミニッツ』より。東京から衝動的に日帰りドライブを満喫するための情報。

Japan 2004
D, I: Tokuma CW: Junichi Kobayashi CL: Starts Publishing Co. S: Bowlgraphics

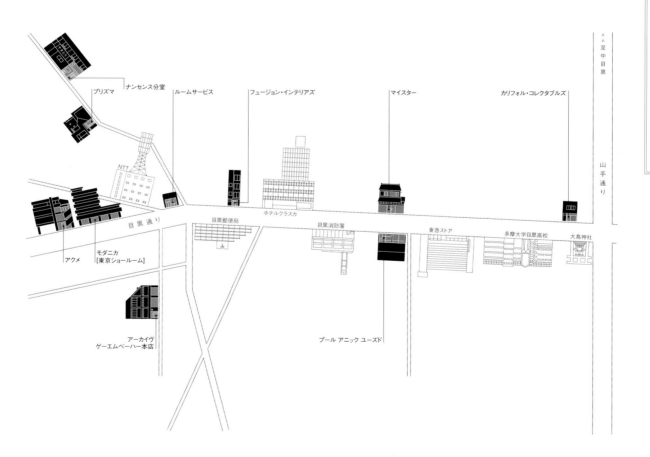

A map introducing interior design shops on Meguro-dori from the magazine "TITLe."

雑誌『TITLe』より。目黒通りのインテリアショップを紹介したマップ。

Japan 2004
AD: Tetsushi Kawamura I: Tokuma DF: Atomosphere, Ltd. CL: Bungeishunju Ltd. S: Bowlgraphics

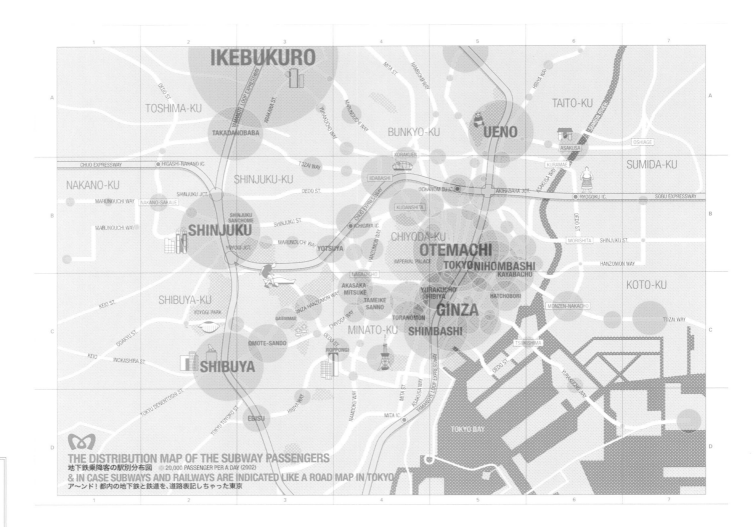

The Tokyo railroad network expressed as road ways also showing the distribution of passengers boarding and alighting at each station, from the magazine "Metro Minutes."

雑誌『メトロミニッツ』より。東京都内の鉄道網を道路に見立てて表現。さらに駅別乗降客の分布も表記。

Japan 2004
AD, D: Takashi Tokuma I: Tokuma DF: Dynamite Brothers Syndicate Co., Ltd. CL: Starts Publishing Co. S: Bowlgraphics

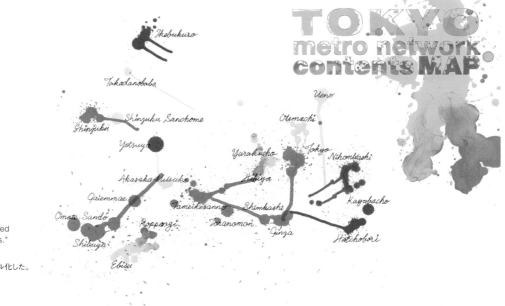

Visualization of the main rail lines and stations related
to topics dealt with in the magazine "Metro Minutes."

雑誌『メトロミニッツ』より。
雑誌内で扱うトピックを中心に主要部の駅と路線をビジュアル化した。

Japan 2003
AD: Shinsuke Koshio D: Miki Shimizu
CL: Starts Publishing Co. S: Sunday-Vision

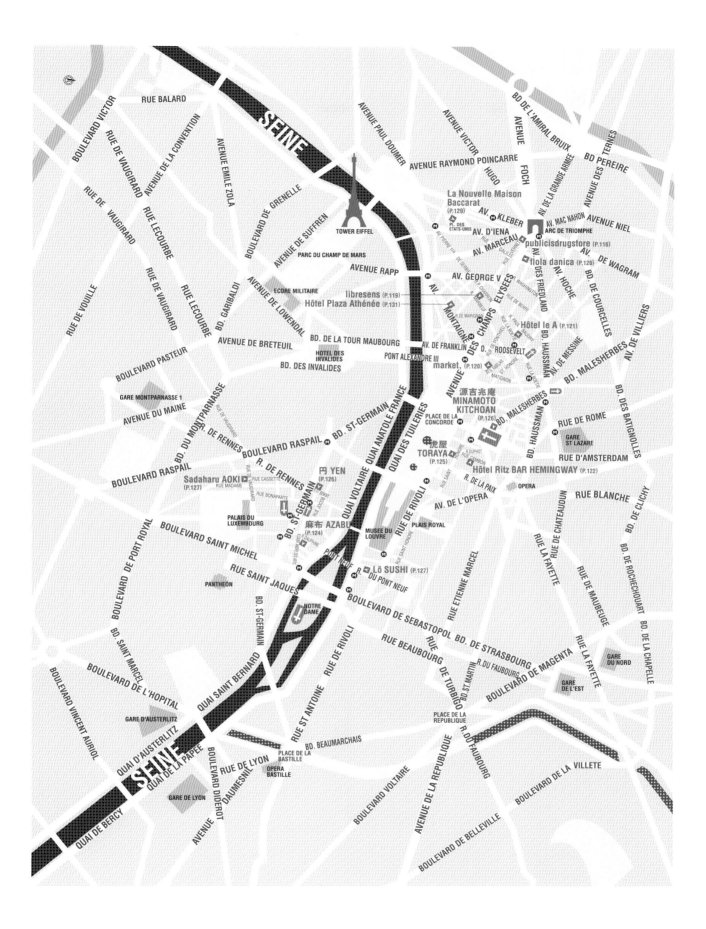

A map of Paris streets from a feature article on Paris in the magazine "Tokyo Calendar."

雑誌『東京カレンダー』より。パリの特集内で使用したパリ市街のマップ。

Japan 2004
AD: Mayuko Horikawa   I: Tokuma   DF: Dynamite Brothers Syndicate Co., Ltd.   CL: Access Publishing Co., Ltd.   S: Bowlgraphics

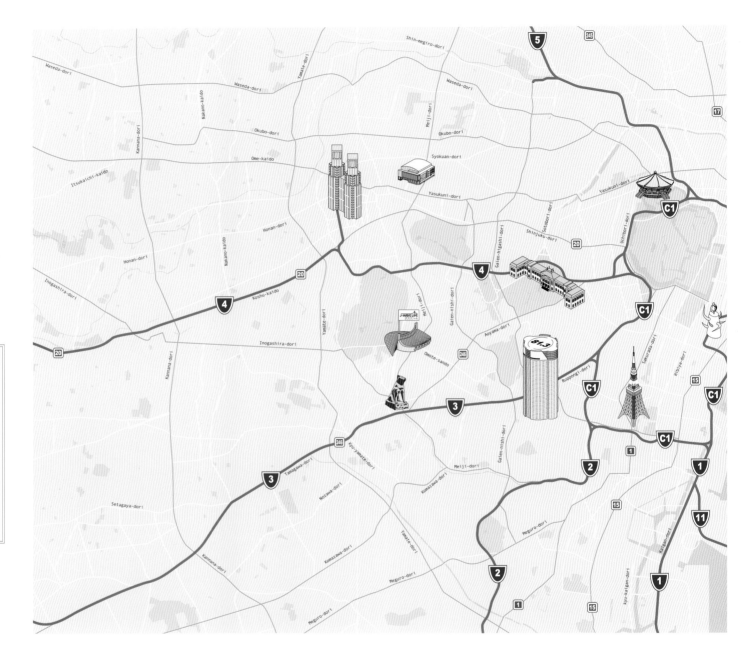

A map of Tokyo centered on the headquarters of a broadcasting company.

放送会社の本社を中心とした東京のマップ。

Japan   2004
AD: Kazunari Shimajiri   D: Mizuna Kojima   I, S: Teppei Watanabe   CW: Toru Ejima / Takaaki Kubota   DF: Sony Music Communications Inc.   CL: J-Wave, Inc.

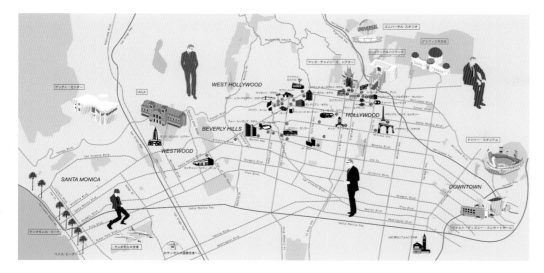

Los Angeles guide map centered around Hollywood.

ハリウッドを中心としたロサンゼルスのガイドマップ。

Japan 2004
I, S: Teppei Watanabe
CL: Shochiku Co., Ltd.

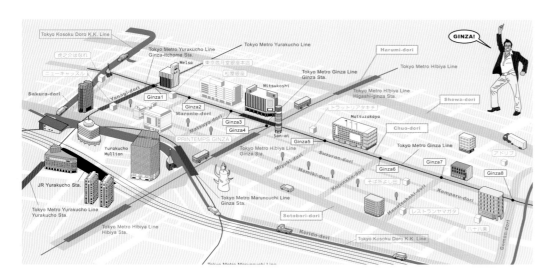

Ginza guide map.

銀座のガイドマップ。

Japan 2004
AD: Aoco (Pangaea) D: Uru-uru
P: Naomichi Seo I, S: Teppei Watanabe
CW: Ayako Otsuka
Compilation: Nobuyuki Hirai
CL: Starts Publishing Co.

Naka-Meguro guide map.

中目黒のガイドマップ。

Japan 2003
AD: Aoco (Pangaea) D: Uru-uru
P: Takashi Misawa / Takashi Nishizawa /
Katsumi Sato I, S: Teppei Watanabe
CW, Compilation: Mihoko Nemoto
CL: Starts Publishing Co.

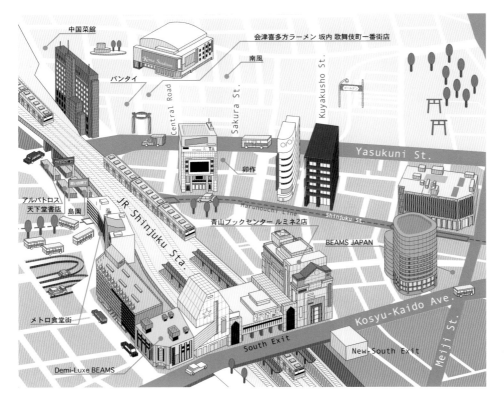

Shinjuku guide map.

新宿のガイドマップ。

Japan 2003
CL: Starts Publishing Corporation   AD: Aoco(Pangaea)
D: Uru-Uru   P: Takashi Nishizawa / Naomichi Seo
I, S: Teppei Watanabe   CW, Kousei: Mihoko Nemoto

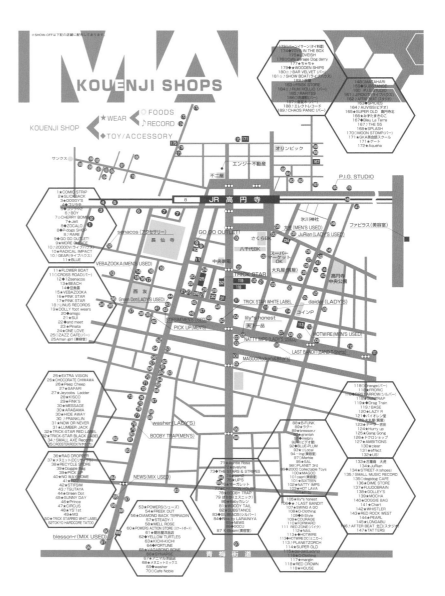

A map indicating stores in Koenji that distribute the free paper "SHOW-OFF."

フリーペーパー『SHOW-OFF』を配布している高円寺内の店舗を示すマップ。

Japan 2000
DF: Lovin' Graphic   CL, S: Show-Off

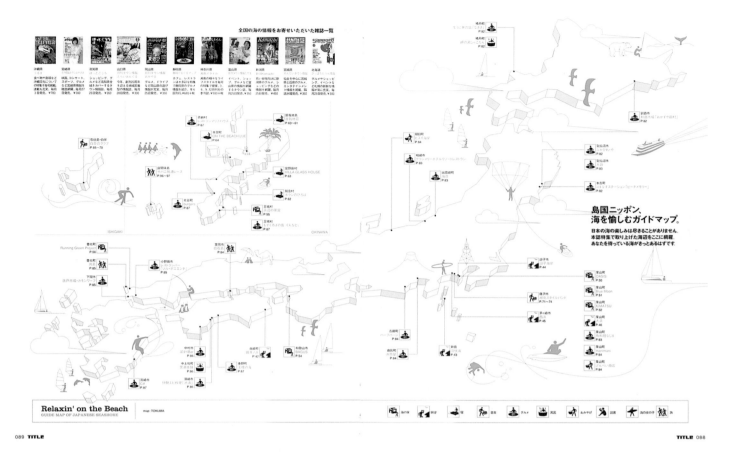

A map showing the distribution of beaches featured in Japan in a special article on beaches in the magazine "TITLe."

雑誌『TITLe』より。海辺の特集内で使用した日本国内の海辺の分布図。

Japan　2003

AD: Tetsushi Kawamura　I: Tokuma　DF: Atmosphere, Ltd.　CL: Bungeisyunju Ltd.　S: Bowlgraphics

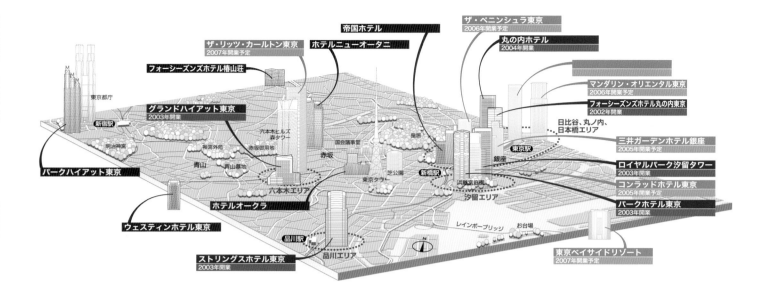

Illustrations of buildings arranged on a map describing the inroads of foreign-owned hotels from the magazine "Weekly Diamond."
雑誌『週刊ダイヤモンド』より。外資系ホテル進出ラッシュを、地図上に建物イラストを配置して説明。

Japan   2004
CD: Hiroyuki Kimura   D: Sachiko Hagiwara   DF, S: Tube Graphics   CL: Diamond Inc.

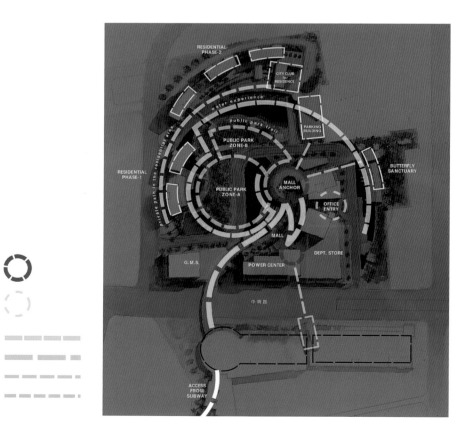

A diagram showing the arrangement of spatial elements related to the various facilities planned within the development area.
開発地区内に計画される多種用途の施設を、空間の環境要素により関連付けた配置を表す分布図。

Japan   2001
CD, AD: Kiharu Tsuge   D: Hikaru Sasaki   DF, S: Tsuge Design Management   CL: Hamano Institute Inc.

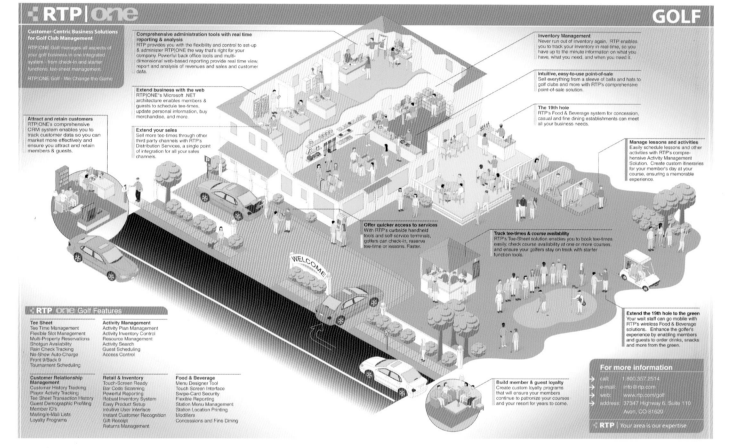

A diagram showing features of a golf resort point-of-sale software package.

ゴルフ・リゾートのセールス・ポイントを伝えるソフトウェア・パッケージの特徴を図解。

USA 2004
D, I, CW, S: William H. Bardel   CL: Resort Technology Partners

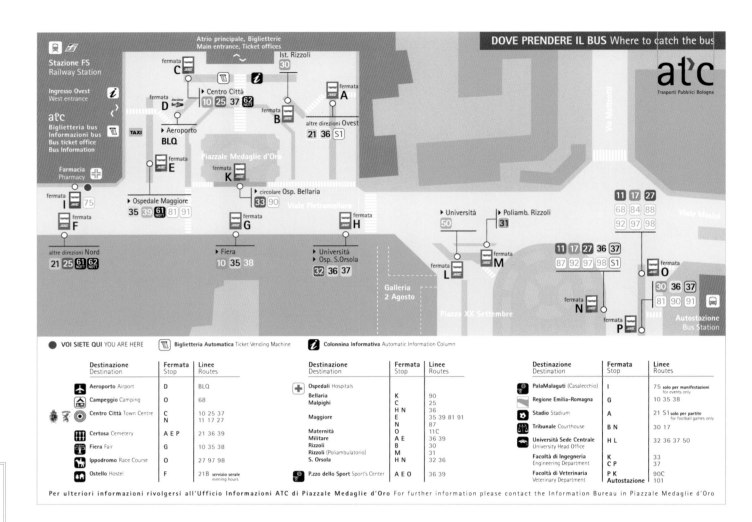

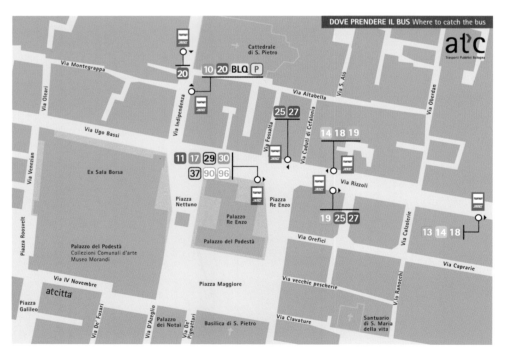

Various diagrams showing time tables, locations of bus stops, route maps of the public transportation.

公共の交通機関の路線図、バス停の場所、時刻表を示す様々な案内図。

Italy 2001

CD: Barbara Cuniberti   D: Elena Corradini / Martina Zucchini   DF, S: Kuni   CL: ATC-Azienda Trasporti Pubblici

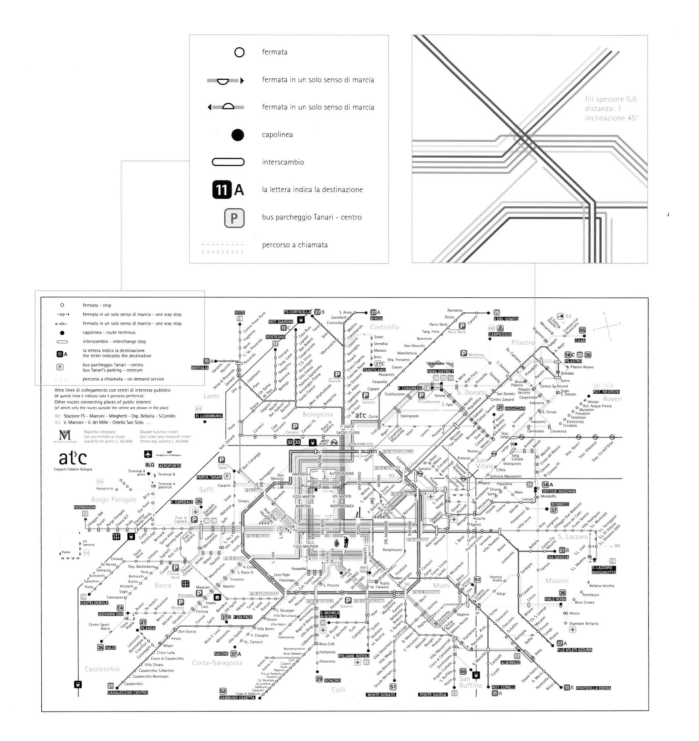

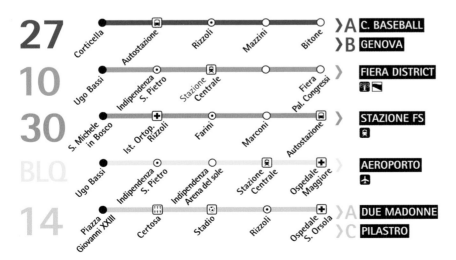

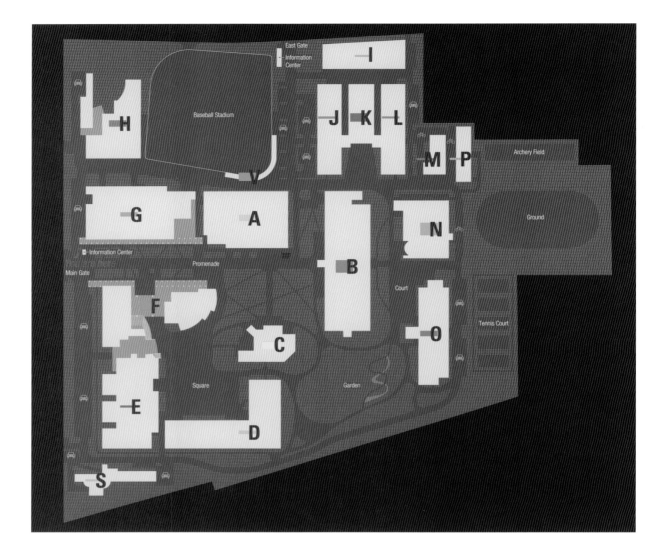

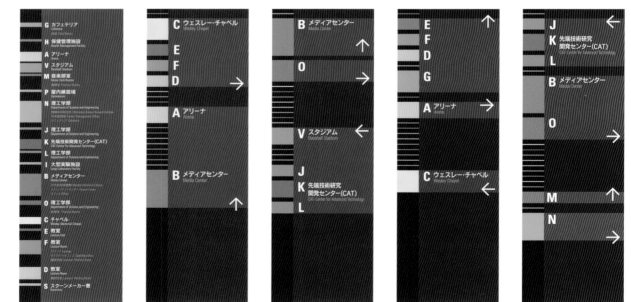

A map and guided diagram of the Aoyama Gakuin University Sagamihara Campus.

青山学院大学相模原キャンパス内のマップと案内表示。

Japan　2002
CD, AD, D, S: Kei Miyazaki　D: Natsuko Hosokawa　DF: KMD Inc.　CL: Aoyama Gakuin University

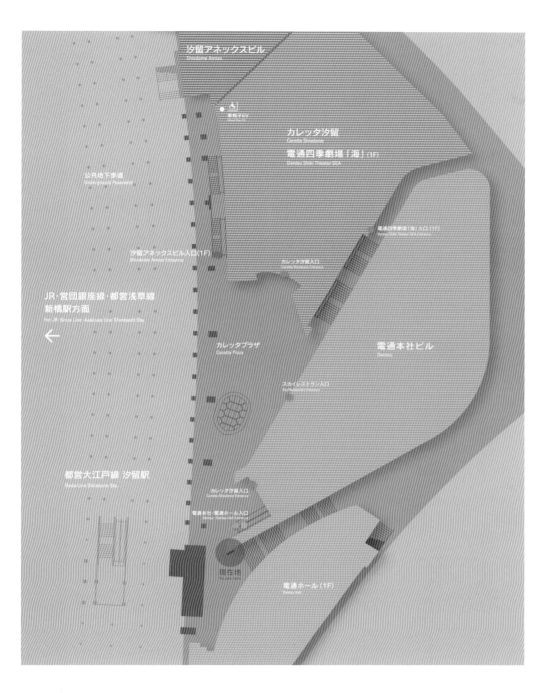

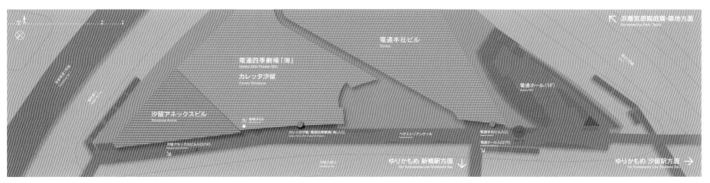

Guide to the area (Shiodome area A) surrounding Dentsu corporate headquarters.

電通本社周辺（汐留A街区）の案内図。

Japan 2002
CD, AD, D, S: Kei Miyazaki   D: Masako Nishikata   DF: KMD Inc.   CL: Dentsu Inc.

This application is less linear and more organic, with Resolve clusters along winding secondary paths. All routes and groups are defined by trusses, flags, or colored screens. Designed to support some collaboration and teamwork, this plan is primarily composed of individual spaces.

Think high.
Make use of overhead space with sliding trusses. A sliding truss connecting two constel-lations creates a threshold that can be constellations together to identify teams and also assist in wayfinding

Making room.
A 4' work surface on a 5' arm leaves room for attaching storage on either side: a ladder shelf or cabinet on one side, a tool rail or monitor pod on the other.

Making more room.
Work surfaces oriented in an "outbound" position create a peninsula off the pole, making the work space feel larger and freeing up infrastructure to support additional storage elements

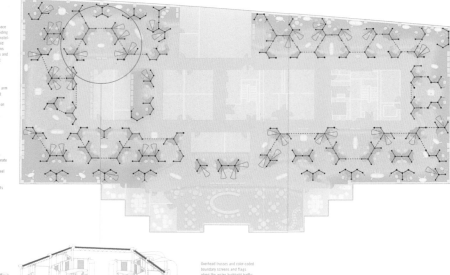

Primary circulation route.

Secondary traffic paths meander through constellations to provide opportunities for chance encounters and impromptu conversations.

Cul-de-sacs offer quiet places for casual meeting

Trusses create a rhythm through the space that aids wayfinding and adds vertical dimension to the environment.

Overhead trusses and color-coded boundary screens and flags along the aisles highlight traffic paths and identify groups

38 DESIGNING RESOLVE ENVIRONMENTS   PLANNING 39

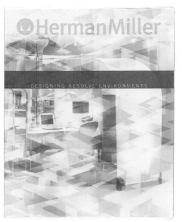

Diagrams indicate floorplan examples to help interior designers and architects in designing office spaces.

インテリア・デザイナーや建築家がオフィス・スペースをデザインする際に役立つフロアプラン。

USA   2000
CD, AD, S: Yang Kim   AD, D: Brian Hauch   P: Herman Miller archives   I: Amy Franceschini   CW: Deb Wierenga   DF: BBK Studio   CL: Herman Miller

ZIG-ZAG

This 2-sided constellation can be extended to create space-efficient layouts within a floor plate of virtually any size or shape. Group floating Zig-Zags to create open, collaborative work areas.

ZIG-ZAG 4
CHUTE
ZIGGY
ZIG-ZAG 5
TRIPOD
POPCORN
ZIG-ZAG 6
BRANCH
ARENA

SHELL

The 3-sided Shell provides some enclosure for concentrated work while remaining open to collaborative efforts. Expanded constellations of Shells perform well as hubs for group areas, creating boundaries that define team space.

SHELL 2
CROWN
SUMO
SHELL 3
SEA SHELL
PEACOCK
PROPELLER
EXTENDED SHELL
CLAM SHELL
SUNFLOWER

Extended Honey
Clustered in groups of four along an expansive window wall, Extended Honey constellations support the computing, meeting, and paper-based work of their multitasking occupants.

EXTENDED HONEY

Dogbone, Extended Honey
Closely placed architectural columns in this long, narrow space are easily accommodated by Dogbone constellations placed at angles and linked with sliding trusses that carry power and telecommunications cables over the entrances to team areas.

DOGBONE

EXTENDED HONEY

340 Madison
Space Plan Studies

Legal – 39,000rsf ◑

Open Plan – 39,000rsf ◑

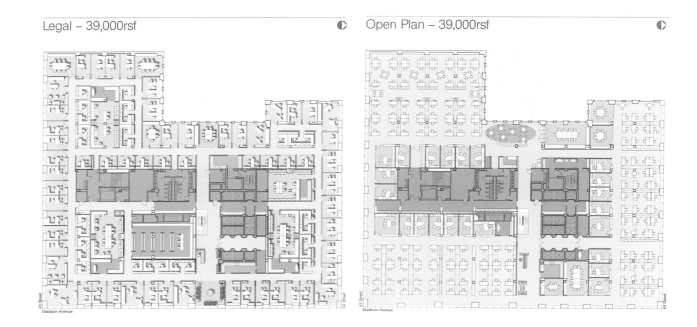

340 Madison
Stacking Plan

22	23,000rsf
21	24,000rsf
20	24,000rsf
19	27,000rsf
18	27,000rsf
17	30,000rsf
16	38,000rsf
15	39,000rsf
14	39,000rsf
12	39,000rsf — Crossover Floor
11	39,000rsf
10	39,000rsf
9	39,000rsf
8	39,000rsf
7	39,000rsf
6	39,000rsf
5	29,000rsf
4	29,000rsf
3	29,000rsf
2	29,000rsf
1	Lobby/Retail
LL	Lower Level

Freight · Hi-Rise · Lo-Rise

Floor guide and plan from an overview book for a major new office buildings in the midtown Manhattan.
マンハッタンのミッドタウンに建つ新しいオフィスビルの案内書から抜粋したフロアガイドとフロアプラン。

USA 2003
CD, D: Graham Hanson   P: Wayne Sorce   CW: Sheldon Werdiger   DF, S: Graham Hanson Design   CL: Macklowe Properties

O ESCRITÓRIO DO FUTURO

Projeto do que pode ser o escritório do século 21, desenvolvido por Piratininga Arquitetos Associados a pedido da Folha; a principal inovação está em alterar o layout do ambiente de trabalho ao longo de um único dia conforme as necessidades específicas da empresa

10:00 PLANEJAMENTO

O escritório se volta ao trabalho em grupo, ao estabelecimento de estratégias e à troca de informações; as salas se moldam para abrigar reuniões e grupos de discussão

Espaços que mudam de função e layout

Espaços que mudam apenas de função

área para planejamento estratégico

recepção

cafeteria

salas para reuniões

sala para equipes de trabalho

sala de leitura

Notebooks e redes sem cabo substituirão os gabinetes de mesa, eliminando o acúmulo de fios nos escritórios

espaço para reunião informal

sala para equipes de trabalho

cabines para trabalhos individuais

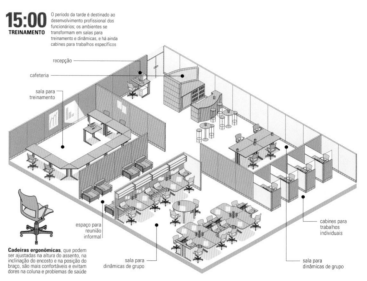

15:00 TREINAMENTO

O período da tarde é destinado ao desenvolvimento profissional dos funcionários; os ambientes se transformam em salas para treinamento e dinâmicas, e há ainda cabines para trabalhos específicos

recepção

cafeteria

sala para treinamento

espaço para reunião informal

Cadeiras ergonômicas, que podem ser ajustadas na altura do assento, na inclinação do encosto e na posição do braço, são mais confortáveis e evitam dores na coluna e problemas de saúde

sala para dinâmicas de grupo

sala para dinâmicas de grupo

cabines para trabalhos individuais

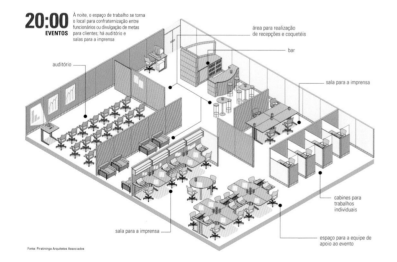

20:00 EVENTOS

À noite, o espaço de trabalho se torna o local para confraternização entre funcionários ou divulgação de metas para clientes; há auditório e salas para a imprensa

auditório

área para realização de recepções e coquetéis

bar

sala para a imprensa

sala para a imprensa

cabines para trabalhos individuais

espaço para a equipe de apoio ao evento

Fonte: Piratininga Arquitetos Associados

Illustration showing the different layouts of office space and explaining that offices will be more dynamic in the future.

オフィス・スペースの様々なレイアウトを紹介。オフィスは将来的にもっとダイナミックになるだろうと予測している。

Brazil 2000

CD, S: Eduardo Asta   CW: Mauricio Puls / Thales de Menezes / Leonardo Cruz   CL: Folha de São Paulo

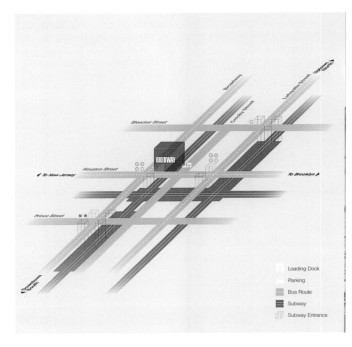

Access

Subway

○ Service between Jamaica–179 Street, Queens and Coney Island–Stillwell Avenue, Brooklyn

○ Service between Forest Hills–71 Avenue, Queens and Lower East Side–2nd Avenue, Manhattan

○ Shuttle service between Grand Street and West 4th Street, Manhattan

○ Service between Astoria–Ditmars Boulevard, Queens and 86 Street, Brooklyn

○ Service between Forest Hills–71 Avenue, Queens and 95 Street–Fort Hamilton, Brooklyn

○ Service between Pelham Bay Park–Bronx and Brooklyn Bridge–City Hall, Manhattan

Bus

M1 Service between Harlem and the East Village or South Ferry

M5 Service between Washington Heights and Greenwich Village

M6 Service between South Ferry and Midtown Manhattan

M21 Local crosstown service between Bellevue Hospital and West Village

Pedestrian

There are three major subway lines and six trains servicing 610 Broadway, including the N, R, 6, F, V and S trains. The MTA records indicate the daily pedestrian turnstile count at the local stations to be approximately 75,000 persons.

Vehicular

610 Broadway is located at the intersection of Houston Street and Broadway with direct access from the North, South and river to river. Traffic counts at this intersection have shown the vehicular hourly volume to be 2,000 cars on Houston Street and 1,200 cars on Broadway.

The building has an interior loading dock and on-site public parking off Crosby Street.

Stacking Plan

Floor	Ceiling	RSF
6	13' – 6"	10,050 plus 3,360sf outdoor terrace
5	15' – 0"	15,350
4	15' – 0"	15,350
3	15' – 0"	15,350
2	15' – 0"	15,350
Ground	19' – 0"	12,000
Cellar	10' – 0"	9,000
Parking 1	9' – 0"	14,750
Parking 2	9' – 0"	15,000

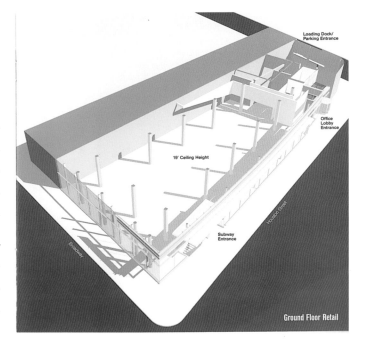

Map from an overview book for a major new showroom building in the SOHO area of New York City.

ニューヨーク市のソーホー地区にある新しいショールームビルの案内書から抜粋したマップとフロアプラン。

USA   2003
CD, D: Graham Hanson   D: Jiranuch Sanguaree   CW: Sheldon Werdiger   DF, S: Graham Hanson Design   CL: Macklowe Properties

With 11 stories above ground and 3 below, Tokyo's first convention & art center is a magnificent venue embracing a glass atrium and four buildings each housing a unique hall.

Four buildings, each housing a unique hall, plus the distinctive atrium of the Glass Building. This is the Tokyo International Forum. 7 Multistoried halls, the Exhibition Hall, and conference rooms cater to a wide range of events and requests. Each of these refined spaces boasts the finest equipment and facilities.

Hall A
Japan's representative hall with seating for 5,012.
A double-level theater-type structure, this hall boasts a range of advanced equipment and is ideal for major events ranging from international conferences to concerts.

Hall B7
Multi-purpose space that can be divided in two.
This highly versatile flat open space is suitable for various events such as conferences, fashion shows and exhibitions.

Hall C
Venue boasting the most advanced audio technology to cater to a range of events.
This triple-level theater-type hall seats 1,502 and is suitable for classical concerts and stage performances.

Hall D7
Hall with a flexible design to give you complete freedom of expression.
Roll-back seats and 25 trussed battens can be configured for alternative performances providing generous freedom of expression in this space.

Hall B5
Social gathering place with kitchen facilities.
Ideal for ceremonies and receptions, this hall features a waiting room for hosts or guests of honor.

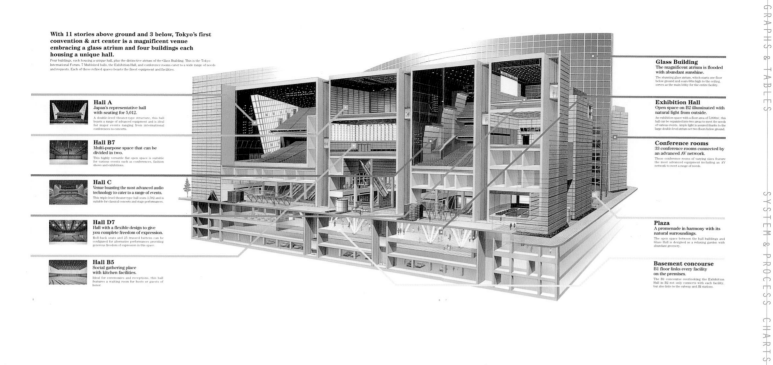

Glass Building
The magnificent atrium is flooded with abundant sunshine.
The stunning glass atrium, which starts one floor below ground and soars 60m high to the ceiling, serves as the main lobby for the entire facility.

Exhibition Hall
Open space on B2 illuminated with natural light from outside.
An exhibition space with a floor area of 5,000㎡, this hall can be separated into two areas to meet the needs of various events. Ample light is assured thanks to the large double-level atrium set two floors below ground.

Conference rooms
33 conference rooms connected by an advanced AV network.
These conference rooms of varying sizes feature the most advanced equipment including an AV network to meet a range of needs.

Plaza
A promenade in harmony with its natural surroundings.
The open space between the hall buildings and Glass Hall is designed as a retaining garden with abundant greenery.

Basement concourse
B1 floor links every facility on the premises.
The B1 concourse overlooking the Exhibition Hall in B2 not only connects with each facility, but also links to the subway and JR stations.

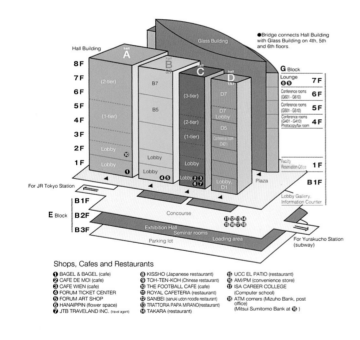

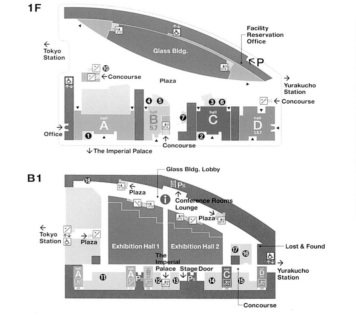

Shops, Cafes and Restaurants

❶ BAGEL & BAGEL (cafe)
❷ CAFE DE MOI (cafe)
❸ CAFE WIEN (cafe)
❹ FORUM TICKET CENTER
❺ FORUM ART SHOP
❻ HANAIPPIN (flower space)
❼ JTB TRAVELAND INC. (travel agent)

❽ KISSHO (Japanese restaurant)
❾ TOH-TEN-KOH (Chinese restaurant)
❿ THE FOOTBALL CAFE (cafe)
⓫ ROYAL CAFETERIA (restaurant)
⓬ SANBEI (sanuki udon noodle restaurant)
⓭ TRATTORIA PAPA MIRANO (restaurant)
⓮ TAKARA (restaurant)

⓯ UCC EL PATIO (restaurant)
⓰ AM/PM (convenience store)
⓱ ISA CAREER COLLEGE
(Computer school)
⓲ ATM corners (Mizuho Bank, post office)
(Mitsui Sumitomo Bank at ⓯)

Guide to conference rooms, halls and facilities in a building.
大規模公共施設「東京国際フォーラム」内のホール、会議室等の案内図。

Japan   2003
DF: McCann-Erickson Inc.   S: Tokyo International Forum Co., Ltd.

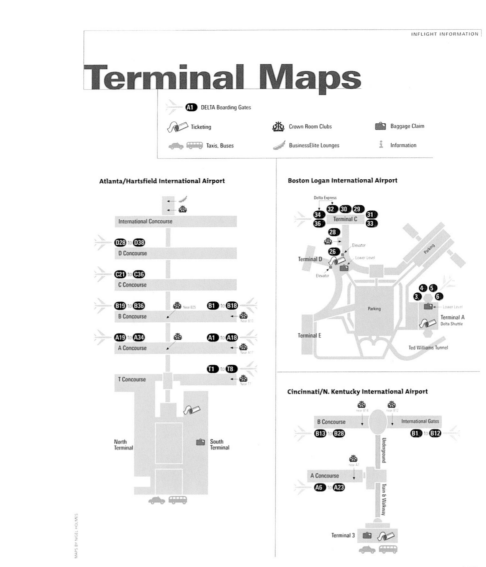

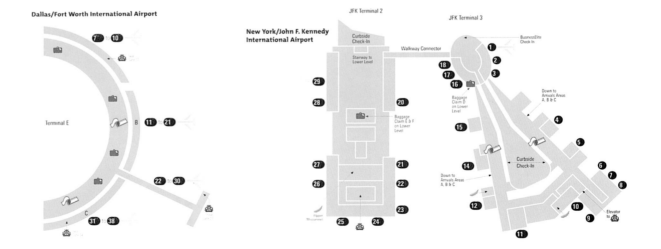

Maps of 6 airport terminals from the in-flight magazine.
機内誌から抜粋した6つの空港ターミナルのマップ。

USA   2000
AD: Ann Harvey   D, I, S: Nigel Holmes   DF: Explanation Graphics   CL: Delta Airlines Sky Magazine

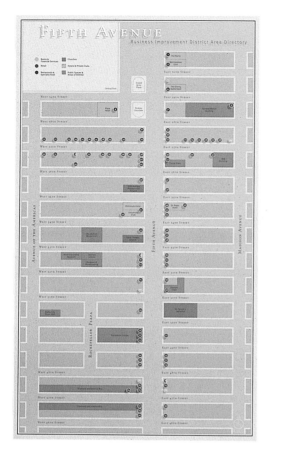

A visitor information map/guide.
来場者のためのインフォメーション・マップ兼ガイド。

USA 2003
D: L. Richard Poulin / Douglas Morris   DF, S: Poulin + Morris Inc.   CL: Fifth Avenue Business Development

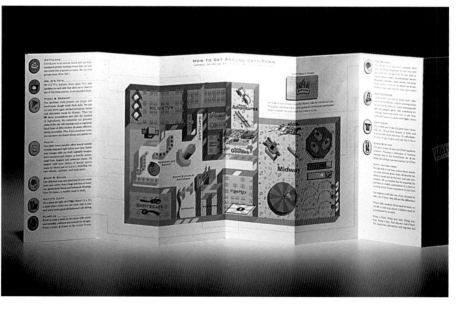

Maps to and around Gattitown, a Mr. Gatti's restaurant that includes buffets, an arcade, and a gift shop.
ビュッフェ、アーケード、ギフトショップを含むレストラン、Gattitownのフロアガイド。

USA 2002
AD, D, CW: Rex Peteet   D: Carrie Echo   DF, S: Sibley Peteet   CL: Mr. Gatti's

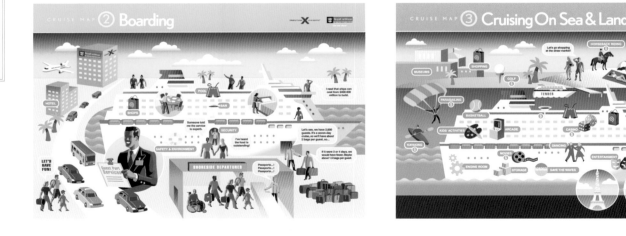

Employee training maps designed to show call-center employees how a cruise "works" from a customer's perspective.
顧客の立場から見たクルーズの流れをコールセンターの従業員に説明するためにデザインされた、研修用のイラストレーション。

USA   2004
CD, S: Sonia Greteman   AD, D: James Strange   DF: Greteman Group   CL: Royal Caribbean Cruises Ltd.

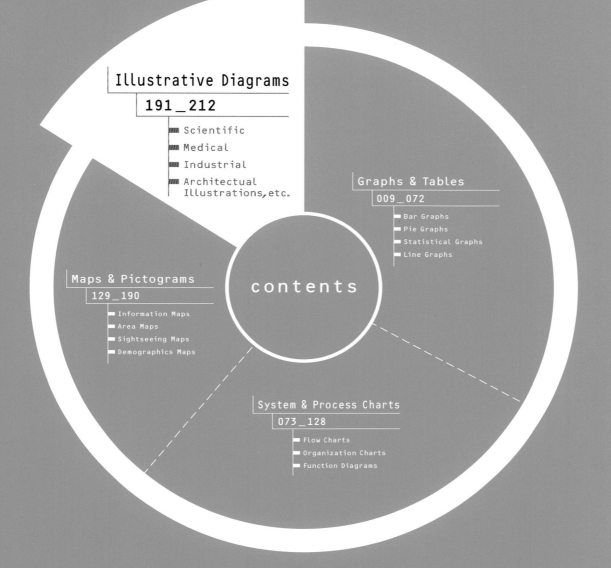

contents

Advanced **PEG Molecule**

In an aqueous medium, the long chain-like PEG molecule is heavily hydrated and in rapid motion. This rapid motion causes the PEG to sweep out a large volume and prevents the approach and interference of other molecules.

〜 PEG
◯ Water
◉ Drug molecule

From the corporate brochure for Nektar Therapeutics, a pharmaceutical company. Charts explain their technologies and drug formulations.
製薬会社のNektar Therapeutics社の会社案内より。同社のテクノロジーや製剤設計を説明するチャート。

USA　2003
CD, AD: Bill Cahan　AD, D: Sharrie Brooks　I: Doug Struthers　CW: Nicole Litchfield　DF, S: Cahan & Associates　CL: Nektar Therapeutics

Advanced PEGylation

The mPEG-SPA Advanced PEGylation reagent is an example of Nektar's clinically proven stable attachment chemistry, which enables improved therapeutic safety and efficacy and decreased dosing frequency.

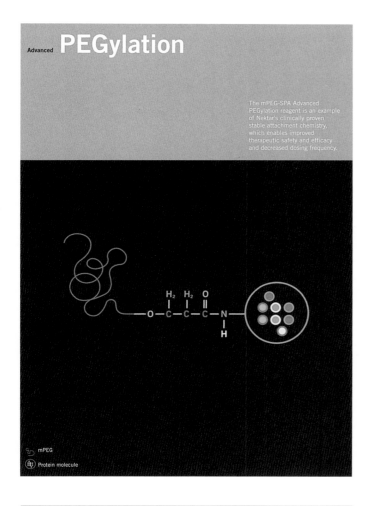

mPEG
Protein molecule

Hydrogel PEG Matrix

Composed of chemically cross-linked or physically associated PEGs that create three-dimensional structures, Nektar Hydrogels degrade slowly over time and can dramatically decrease dosing frequency by prolonging drug absorption and release.

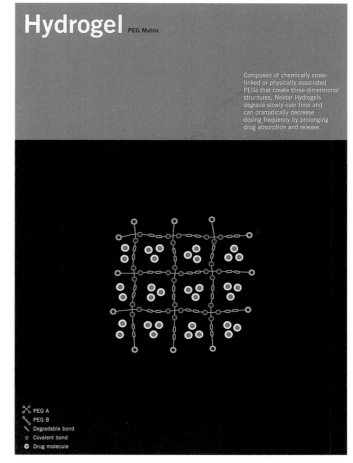

PEG A
PEG B
Degradable bond
Covalent bond
Drug molecule

Particle Engineering

In order to effectively administer therapeutics to the deep lung, research indicates that drug particles must have a small, controlled size of under five microns and be highly dispersible. Nektar optimizes particles for efficient and reproducible pulmonary delivery.

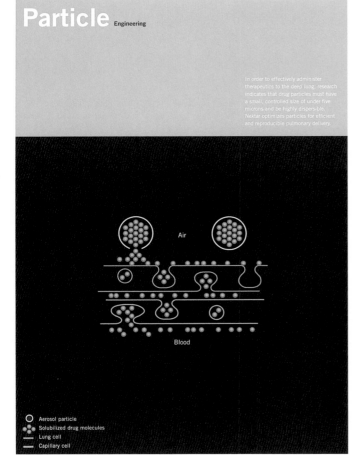

Aerosol particle
Solubilized drug molecules
Lung cell
Capillary cell

Amorphous Formulations

Nektar applies innovative screening and modeling methods to determine long-term stability of amorphous formulations, including the formulation's ability to withstand the range of environmental conditions experienced during storage and patient use.

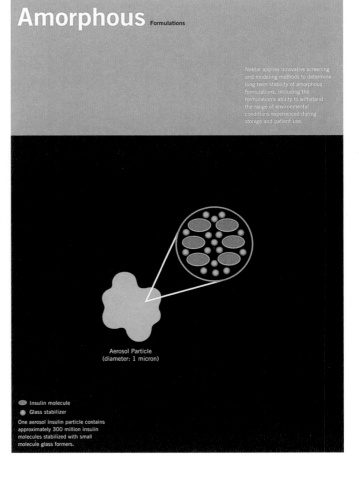

Aerosol Particle
(diameter: 1 micron)

Insulin molecule
Glass stabilizer

One aerosol insulin particle contains approximately 300 million insulin molecules stabilized with small molecule glass formers.

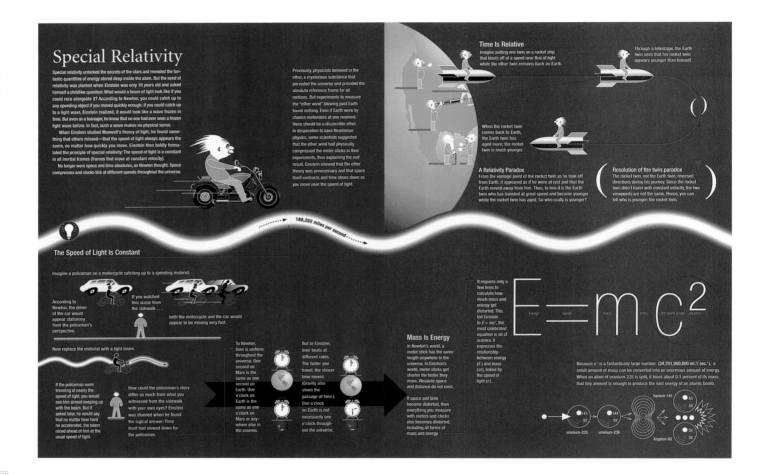

A series of diagrams from a magazine article. Explaining Einstein's theories.

雑誌の記事から抜粋。アインシュタインの理論を説明する図。

USA　2004
CD: Michael Mrak　AD: John Gilman　D, I, S: Nigel Holmes　CW: Michio Kaku　DF: Explanation Graphics　CL: Discover

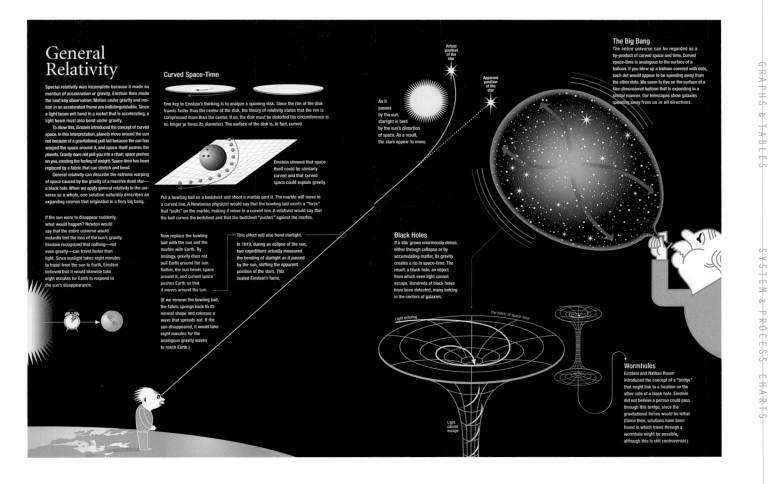

General Relativity

Special relativity was incomplete because it made no mention of acceleration or gravity. Einstein then made the next key observation: Motion under gravity and motion in an accelerated frame are indistinguishable. Since a light beam will bend in a rocket that is accelerating, a light beam must also bend under gravity.

To show this, Einstein introduced the concept of curved space. In this interpretation, planets move around the sun not because of a gravitational pull but because the sun has warped the space around it, and space itself pushes the planets. Gravity does not pull you into a chair; space pushes on you, creating the feeling of weight. Space-time has been replaced by a fabric that can stretch and bend.

General relativity can describe the extreme warping of space caused by the gravity of a massive dead star—a black hole. When we apply general relativity to the universe as a whole, one solution naturally describes an expanding cosmos that originated in a fiery big bang.

If the sun were to disappear suddenly, what would happen? Newton would say that the entire universe would instantly feel the loss of the sun's gravity. Einstein recognized that nothing—not even gravity—can travel faster than light. Since sunlight takes eight minutes to travel from the sun to Earth, Einstein believed that it would likewise take eight minutes for Earth to respond to the sun's disappearance.

Curved Space-Time

One key to Einstein's thinking is to analyze a spinning disk. Since the rim of the disk travels faster than the center of the disk, the theory of relativity states that the rim is compressed more than the center. If so, the disk must be distorted (its circumference is no longer pi times its diameter). The surface of the disk is, in fact, curved.

Einstein showed that space itself could be similarly curved and that curved space could explain gravity.

Put a bowling ball on a bedsheet and shoot a marble past it. The marble will move in a curved line. A Newtonian physicist would say that the bowling ball exerts a "force" that "pulls" on the marble, making it move in a curved line. A relativist would say that the ball curves the bedsheet and that the bedsheet "pushes" against the marble.

Now replace the bowling ball with the sun and the marble with Earth. By analogy, gravity does not pull Earth around the sun. Rather, the sun bends space around it, and curved space pushes Earth so that it moves around the sun.

(If we remove the bowling ball, the fabric springs back to its normal shape and releases a wave that spreads out. If the sun disappeared, it would take eight minutes for the analogous gravity waves to reach Earth.)

This effect will also bend starlight. In 1919, during an eclipse of the sun, two expeditions actually measured the bending of starlight as it passed by the sun, shifting the apparent position of the stars. This sealed Einstein's fame.

Actual position of the star

Apparent position of the star

As it passes by the sun, starlight is bent by the sun's distortion of space. As a result, the stars appear to move.

The Big Bang

The entire universe can be regarded as a by-product of curved space and time. Curved space-time is analogous to the surface of a balloon. If you blew up a balloon covered with dots, each dot would appear to be speeding away from the other dots. We seem to live on the surface of a four-dimensional balloon that is expanding in a similar manner. Our telescopes show galaxies speeding away from us in all directions.

Black Holes

If a star grows enormously dense, either through collapse or by accumulating matter, its gravity creates a rip in space-time. The result: a black hole, an object from which even light cannot escape. Hundreds of black holes have been detected, many lurking in the centers of galaxies.

Light entering

The fabric of space-time

Light cannot escape

Wormholes

Einstein and Nathan Rosen introduced the concept of a "bridge" that might link to a location on the other side of a black hole. Einstein did not believe a person could pass through this bridge, since the gravitational forces would be lethal. (Since then, solutions have been found in which travel through a wormhole might be possible, although this is still controversial.)

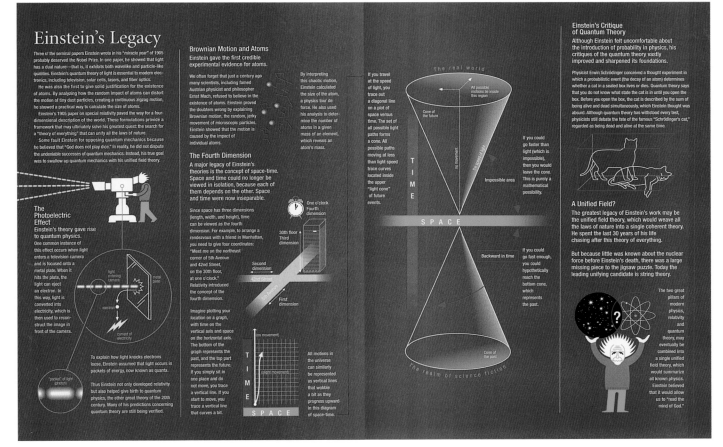

Einstein's Legacy

Three of the seminal papers Einstein wrote in his "miracle year" of 1905 probably deserved the Nobel Prize. In one paper, he showed that light has a dual nature—that is, it exhibits both wavelike and particle-like qualities. Einstein's quantum theory of light is essential to modern electronics, including television, solar cells, lasers, and fiber optics.

He was also the first to give solid justification for the existence of atoms. By analyzing how the random impact of atoms can distort the motion of tiny dust particles, creating a continuous zigzag motion, he showed a practical way to calculate the size of atoms.

Einstein's 1905 paper on special relativity paved the way for a four-dimensional description of the world. These formulations provide a framework that may ultimately solve his greatest quest: the search for a "theory of everything" that can unify all the laws of nature.

Some fault Einstein for opposing quantum mechanics because he believed that "God does not play dice." In reality, he did not dispute the undeniable successes of quantum mechanics. Instead, his true goal was to swallow up quantum mechanics with his unified field theory.

The Photoelectric Effect

Einstein's theory gave rise to quantum physics. One common instance of this effect occurs when light enters a television camera and is focused onto a metal plate. When it hits the plate, the light can eject an electron. In this way, light is converted into electricity, which is then used to reconstruct the image in front of the camera.

light entering camera

metal plate

electron

current of electricity

To explain how light knocks electrons loose, Einstein assumed that light occurs in packets of energy, now known as quanta.

"packet" of light (photon)

Thus Einstein not only developed relativity but also helped give birth to quantum physics, the other great theory of the 20th century. Many of his predictions concerning quantum theory are still being verified.

Brownian Motion and Atoms

Einstein gave the first credible experimental evidence for atoms.

We often forget that just a century ago many scientists, including famed Austrian physicist and philosopher Ernst Mach, refused to believe in the existence of atoms. Einstein proved the doubters wrong by explaining Brownian motion, the random, jerky movement of microscopic particles. Einstein showed that the motion is caused by the impact of individual atoms.

By interpreting this chaotic motion, Einstein calculated the size of the atom, a physics tour de force. He also used his analysis to determine the number of atoms in a given mass of an element, which reveals an atom's mass.

The Fourth Dimension

A major legacy of Einstein's theories is the concept of space-time. Space and time could no longer be viewed in isolation, because each of them depends on the other. Space and time were now inseparable.

Since space has three dimensions (length, width, and height), time can be viewed as the fourth dimension. For example, to arrange a rendezvous with a friend in Manhattan, you need to give four coordinates: "Meet me on the northeast corner of 5th Avenue and 42nd Street, on the 30th floor, at one o'clock." Relativity introduced the concept of the fourth dimension.

Imagine plotting your location on a graph, with time on the vertical axis and space on the horizontal axis. The bottom of the graph represents the past, and the top part represents the future. If you simply sit in one place and do not move, you trace a vertical line. If you start to move, you trace a vertical line that curves a bit.

One o'clock Fourth dimension

30th floor Third dimension

Second dimension

First dimension

TIME (no movement)

(slight movement)

SPACE

All motions in the universe can similarly be represented as vertical lines that wobble a bit as they progress upward in this diagram of space-time.

The real world

Cone of the future

All possible motions lie inside this region

TIME

SPACE

If you travel at the speed of light, you trace out a diagonal line on a plot of space versus time. The set of all possible light paths forms a cone. All possible paths moving at less than light speed trace curves located inside the upper "light cone" of future events.

If you could go faster than light (which is impossible), then you would leave the cone. This is purely a mathematical possibility.

Impossible area

Backward in time

If you could go fast enough, you could hypothetically reach the bottom cone, which represents the past.

Cone of the past

The realm of science fiction

Einstein's Critique of Quantum Theory

Although Einstein felt uncomfortable about the introduction of probability in physics, his critiques of the quantum theory vastly improved and sharpened its foundations.

Physicist Erwin Schrödinger conceived a thought experiment in which a probabilistic event (the decay of an atom) determines whether a cat in a sealed box lives or dies. Quantum theory says that you do not know what state the cat is in until you open the box. Before you open the box, the cat is described by the sum of being alive and dead simultaneously, which Einstein thought was absurd. Although quantum theory has withstood every test, physicists still debate the fate of the famous "Schrödinger's cat," regarded as being dead and alive at the same time.

A Unified Field?

The greatest legacy of Einstein's work may be the unified field theory, which would weave all the laws of nature into a single coherent theory. He spent the last 30 years of his life chasing after this theory of everything.

But because little was known about the nuclear force before Einstein's death, there was a large missing piece to the jigsaw puzzle. Today the leading unifying candidate is string theory.

The two great pillars of modern physics, relativity and quantum theory, may eventually be combined into a single unified field theory, which would summarize all known physics. Einstein believed that it would allow us to "read the mind of God."

The Java That Really Did Change the World

On average, everyone in the **U.S.** drinks a cup and a half of coffee daily:
(That's far less than folks in the **Netherlands;** they down four cups a day: .)
Here's why we humans like caffeine so much (and why spiders don't).

BY NIGEL HOLMES

What is caffeine?
Caffeine is a stimulant found in more than 60 plants, including coffee beans and tea leaves, but also guarana seeds and some holly. In its pure form, it is a white, bitter-tasting crystalline powder. The chemical structure, first identified in 1819, is nearly identical to that of **adenosine,** a chemical in the brain that slows activity and helps to regulate sleep and wakefulness.

A very short history.
The Chinese discovered the effects of caffeine, in the form of medicinal tea, some 5,000 years ago, and legend has it that 15th-century Sufis in Yemen drank coffee to stay awake during night prayers. Coffee was introduced to Europe at the beginning of the 1600s. By the early 1700s, **Bach** had written his "Coffee Cantata" operetta while intellectuals such as Voltaire and Rousseau, frequenters of Paris's many coffeehouses, praised the drink's ability to keep them Enlightened.

How does caffeine work?
Since the molecular structure of caffeine is so similar to that of adenosine, caffeine can "pose" as adenosine in the flow of messages from one brain cell to the next.

When there's no caffeine present, adenosine (⊙) can flow unrestricted from one brain cell to receptors on the adjoining cell.

end of one brain cell

receptor sites on next brain cell

But when caffeine (◎) is present, it fits perfectly into the receptors, fooling the brain cell and effectively suppressing the calming action of the adenosine.

With the adenosine blocked, more neurons start firing in the brain. This increased activity triggers the production of adrenaline, which causes your pupils to dilate, your heart to beat faster, and your blood pressure to rise. Your liver releases fatty acids and sugar into the bloodstream, giving you extra energy.

Caffeine is very efficient.
Because of the good molecular "fit," one cup of coffee (with 200 mg of caffeine in it) has a stronger, though different, physiological effect than one beer, which contains about 14,000 mg of alcohol.

How long does it stay in your system?
The average half-life of caffeine in your body is six hours. That means that if you have a cup of coffee with 200 mg of caffeine in it at 3 p.m., there will still be 100 mg of caffeine left in your body at 9 p.m.

100 mg   200 mg

How much caffeine is in...

... milk chocolate? (1 ounce)
■ 6 milligrams

... cola? (12-ounce can)
36 mg

... Anacin? (2 tablets)
64 mg

... Jolt? (12-ounce can)
71.5 mg

... tea? (8-ounce cup)
20 mg ←brewed weak   strong 110 mg

... coffee? (8-ounce cup)
brewed weak 65mg   brewed strong 200 mg

... Vivarin? (1 tablet)
200 mg

Is caffeine really a drug?
The International Olympic Committee thinks so: It lists caffeine as a "doping agent." The limit, 12 micrograms of caffeine per milliliter of blood, is the equivalent of drinking at least six cups of coffee in half an hour.

Smoking doubles the rate at which your body metabolizes caffeine.

Don't forget that a "grande" can refer to a container that holds anywhere from 12 to 20 ounces.

If I were a spider, would coffee help me make a better web?
No. In a 1965 study on the effect of drugs on arachnids, a German researcher analyzed the web-making of spiders that were under the influence of caffeine.

Normal web   Caffeine web

SOURCES: National Coffee Assn.; *The World of Caffeine,* Bennett Alan Weinberg and Bonnie K. Bealer; Duke University Medical Center; International Food Information Council; International Olympic Committee; *A Spider's Web,* Peter N. Witt et al.

Diagrams explaining how caffeine affects the brain.

カフェインがどのように脳に影響を与えるかを図解したもの。

USA 2002

CD: Susan Casey   AD: Susan Scandrett   D, I, CW, S: Nigel Holmes   DF: Explanation Graphics   CL: E-Company

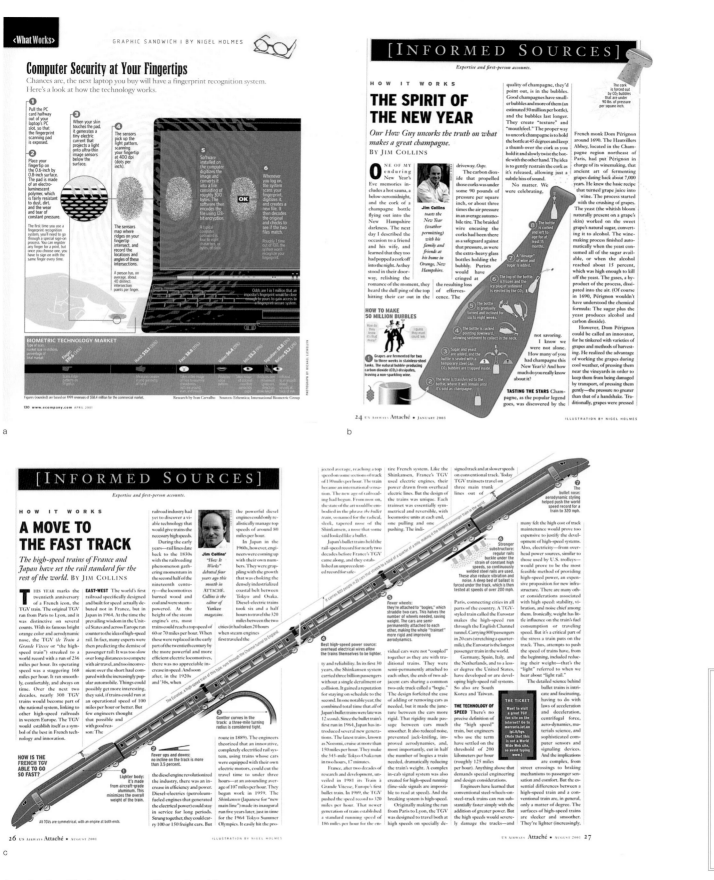

An explanation of the fingerprint recognition system. (a)
Diagram showing the process of champagne making. (b)
Illustration accompanying an article about the French TGV train. How is french TGV to go so fast? (c)

指紋識別システムに関する説明図。 (a)
シャンパンができるまでの過程図。 (b)
TGV（フランス新幹線）がなぜ速く走れるのかを図解。 (c)

USA　2001 (a, c) / 2003 (b)
CD: Susan Casey (a)　AD: Susan Scandrett (a) / Holly Holliday (b, c)　D, I, S: Nigel Holmes　CW: Nigel Holmes (a)　DF: Explanation Graphics
CL: E-Company (a) / Attaché Magazine (b, c)

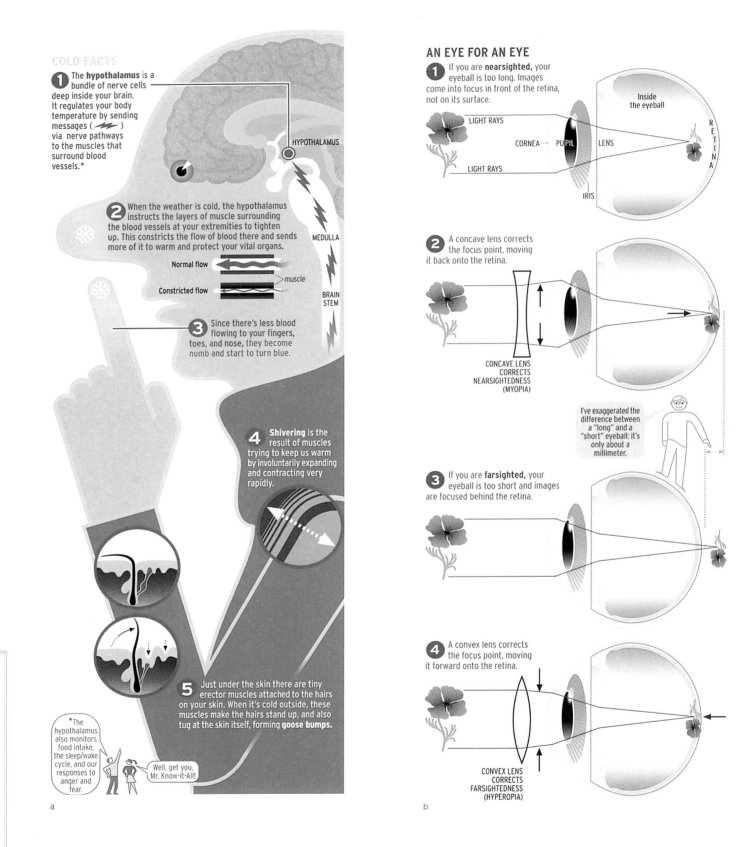

a

b

Illustration explains the facts on common cold symptom. (a)
How an eye focuses. (b)

風邪の症状に関する事実を説明するイラストレーション。 (a)
眼球が焦点を合わせるしくみを説明するイラストレーション。 (b)

USA　2001 (a) / 2003 (b) / 2004 (c, d)
AD: Holly Holliday　D, I, S: Nigel Holmes　DF: Explanation Graphics　CL: Attaché Magazine

A SWEET STREAM

1 In summer, the leaves of sugar maples absorb sunlight and carbon dioxide, eventually converting them into sucrose. This is dissolved in the sap, and in the fall stored as starch in the roots.

Noisy crows herald the start of sugaring.

2 In late winter, the cycle of freezing nights and 40° days creates pressure in the tree. This starts the sap flowing to and from each branch and twig.

Spout (with a hook to hold the bucket) is set at a slight downward angle.

3 7/16" holes are drilled into the trunk to a depth of about 3" and spouts are tapped in. Trees with a 10" diameter typically get one spout; those with 25" diameters get up to four spouts.

4 The buckets of sap are poured into a collecting tank.

Some people still use horses to drag the collecting tank to the sugarhouse, but others bypass this stage by attaching plastic tubes to the spouts and letting gravity transfer the sap directly from the tree to the sugarhouse.

5 In the sugarhouse, the sap goes into the evaporator, where water is burned off, leaving syrup. On average, about 40 gallons of sap makes one gallon of syrup.

Some maples have produced sap for centuries.

Yes, you can still see marks left by the spouts.

The sound of woodpeckers drumming against the galvanized collecting buckets marks the end of the season. It's time to take the spouts out (gently, so the trees heal) and wait for another year.

c

PROJECTING A GOOD IMAGE

1 A seven-foot-wide horizontal **platter** contains the entire movie. That's about two miles of celluloid for a two-hour film.

2 The projectionist threads the film through a series of **rollers** so that it runs vertically through the projector.

3 As the film moves from one frame to another, a revolving **shutter** blocks out the projected light for a fraction of a second.

4 The **light source** is a xenon-gas bulb.

5 Synchronized with the shutter, an intermittent **sprocket-wheel** turns just enough to advance the film one frame at a time, so that the audience is in fact seeing a succession of still images. But the frames pass at such speed that the eye is fooled into seeing continuous movement. This is known as "persistence of vision."

There are 16 frames in every foot of film, and the film is projected at a speed of 24 frames per second.

So that means that a strip of film the height of this page contains only about half a second of the movie!

Shhhhh!

6 After passing through the projector, the film is wound onto a **second platter**, which is positioned directly under the first.

d

Informational graphics describing how movies are projected. (c)
Illustration explaining the process of maple syrup production. (d)

メイプル・シロップの製造過程を説明するイラストレーション。 (c)
映画がどのように映し出されるかを説明するグラフィック。 (d)

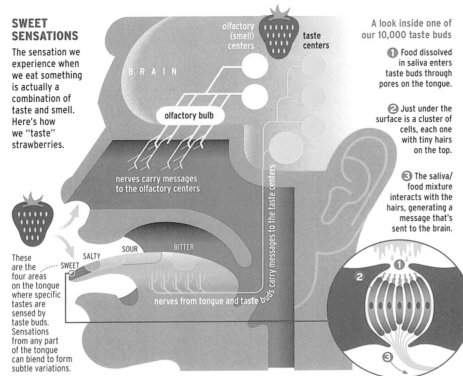

SWEET SENSATIONS

The sensation we experience when we eat something is actually a combination of taste and smell. Here's how we "taste" strawberries.

olfactory (smell) centers

taste centers

BRAIN

olfactory bulb

nerves carry messages to the olfactory centers

These are the four areas on the tongue where specific tastes are sensed by taste buds. Sensations from any part of the tongue can blend to form subtle variations.

SALTY   SOUR   BITTER
SWEET

nerves from tongue and taste buds

nerves carry messages to the taste centers

A look inside one of our 10,000 taste buds

1 Food dissolved in saliva enters taste buds through pores on the tongue.

2 Just under the surface is a cluster of cells, each one with tiny hairs on the top.

3 The saliva/food mixture interacts with the hairs, generating a message that's sent to the brain.

a

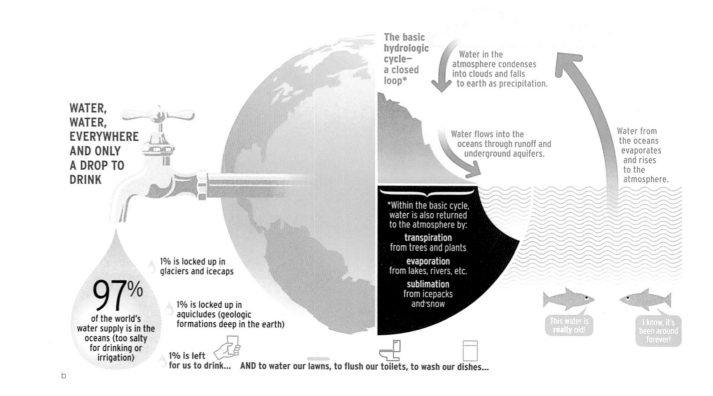

WATER, WATER, EVERYWHERE AND ONLY A DROP TO DRINK

The basic hydrologic cycle— a closed loop*

Water in the atmosphere condenses into clouds and falls to earth as precipitation.

Water flows into the oceans through runoff and underground aquifers.

Water from the oceans evaporates and rises to the atmosphere.

97% of the world's water supply is in the oceans (too salty for drinking or irrigation)

1% is locked up in glaciers and icecaps

1% is locked up in aquicludes (geologic formations deep in the earth)

1% is left for us to drink... AND to water our lawns, to flush our toilets, to wash our dishes...

*Within the basic cycle, water is also returned to the atmosphere by:
transpiration from trees and plants
evaporation from lakes, rivers, etc.
sublimation from icepacks and snow

This water is really old!   I know, it's been around forever!

b

Illustration explaining the mechanism for gustatory and olfactory sensation. How we "taste" strawberries. (a)
An explanation of the basic hydrologic cycle. (b)

味覚と嗅覚の仕組みを説明する図。どうやってイチゴを味わうか。 (a)
基本的な水の循環の説明図。 (b)

USA 2002 (a) / 2003 (b)
AD: Holly Holliday   D, I, S: Nigel Holmes   DF: Explanation Graphics   CL: Attaché Magazine

2

MONKS, VEGETABLES & GENES

It all began when a quiet monk named Mendel decided to study his vegetables instead of just eating them.

Living in a quiet monastery in Moravia, a country that no longer exists, Mendel puttered around the garden experimenting with various types of peas.

He found that **when** **peas have sex,** some characteristics are dominant and some tend to disappear for a generation. From this he deduced that you can statistically predict what the next generations will look like.

Mendel published, joined management, retired, and perished. It took decades until researchers discovered his work and began to build a pyramid of knowledge based on "Mendelian Genetics."

(So we can begin to understand why someone has blonde or red hair; why only one brother is tall and thin; why your sister is good looking while you…)

The Monk in the Garden
Robin Marantz Henig

a

3

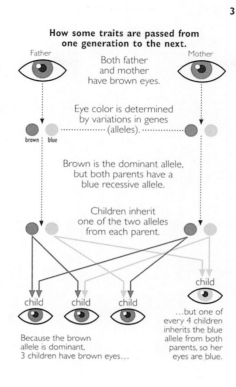

How some traits are passed from one generation to the next.

Father — Mother

Both father and mother have brown eyes.

brown : blue

Eye color is determined by variations in genes (alleles).

Brown is the dominant allele, but both parents have a blue recessive allele.

Children inherit one of the two alleles from each parent.

child child child child

Because the brown allele is dominant, 3 children have brown eyes…

…but one of every 4 children inherits the blue allele from both parents, so her eyes are blue.

The smallest ever
GUIDE TO LIFE SCIENCES
(for busy people)

JUAN ENRIQUEZ • RODRIGO MARTINEZ
Life Sciences Project, Harvard Business School

NIGEL HOLMES
Designer

Produced by
THE VAN HEYST GROUP

6

SIZE MATTERS: quarks to the universe

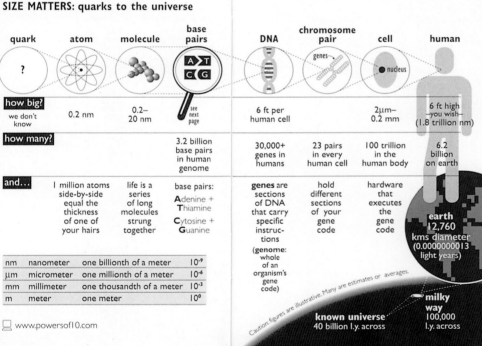

	quark	atom	molecule	base pairs	DNA	chromosome pair	cell	human
how big?	we don't know	0.2 nm	0.2– 20 nm	see next page	6 ft per human cell		2μm– 0.2 mm	6 ft high –you wish– (1.8 trillion nm)
how many?				3.2 billion base pairs in human genome	30,000+ genes in humans	23 pairs in every human cell	100 trillion in the human body	6.2 billion on earth
and...	1 million atoms side-by-side equal the thickness of one of your hairs	life is a series of long molecules strung together	base pairs: **A**denine + **T**hiamine **C**ytosine + **G**uanine	**genes** are sections of DNA that carry specific instruc- tions (genome: whole of an organism's gene code)	hold different sections of your gene code	hardware that executes the gene code	

nm	nanometer	one billionth of a meter	10^{-9}
μm	micrometer	one millionth of a meter	10^{-6}
mm	millimeter	one thousandth of a meter	10^{-3}
m	meter	one meter	10^{0}

www.powersof10.com

7

earth
12,760 kms diameter (0.0000000013 light years)

Caution: figures are illustrative. Many are estimates or averages.

known universe 40 billion l.y. across

milky way 100,000 l.y. across

b

A series of diagrams from the little book explaining the human genome. How some traits are passed from one generation to the next. (a)
Size matters : quarks to the universe. (b)

ヒトゲノムを説明する小冊子から抜粋した一連のダイアグラム。ある体質が次の世代に受け継がれる仕組み。 (a)
クォークから宇宙までの大きさを表すダイアグラム。 (b)

USA 2003
CD, AD, D, I, S: Nigel Holmes   CW: Juan Enriquez / Rodrigo Martinez   DF: Explanation Graphics   CL: Van Heyst Group

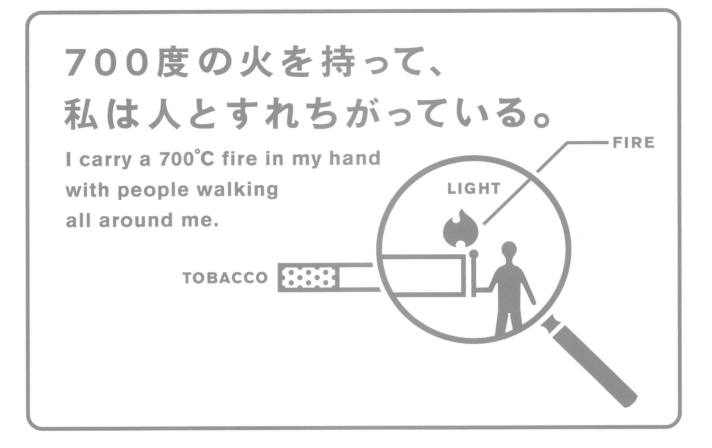

７００度の火を持って、私は人とすれちがっている。

I carry a 700°C fire in my hand with people walking all around me.

FIRE

LIGHT

TOBACCO

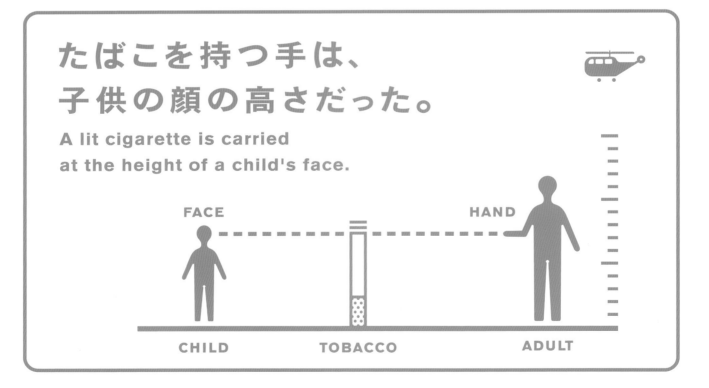

たばこを持つ手は、子供の顔の高さだった。

A lit cigarette is carried at the height of a child's face.

FACE

HAND

CHILD   TOBACCO   ADULT

A diagram designed to stimulate awareness, thought and action by presenting various scenes of thoughtless smoking manners.

何気なく行ってしまう喫煙マナー行動について多くのシーンを紹介し、気づき、考え、行動することを促すためのイラストレーション。

Japan   2004
CD: Hiroshi Aizawa   AD, I: Bunpei Yorifuji   D: Takuya Shibata   CW: Kinya Okamoto   DF: Bunpei Ginza   CL, S: Japan Tobacco Inc.

私に手を振る人がいた。
煙を払う仕草だった。

A person was waving at me.
He was waving away
my smoke.

SMOKE

HAND WAVING

PROTECTION

スタンド灰皿。火を消さないで
入れるのは、煙をふやす行為だ。

Stand ashtrays.
Disposing of a lit cigarette
in one just creates
more smoke.

TOBACCO

STAND ASHTRAY

INCINERATOR

煙の行方。本人だけが、
他人事だった。

Where does the smoke go?
Only the person producing
it is unconcerned.

ROUTE
OF
SMOKE

SMOKER　　NEGLECT

吸いがらを
排水溝に捨てた。
というか隠した。

I threw my cigarette butt
into the drain. That is to say,
I hid it in the drain.

DROP

TOBACCO

SEWER

体はよけた。
それでも煙は
ぶつかった。

I moved to avoid him.
But my smoke didn't.

SMOKE

SIDE STEP

TOBACCO

日本一、
目につくゴミは、
吸いがらかも。

Probably the kind of litter
I see most often in Japan
is cigarette butts.

TOSS AWAY

TOBACCO

TOSS AWAY

JAPAN

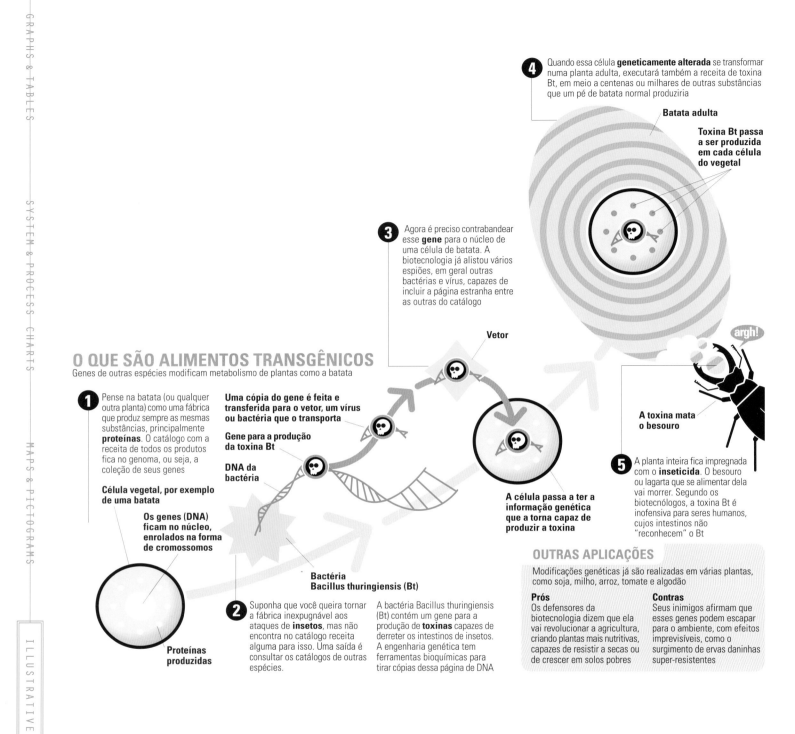

O QUE SÃO ALIMENTOS TRANSGÊNICOS
Genes de outras espécies modificam metabolismo de plantas como a batata

4 Quando essa célula **geneticamente alterada** se transformar numa planta adulta, executará também a receita de toxina Bt, em meio a centenas ou milhares de outras substâncias que um pé de batata normal produziria

Batata adulta

Toxina Bt passa a ser produzida em cada célula do vegetal

3 Agora é preciso contrabandear esse **gene** para o núcleo de uma célula de batata. A biotecnologia já alistou vários espiões, em geral outras bactérias e vírus, capazes de incluir a página estranha entre as outras do catálogo

Vetor

1 Pense na batata (ou qualquer outra planta) como uma fábrica que produz sempre as mesmas substâncias, principalmente **proteínas**. O catálogo com a receita de todos os produtos fica no genoma, ou seja, a coleção de seus genes

Uma cópia do gene é feita e transferida para o vetor, um vírus ou bactéria que o transporta

Gene para a produção da toxina Bt

DNA da bactéria

Célula vegetal, por exemplo de uma batata

Os genes (DNA) ficam no núcleo, enrolados na forma de cromossomos

A toxina mata o besouro

argh!

5 A planta inteira fica impregnada com o **inseticida**. O besouro ou lagarta que se alimentar dela vai morrer. Segundo os biotecnólogos, a toxina Bt é inofensiva para seres humanos, cujos intestinos não "reconhecem" o Bt

A célula passa a ter a informação genética que a torna capaz de produzir a toxina

Bactéria Bacillus thuringiensis (Bt)

Proteínas produzidas

2 Suponha que você queira tornar a fábrica inexpugnável aos ataques de **insetos**, mas não encontra no catálogo receita alguma para isso. Uma saída é consultar os catálogos de outras espécies.

A bactéria Bacillus thuringiensis (Bt) contém um gene para a produção de **toxinas** capazes de derreter os intestinos de insetos. A engenharia genética tem ferramentas bioquímicas para tirar cópias dessa página de DNA

OUTRAS APLICAÇÕES

Modificações genéticas já são realizadas em várias plantas, como soja, milho, arroz, tomate e algodão

Prós
Os defensores da biotecnologia dizem que ela vai revolucionar a agricultura, criando plantas mais nutritivas, capazes de resistir a secas ou de crescer em solos pobres

Contras
Seus inimigos afirmam que esses genes podem escapar para o ambiente, com efeitos imprevisíveis, como o surgimento de ervas daninhas super-resistentes

Will transgenic foods be the final solution to hunger? Diagrams explaining what is transgenic foods, and creating a starting point for readers to think about this question.

遺伝子組み換え食品は飢餓の最終的な解決策になるのだろうか？ 遺伝子組み換え食品とは何かを説明し、読者がこの問題について考えるための出発点となる図。

Brazil   2000
CD, S: Eduardo Asta   CW: Mauricio Puls / Thales de Menezes / Leonardo Cruz   CL: Folha de São Paulo

O PRESENTE E O FUTURO NA CONSTRUÇÃO CIVIL

═══ A R T E S A N A L ═══   ═══ I N D U S T R I A L ═══

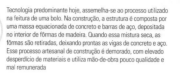

Tecnologia predominante hoje, assemelha-se ao processo utilizado na feitura de uma bolo. Na construção, a estrutura é composta por uma massa equacionada de concreto e barras de aço, depositada no interior de fôrmas de madeira. Quando essa mistura seca, as fôrmas são retiradas, deixando prontas as vigas de concreto e aço. Esse processo artesanal de construção é demorado, com elevado desperdício de materiais e utiliza mão-de-obra pouco qualidade e mal remunerada

Já utilizada hoje em menor escala, a tecnologia dos pré-fabricados é a principal tendência na construção para o futuro. Seu sistema assemelha-se mais a um jogo infantil com pequenas peças de plástico de montar. Todos os componentes vêm finalizados da fábrica e nas dimensões exatas, prontos para serem montados, no canteiro de obras. Há redução do tempo de duração da obra, do desperdício de materiais e da mão-de-obra, que deverá ter melhor qualificação

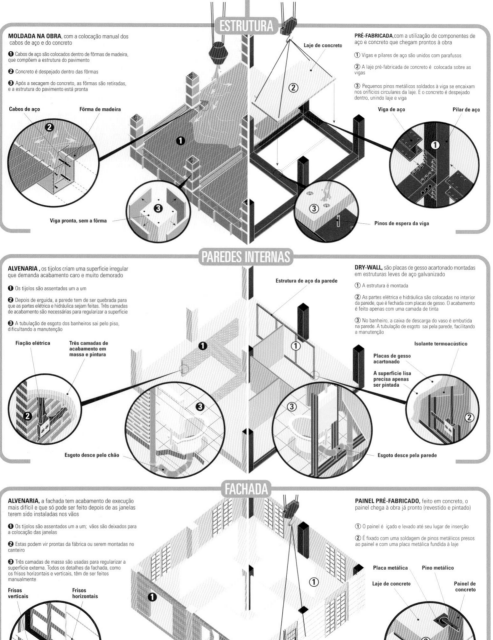

ESTRUTURA

MOLDADA NA OBRA, com a colocação manual dos cabos de aço e do concreto

① Cabos de aço são colocados dentro de fôrmas de madeira, que compõem a estrutura do pavimento

② Concreto é despejado dentro das fôrmas

③ Após a secagem do concreto, as fôrmas são retiradas, e a estrutura do pavimento está pronta

Cabos de aço · Fôrma de madeira

Viga pronta, sem a fôrma

PRÉ-FABRICADA, com a utilização de componentes de aço e concreto que chegam prontos à obra

① Vigas e pilares de aço são unidos com parafusos

② A laje pré-fabricada de concreto é colocada sobre as vigas

③ Pequenos pinos metálicos soldados à viga se encaixam nos orifícios circulares da laje. E o concreto é despejado dentro, unindo laje e viga

Laje de concreto

Viga de aço · Pilar de aço

Pinos de espera da viga

PAREDES INTERNAS

ALVENARIA, os tijolos criam uma superfície irregular que demanda acabamento caro e muito demorado

① Os tijolos são assentados um a um

② Depois de erguida, a parede tem de ser quebrada para que as partes elétrica e hidráulica sejam feitas. Três camadas de acabamento são necessárias para regularizar a superfície

③ A tubulação de esgoto dos banheiros sai pelo piso, dificultando a manutenção

Fiação elétrica · Três camadas de acabamento em massa e pintura

Esgoto desce pelo chão

DRY-WALL, são placas de gesso acartonado montadas em estruturas leves de aço galvanizado

① A estrutura é montada

② As partes elétrica e hidráulica são colocadas no interior da parede, que é fechada com placas de gesso. O acabamento é feito apenas com uma camada de tinta

③ No banheiro, a caixa de descarga do vaso é embutida na parede. A tubulação de esgoto sai pela parede, facilitando a manutenção

Estrutura de aço da parede

Isolante termoacústico

Placas de gesso acartonado

A superfície lisa precisa apenas ser pintada

Esgoto desce pela parede

FACHADA

ALVENARIA, a fachada tem acabamento de execução mais difícil e que só pode ser feito depois de as janelas terem sido instaladas nos vãos

① Os tijolos são assentados um a um; vãos são deixados para a colocação das janelas

② Estas podem vir prontas da fábrica ou serem montadas no canteiro

③ Três camadas de massa são usadas para regularizar a superfície externa. Todos os detalhes da fachada, como os frisos horizontais e verticais, têm de ser feitos manualmente

Frisos verticais · Frisos horizontais

PAINEL PRÉ-FABRICADO, feito em concreto, o painel chega à obra já pronto (revestido e pintado)

① O painel é içado e levado até seu lugar de inserção

② É fixado com uma soldagem de pinos metálicos presos ao painel e com uma placa metálica fundida à laje

Placa metálica · Pino metálico

Laje de concreto · Painel de concreto

Fonte: Revista AU, catálogos técnicos e entrevistas com construtoras

From a newspaper article that says a house will be built as a car in the future.
Illustration explaining the difference between the present and future construction process step by step.

将来、住宅が車の様に組み立てられるようになるという新聞記事のイラスト。現在と将来の建築プロセスの違いを順を追って説明している。

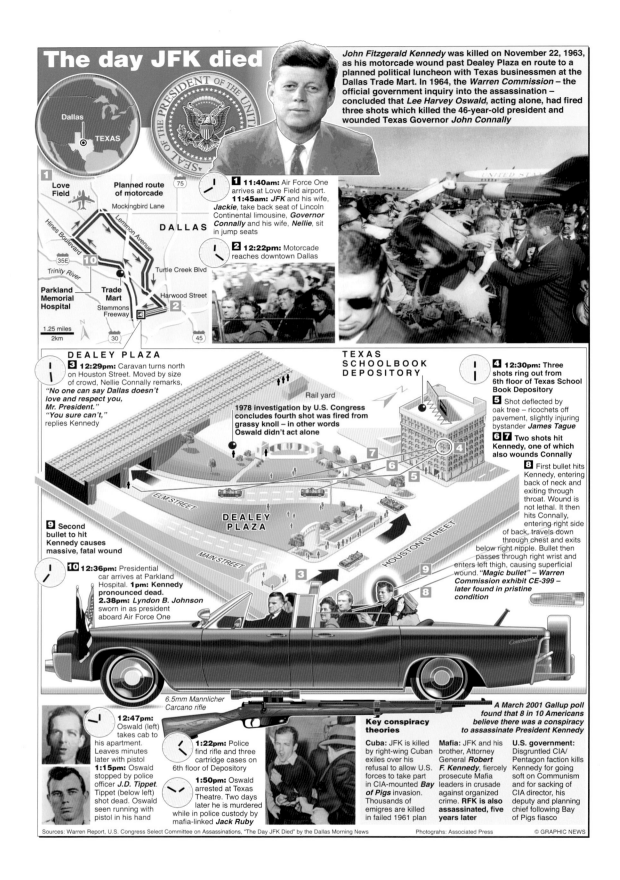

40th anniversary of President John F. Kennedy's assassination. Graphic shows chronology of events in Dallas and details main conspiracy theories. 8 in 10 Americans believe there was a conspiracy to kill JFK.

ジョン・F・ケネディ元大統領暗殺の40周年。ダラスでの出来事を順を追って紹介し、主な陰謀説を解説する図。
アメリカ人の10人のうち8人がJFKを殺害する陰謀があったと信じている。

UK 2003

Creative Team: Duncan Mil / Phi Bainbridge / Jordi Bou / Mark McLellan   Copywriter & Research: Julie Mullins
DF, S: Graphic News Ltd.   CL: Various Newspapers & Magazines

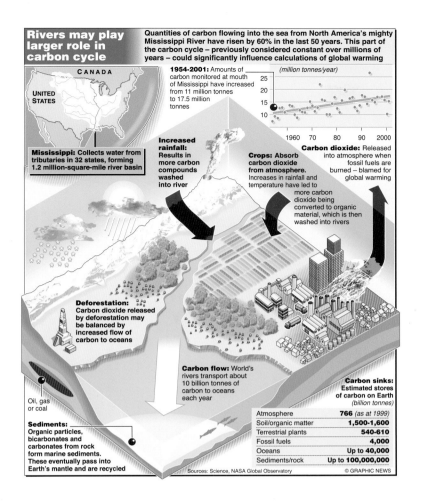

Rivers may play larger role in carbon cycle

Quantities of carbon flowing into the sea from North America's mighty Mississippi River have risen by 60% in the last 50 years. This part of the carbon cycle – previously considered constant over millions of years – could significantly influence calculations of global warming

1954-2001: Amounts of carbon monitored at mouth of Mississippi have increased from 11 million tonnes to 17.5 million tonnes

(million tonnes/year)

25
20
15
10

1960 70 80 90 2000

Increased rainfall: Results in more carbon compounds washed into river

Crops: Absorb carbon dioxide from atmosphere. Increases in rainfall and temperature have led to more carbon dioxide being converted to organic material, which is then washed into rivers

Carbon dioxide: Released into atmosphere when fossil fuels are burned – blamed for global warming

Mississippi: Collects water from tributaries in 32 states, forming 1.2 million-square-mile river basin

Deforestation: Carbon dioxide released by deforestation may be balanced by increased flow of carbon to oceans

Carbon flow: World's rivers transport about 10 billion tonnes of carbon to oceans each year

Oil, gas or coal

Sediments: Organic particles, bicarbonates and carbonates from rock form marine sediments. These eventually pass into Earth's mantle and are recycled

Carbon sinks: Estimated stores of carbon on Earth *(billion tonnes)*

Atmosphere	**766** *(as at 1999)*
Soil/organic matter	1,500-1,600
Terrestrial plants	540-610
Fossil fuels	4,000
Oceans	Up to 40,000
Sediments/rock	Up to 100,000,000

CANADA
UNITED STATES

Sources: Science, NASA Global Observatory   © GRAPHIC NEWS

ミシシッピ川から海へと流れ込んだ炭酸ガスの量は、過去半世紀で60%上昇した。図表は、以前は何百万年以上も継続していたと考えられていた炭酸ガスの循環が、地球温暖化の問題にどのような影響を与えているかを示している。

Quantities of carbon flowing into the sea from Mississippi River have risen by 60% in the last half century.
Graphic shows how this part of the carbon cycle previously considered constant over millions of years could significantly influence calculations of global warming.

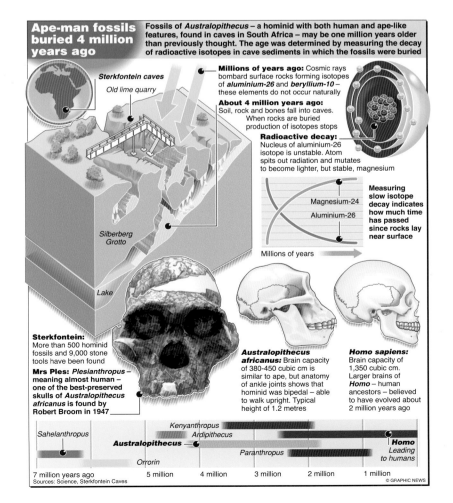

Ape-man fossils buried 4 million years ago

Fossils of *Australopithecus* – a hominid with both human and ape-like features, found in caves in South Africa – may be one million years older than previously thought. The age was determined by measuring the decay of radioactive isotopes in cave sediments in which the fossils were buried

Sterkfontein caves

Old lime quarry

Millions of years ago: Cosmic rays bombard surface rocks forming isotopes of *aluminium-26* and *beryllium-10* – these elements do not occur naturally

About 4 million years ago: Soil, rock and bones fall into caves. When rocks are buried production of isotopes stops

Radioactive decay: Nucleus of aluminium-26 isotope is unstable. Atom spits out radiation and mutates to become lighter, but stable, magnesium

Magnesium-24
Aluminium-26

Measuring slow isotope decay indicates how much time has passed since rocks lay near surface

Millions of years

Silberberg Grotto

Lake

Sterkfontein: More than 500 hominid fossils and 9,000 stone tools have been found

Mrs Ples: *Plesianthropus* – meaning almost human – one of the best-preserved skulls of *Australopithecus africanus* is found by Robert Broom in 1947

Australopithecus africanus: Brain capacity of 380-450 cubic cm is similar to ape, but anatomy of ankle joints shows that hominid was bipedal – able to walk upright. Typical height of 1.2 metres

Homo sapiens: Brain capacity of 1,350 cubic cm. Larger brains of *Homo* – human ancestors – believed to have evolved about 2 million years ago

Kenyanthropus
Sahelanthropus
Ardipithecus
Australopithecus
Paranthropus
Homo Leading to humans
Orrorin

7 million years ago   5 million   4 million   3 million   2 million   1 million
Sources: Science, Sterkfontein Caves   © GRAPHIC NEWS

New Australopithecus fossils from caves in South-Africa— along with a nearly complete skeleton discovered there in 1997— may have been buried about 4 million years ago, as much as 1 million years earlier than previously thought.

南アフリカの洞くつで1997年に発見されたほぼ完全な骨格に加えて、新たに発見されたアウストラロピテクスの化石は、以前考えられていたよりも100万年近くさかのぼる、400万年前に埋葬されていた可能性があることを示す図。

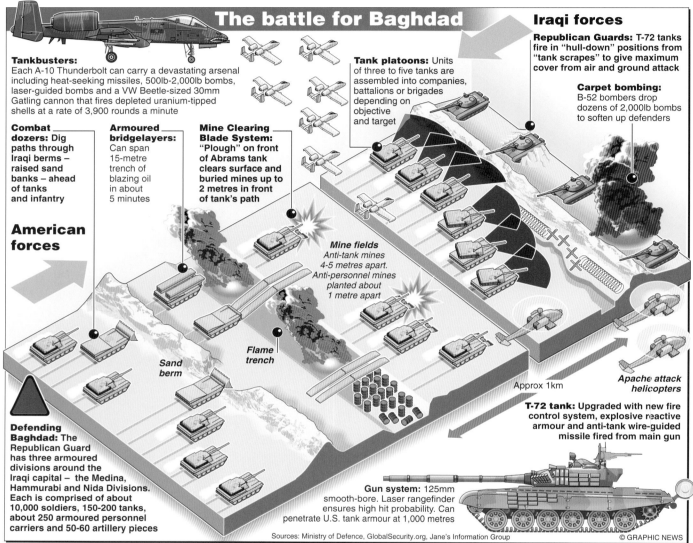

The battle for Baghdad

Iraqi forces

Republican Guards: T-72 tanks fire in "hull-down" positions from "tank scrapes" to give maximum cover from air and ground attack

Carpet bombing: B-52 bombers drop dozens of 2,000lb bombs to soften up defenders

Tank platoons: Units of three to five tanks are assembled into companies, battalions or brigades depending on objective and target

Tankbusters: Each A-10 Thunderbolt can carry a devastating arsenal including heat-seeking missiles, 500lb-2,000lb bombs, laser-guided bombs and a VW Beetle-sized 30mm Gatling cannon that fires depleted uranium-tipped shells at a rate of 3,900 rounds a minute

Combat dozers: Dig paths through Iraqi berms – raised sand banks – ahead of tanks and infantry

Armoured bridgelayers: Can span 15-metre trench of blazing oil in about 5 minutes

Mine Clearing Blade System: "Plough" on front of Abrams tank clears surface and buried mines up to 2 metres in front of tank's path

American forces

Mine fields
Anti-tank mines 4-5 metres apart. Anti-personnel mines planted about 1 metre apart

Flame trench

Sand berm

Approx 1km

Apache attack helicopters

T-72 tank: Upgraded with new fire control system, explosive reactive armour and anti-tank wire-guided missile fired from main gun

Defending Baghdad: The Republican Guard has three armoured divisions around the Iraqi capital – the Medina, Hammurabi and Nida Divisions. Each is comprised of about 10,000 soldiers, 150-200 tanks, about 250 armoured personnel carriers and 50-60 artillery pieces

Gun system: 125mm smooth-bore. Laser rangefinder ensures high hit probability. Can penetrate U.S. tank armour at 1,000 metres

Sources: Ministry of Defence, GlobalSecurity.org, Jane's Information Group

© GRAPHIC NEWS

Graphic shows likely tactics to be adopted by U.S. forces attempting to dislodge Republican Guards defending Bughdad.

バグダッドを守るイラク共和国防衛軍の撤退をもくろむ、米軍が採択したと思われる計画を説明する図。

UK 2003

Creative Team: Duncan Mil / Phi Bainbridge / Jordi Bou / Mark McLellan　Copywriter & Research: Julie Mullins　DF, S: Graphic News Ltd.　CL: Various Newspapers & Magazines

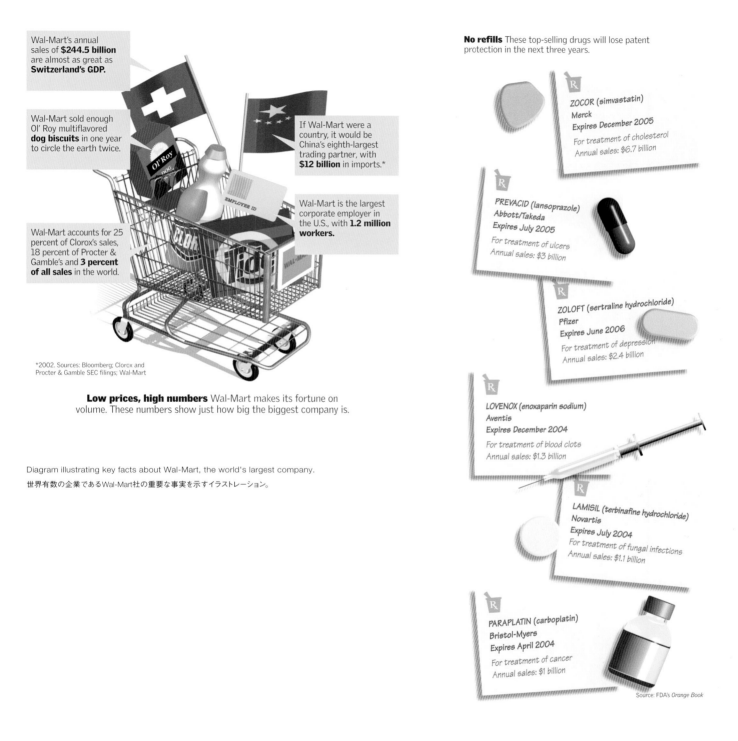

Wal-Mart's annual sales of **$244.5 billion** are almost as great as **Switzerland's GDP.**

Wal-Mart sold enough Ol' Roy multiflavored **dog biscuits** in one year to circle the earth twice.

If Wal-Mart were a country, it would be China's eighth-largest trading partner, with **$12 billion** in imports.*

Wal-Mart is the largest corporate employer in the U.S., with **1.2 million workers.**

Wal-Mart accounts for 25 percent of Clorox's sales, 18 percent of Procter & Gamble's and **3 percent of all sales** in the world.

*2002. Sources: Bloomberg; Clorox and Procter & Gamble SEC filings; Wal-Mart

Low prices, high numbers Wal-Mart makes its fortune on volume. These numbers show just how big the biggest company is.

Diagram illustrating key facts about Wal-Mart, the world's largest company.
世界有数の企業であるWal-Mart社の重要な事実を示すイラストレーション。

No refills These top-selling drugs will lose patent protection in the next three years.

ZOCOR (simvastatin)
Merck
Expires December 2005
For treatment of cholesterol
Annual sales: $6.7 billion

PREVACID (lansoprazole)
Abbott/Takeda
Expires July 2005
For treatment of ulcers
Annual sales: $3 billion

ZOLOFT (sertraline hydrochloride)
Pfizer
Expires June 2006
For treatment of depression
Annual sales: $2.4 billion

LOVENOX (enoxaparin sodium)
Aventis
Expires December 2004
For treatment of blood clots
Annual sales: $1.3 billion

LAMISIL (terbinafine hydrochloride)
Novartis
Expires July 2004
For treatment of fungal infections
Annual sales: $1.1 billion

PARAPLATIN (carboplatin)
Bristol-Myers
Expires April 2004
For treatment of cancer
Annual sales: $1 billion

Source: FDA's *Orange Book*

Diagram illustrating drug patents expiration dates.
医薬品の特許期限を表したイラストレーション。

USA   2004
AD: Carol Macrini   D, I, S: Eliot Bergman   CL: Bloomberg Markets Magazine

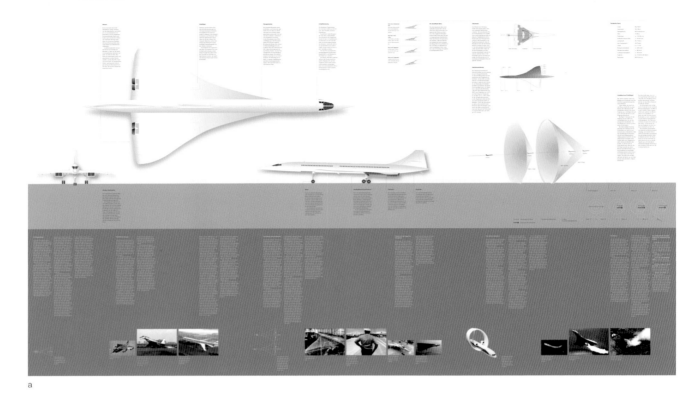

a

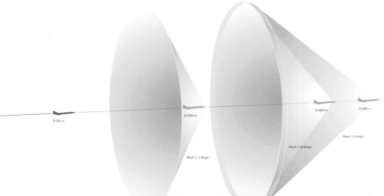

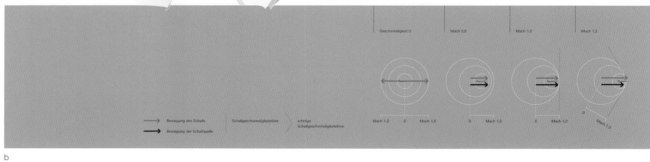

b

A poster deals with the plane's technology and explains supersonic flight in almost three-dimensional representation.
The bottom segment presents the history of the Concorde. (a)
Graphic explanation of supersonic flight in almost three-dimensional representation. (b)

航空技術に関するポスター。コンコルドを立体的な表現を用いて説明している。下の部分では歴史を紹介。 (a)
超音速飛行を立体的な表現を用いて説明したグラフィック。 (b)

Germany   2001
D, I: Lars Wentrup   DF, S: Nieschlag + Wentrup

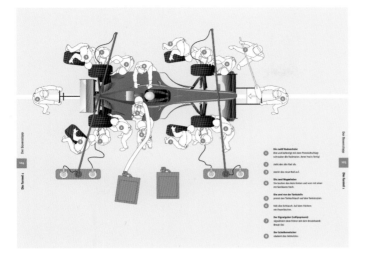

The logistics of a pit stop during a Formula 1 car racing.

F1レース中のピット・ストップの後方支援を表す図。

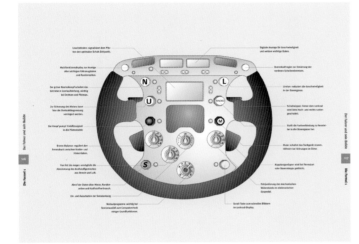

A steering wheel of a Formula 1 racing car and its functions.

F1のレーシング・カーのハンドルと、その性能を説明する図。

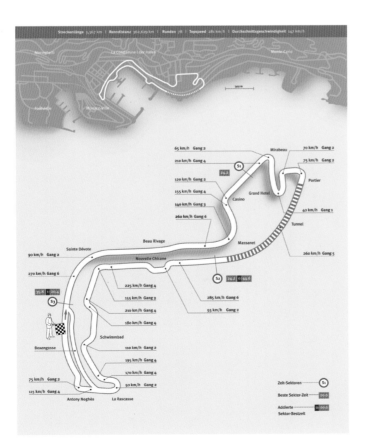

Illustration showing the location of the course in the city of Monaco and the course in detail with additional information.

モナコのレーシング・コースの位置や、
コース中の詳しい情報を示すイラストレーション。

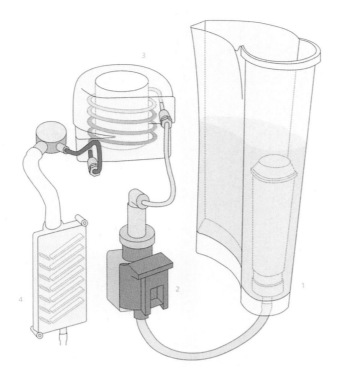

1> The removable water tank lasts a long time between fillings (at a recommended 40 ml per cup) and you can check water level at a glance. Always use cool water that is filtered or bottled, never distilled or softened.

2> The pump delivers 15 bars of pressure (good for two cups) instantaneously and ensures an ideal 25 to 30 seconds for extraction (i.e., when water is in contact with the grounds). If extraction time is too fast, espresso will taste bitter and have little or no crema; too slow, and it will taste burnt.

3> With Thermobloc technology, water is forced through an ultra-compact labyrinth of stainless steel (not aluminum) heating pipes to immediately reach an optimum 92°C. If the water is too cool, the espresso will be weak; too hot, and the grounds will be scalded.

4> Excess water is directed into the drip tray; it doesn't sit in the machine, so each new cup always uses fresh water.

Diagrams indicate how to position the Krups line of espresso makers thoughtfully designed for coffee enthusiasts.

コーヒー好きのために工夫してデザインされたエスプレッソ・メーカー、Krupsシリーズの設置方法を図解。

Canada 2004
CD, AD: Frank Viva   D, I: Todd Temporale   P: Ron Baxter Smith / Hill Peppard   CW: Doug Dolan   DF, S: Viva Dolan Communications & Design Inc.   CL: Groupe Seb

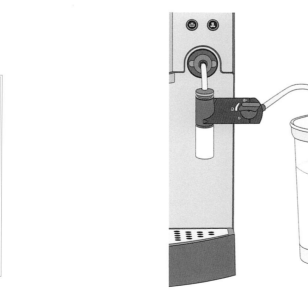

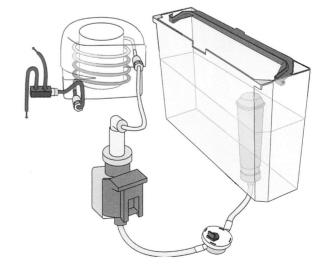

Diagrams are used in a brochure about Krups espresso machines to reinforce the high level of engineering.

ブローシャーに使用したKrupsエスプレッソ・マシンの高度な技術を強調するための図。

Canada 2004
CD, AD: Frank Viva   D, I: Todd Temporale   DF, S: Viva Dolan Communications & Design Inc.   CL: Groupe Seb

STUDENT'S
WORKS

Students' works from the Diagram Design course
in the Department of Visual Communication Design at Musashino Art University

武蔵野美術大学視覚伝達デザイン学科ダイアグラムデザインコース学生作品

Several years ago I initiated a Diagram Design course at the Department of Visual Communication Design at Musashino Art University. In today's society, we live our everyday lives surrounded by a variety of media and information. In my class I classify diagrams into six categories—tables, graphs, schematics, pictograms, illustrations, and maps—and challenge students to express divers information diagrammatically.

In the first semester students study the fundamentals of diagrammatic expression; in the second they hone in on specific themes, applying and developing them as graphic works. The inspirational work is analog; the finish work is generated on computer. Students also monitor each other's work in progress. By scrutinizing other people's ideas, their own design becomes more logical. They also collect their own data, the analysis and organization of which leads to original ideas and concepts. At the end, we critique the works in terms of expressing a visual language, function, and aesthetic sensibilities.

As part of basic graphic training, the diagrams course expands the way students think and aides in refining their design abilities.

*The works shown here represent students' solutions to assignments given in my Diagram Design course.

武蔵野美術大学視覚伝達デザイン学科コースでは数年前から「ダイアグラムデザインコース」を新設しました。私たちは今、日常の社会で多種多様のメディアと情報に囲まれて生きています。授業ではダイアグラムを6つ（①表組　②図表　③図式　④図譜　⑤図解　⑥地図）のカテゴリーに分類し、さまざまなデータを図的に表現することを課題としています。

前半では基本を学び、後半ではテーマを絞り込み、応用と展開で作品化しています。インスピレーションはアナログで、フィニッシュはコンピュータで仕上げます。また、これらの作業はお互いにその場でチェックし合います。他の人の考えを黙過せず凝視することによって論理的なデザインに到達します。データの収集は学生の個人作業で分類・整理させ、発想と結び付けていきます。

最後に、デザインされた作品が視覚言語や機能性や美しさを表現できたかを決定します。

このダイアグラムの授業はグラフィックデザインの基礎トレーニングとして学生たちの発想を広げ、同時に高度なデザイン能力を引き出すために役立ちます。

*ここに掲載された作品は「ダイアグラムデザインコース」授業課題です。

Tetsuya Ohta : graphic designer

Graduated from Kuwasawa Design Laboratory in 1963. After working at Ikko Tanaka Design Office, established the present Ohta Tetsuya Design Office in 1975. His Diagram exhibitions were held at Ginza Graphic Gallery (ggg) in 1991, and Morisawa Typography Space (MOTS) in 2000. Among the awards he has received are: the Ministry of International Trade and Industry Award of the Japan Book Design Concours, and the Tokyo TDC Award in 1991; the ADC Award and Hiroshi Hara Award in 1992; and the Ministry of Education, Culture, Sports, Science and Technology Award of the Japan Book Design Concours in 2002. In 1989 he published "Changes in Logos and Trademarks in Japan" and "Iro no mihoncho (Color Swatchbook)." He teaches the Diagram Design course in the Department of Visual Communication Design at Musashino Art University.

太田徹也（グラフィックデザイナー）

1963年桑沢デザイン研究所卒。田中一光デザイン室を経て1975年太田徹也デザイン室設立、現在に至る。1991年「ダイアグラム展」ギンザグラフィックギャラリー（ggg）、2000年「ダイアグラム展」モリサワ・タイポグラフィ・スペース（MOTS）。1991年全国装幀コンクール、カタログポスター展「通産大臣賞」、東京タイポディレクターズクラブ「会員・銅賞」、1992年東京アートディレクターズクラブ「ADC賞」「原弘賞」、2002年全国装幀コンクール「文部科学大臣賞」などを受賞。1989年『CI＝マーク・ロゴの変遷』六耀社、『色の見本帖』ごま書房（共著）を出版。武蔵野美術大学視覚伝達デザイン学科ダイアグラムデザインコース講師。

A correlation graph of characters in the TV anime series "Kyojin no Hoshi."
テレビアニメ『巨人の星』における人物相関図。

D: Takuya Nagami

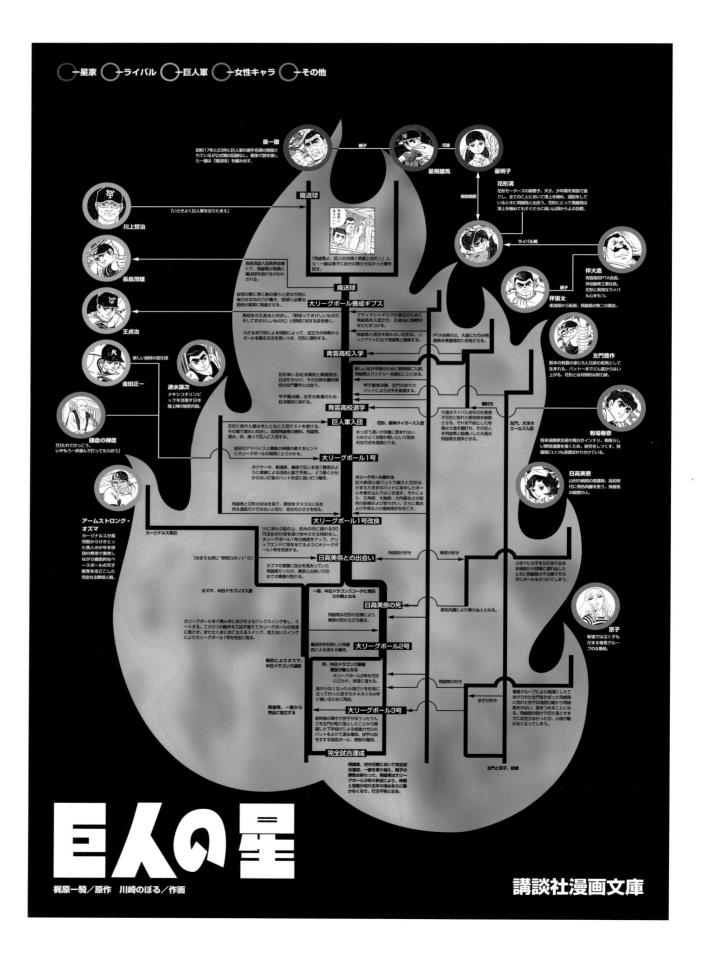

A map expressing the sounds heard en route from home to school.
自宅から学校までの通学途中に耳にする音を表現したサウンドマップ。

D: Misato Yasui

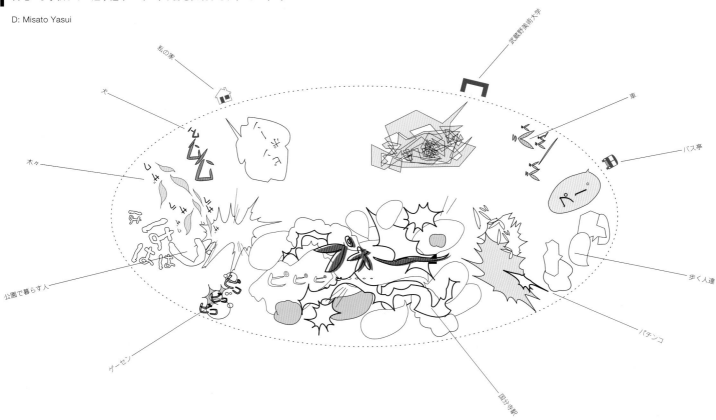

A diagram expressing the surrounds encountered when walking from home to school.
自宅から学校まで歩いたときの周囲の環境を表現したダイアグラム。

D: Arata Yabuuchi

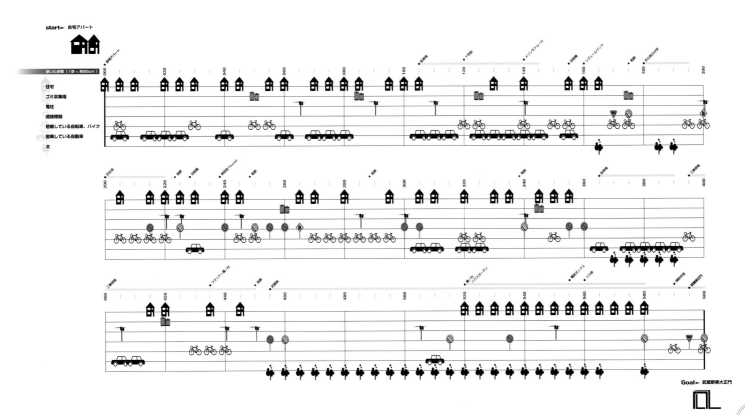

A map expressing the sounds heard en route from home to school.
自宅から学校までの通学途中に耳にする音を表現したサウンドマップ。

D: Inka Shinbo

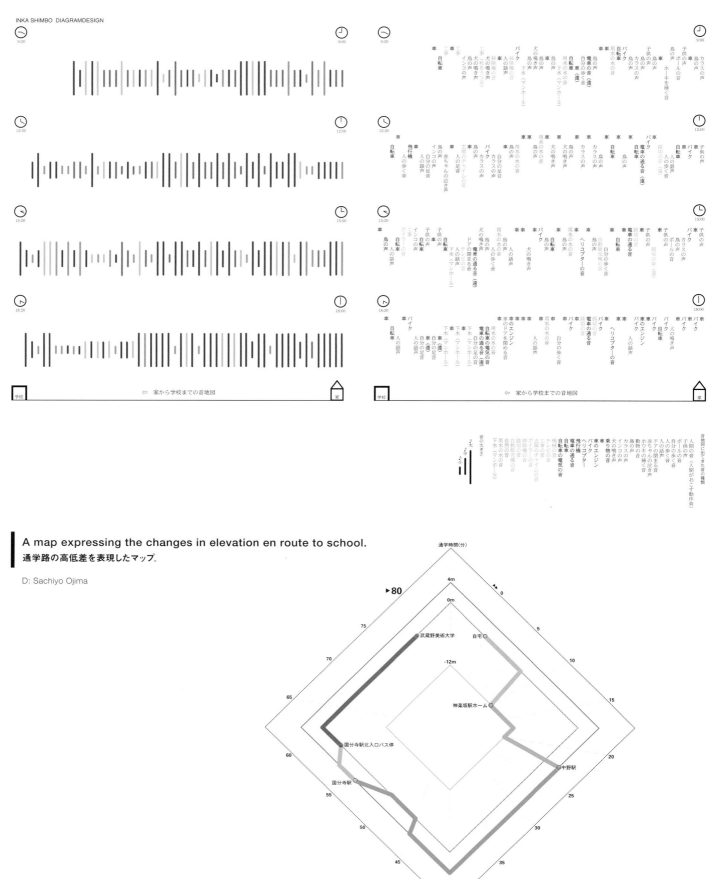

A map expressing the changes in elevation en route to school.
通学路の高低差を表現したマップ。

D: Sachiyo Ojima

A map expressing the number of steps between home and school.
自宅から学校までの歩数を表現したマップ。

D: Natsuko Otaka

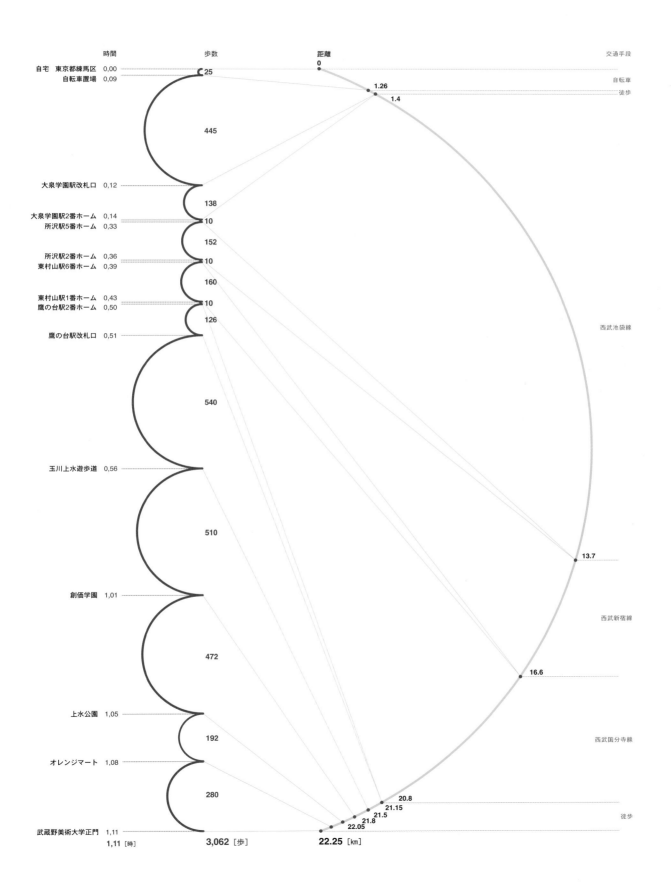

時間   歩数   距離   交通手段

自宅　東京都練馬区　0,00 — 25 — 0
自転車置場　0,09 — 1.26 — 自転車
1.4 — 徒歩
445
大泉学園駅改札口　0,12 — 138
大泉学園駅2番ホーム　0,14 — 10
所沢駅5番ホーム　0,33 — 152
所沢駅2番ホーム　0,36 — 10
東村山駅6番ホーム　0,39 — 160
東村山駅1番ホーム　0,43 — 10
鷹の台駅2番ホーム　0,50 — 126
鷹の台駅改札口　0,51
540
西武池袋線
玉川上水遊歩道　0,56
510
13.7
創価学園　1,01
西武新宿線
472
16.6
上水公園　1,05
192
西武国分寺線
オレンジマート　1,08
280
20.8
21.15
21.5
21.8
22.05
徒歩
武蔵野美術大学正門　1,11
1,11 [時]   3,062 [歩]   22.25 [km]

A map showing nationwide time differences for the first sunrise of 2004 using Tokyo as the standard.
2004年元旦の初日の出、東京を基準とした日本各地の時間差を表したマップ。

D: Kei Minemura

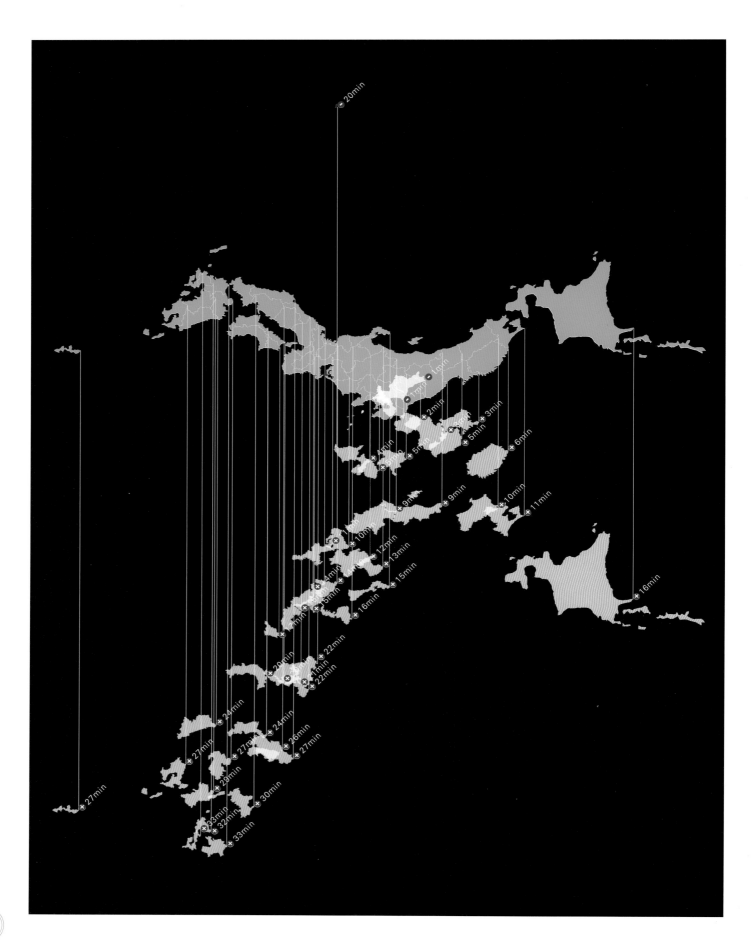

A map showing population density and rate of increase by prefecture.
都道府県別の人口密度と人口増加率を表すマップ。

D: Yayoi Yamamoto

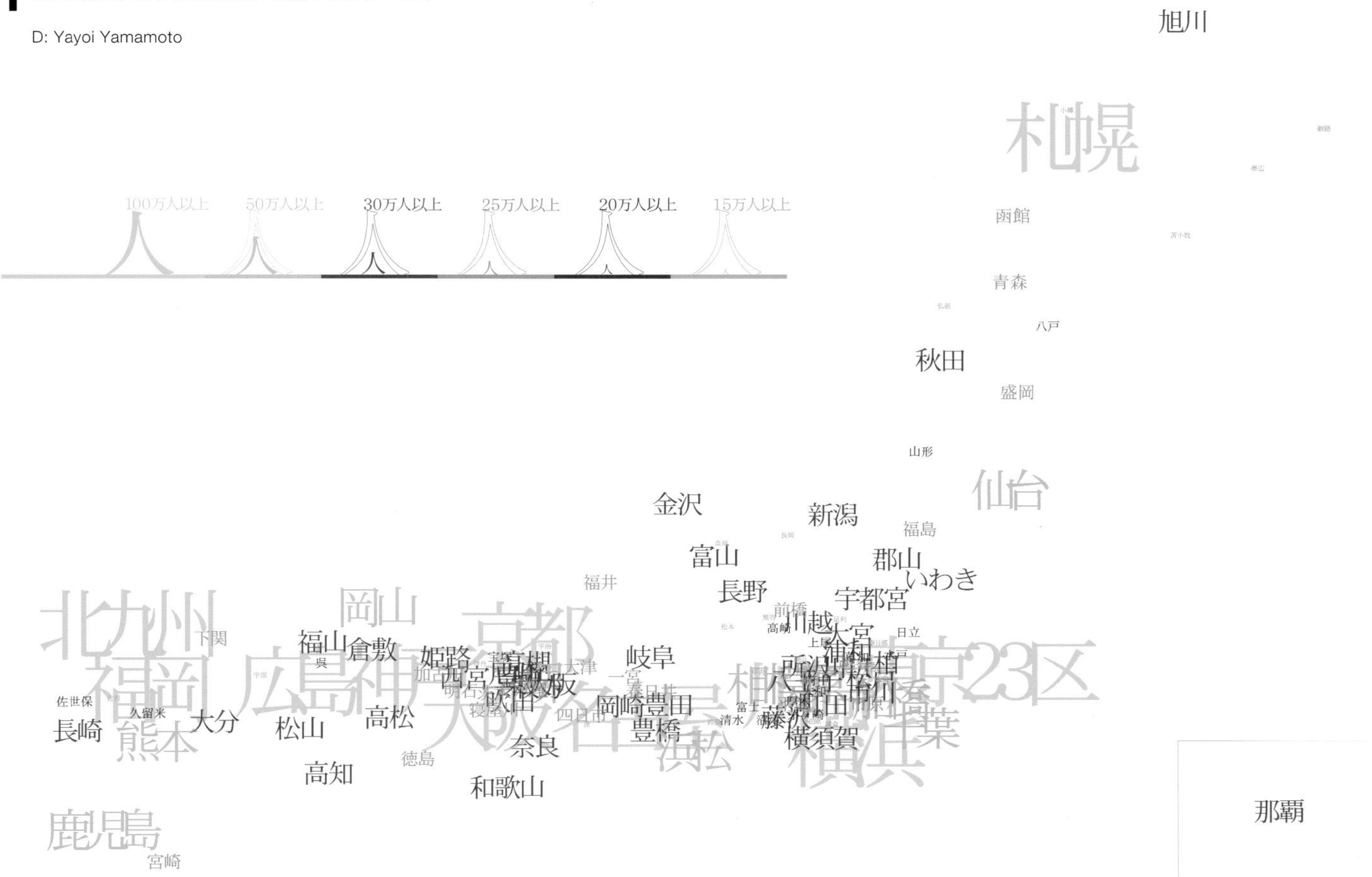

旭川
札幌
函館
青森
八戸
秋田
盛岡
山形
仙台
福島
新潟
金沢
富山
長野
福井
郡山　いわき
宇都宮
川越
前橋
高崎
大宮
日立
北九州　岡山　京都
福岡　広島　神　大阪　名古屋　静岡　横浜　東京23区
下関
佐世保　久留米　大分　松山　高松
長崎　熊本
浜松　横須賀
和歌山　奈良　岡崎　豊田
豊橋
高知　徳島
鹿児島
宮崎
那覇

A map showing the surface area of major lakes in Japan.
日本国内の主要な湖の面積を表すマップ。

D: Ricaco Nagashima

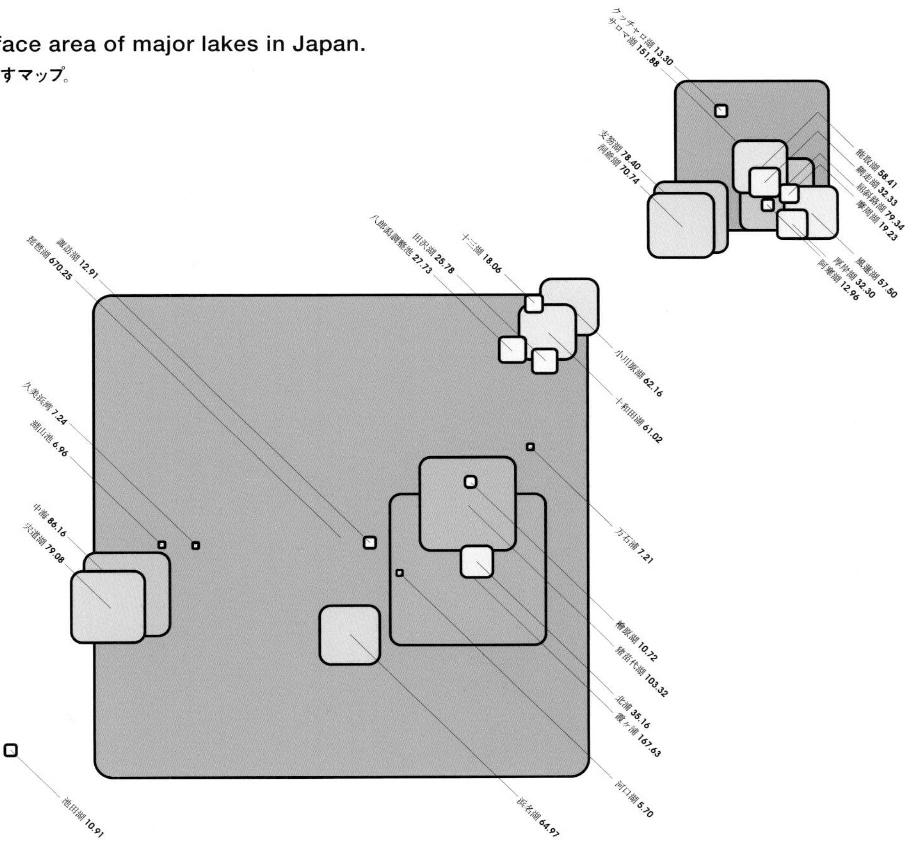

クッチャロ湖 13.30
サロマ湖 151.88
能取湖 58.41
濤沸湖 32.33
温根沼 79.34
厚岸湖 19.23
風蓮湖 78.40
阿寒湖 70.74
摩周湖 57.50
屈斜路湖 12.30

琵琶湖 670.25
諏訪湖 12.91
八郎潟調整池 27.73
田沢湖 25.78
十三湖 18.06
小川原湖 62.16
十和田湖 61.02
久美浜湾 7.24
湖山池 6.96
中海 86.16
宍道湖 79.08
万石浦 7.21
榛名湖 10.72
猪苗代湖 103.32
北浦 35.16
霞ヶ浦 167.63
河口湖 5.70
浜名湖 64.97
池田湖 10.91

A map showing scale of earthquakes occurring in Japan.
日本で起きた地震の規模を表したマップ。

D: Hideki Sugimoto

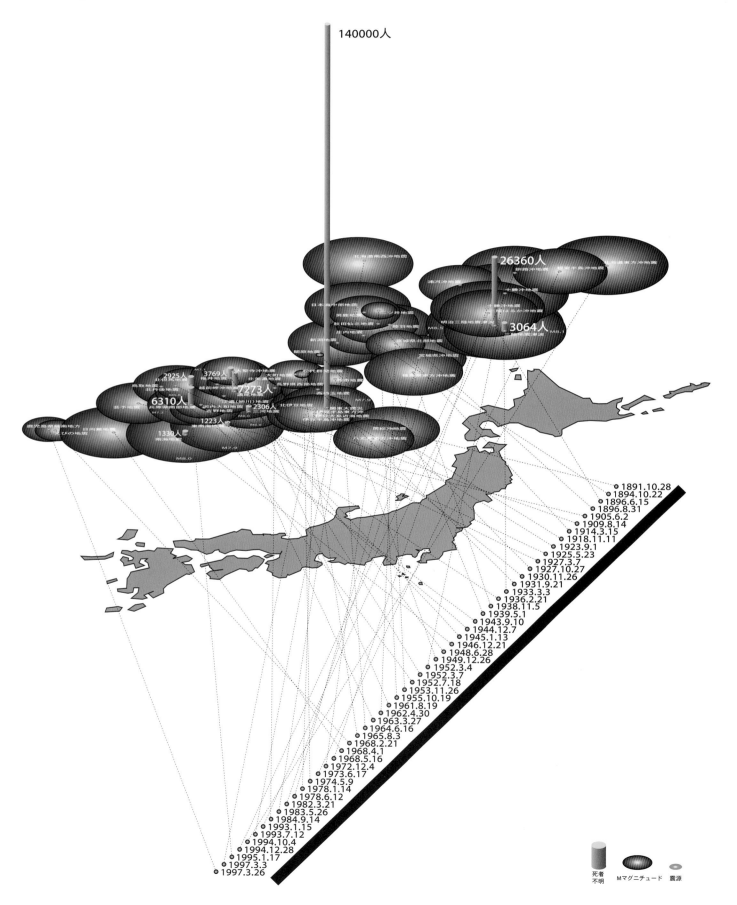

140000人

26360人

3064人

2925人
3769人
7273人
6310人
2306人
1223人
1330人

1891.10.28
1894.10.22
1896.6.15
1896.8.31
1905.6.2
1909.8.14
1914.3.15
1918.11.11
1923.9.1
1925.5.23
1927.3.7
1927.10.27
1930.11.26
1931.9.21
1933.3.3
1936.2.21
1938.11.5
1939.5.1
1943.9.10
1944.12.7
1945.1.13
1946.12.21
1948.6.28
1949.12.26
1952.3.4
1952.3.7
1952.7.18
1953.11.26
1955.10.19
1961.8.19
1962.4.30
1963.3.27
1964.6.16
1965.8.3
1968.2.21
1968.4.1
1968.5.16
1972.12.4
1973.6.17
1974.5.9
1978.1.14
1978.6.12
1982.3.21
1983.5.26
1984.9.14
1993.1.15
1993.7.12
1994.10.4
1994.12.28
1995.1.17
1997.3.3
1997.3.26

死者
不明　　Mマグニチュード　震源

A map showing the severity of acid rain worldwide.
世界の酸性雨の状況を表すマップ。

D: Nakazo Katayama

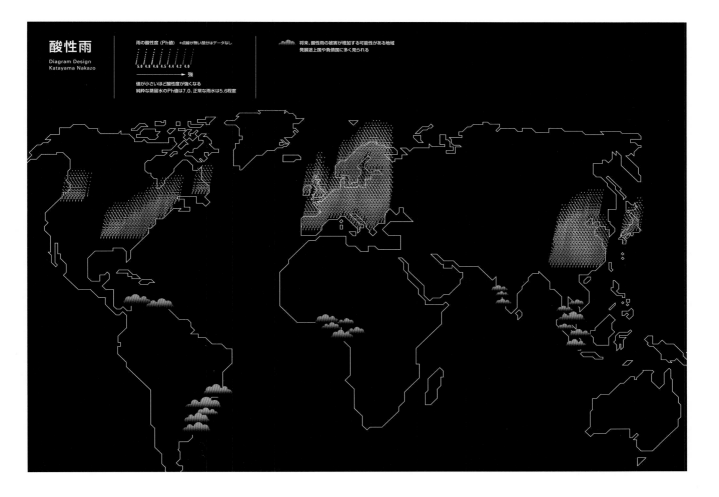

酸性雨
Diagram Design
Katayama Nakazo

雨の酸性度 (Ph値) ※点線が無い部分はデータなし

5.0 4.8 4.6 4.5 4.4 4.2 4.0
→ 強

値が小さいほど酸性度が強くなる
純粋な蒸留水のPh値は7.0、正常な雨水は5.6程度

将来、酸性雨の被害が増加する可能性がある地域
発展途上国や負債国に多く見られる

A map showing the severity of pollution of Japanese rivers.
日本国内の河川の水質汚濁状況を表すマップ。

D: Satoko Shoda

BOD年度平均値 [単位:mg／L]

BOD:生物化学的酸素要求量。Biochemical oxygen demand の略で
微生物が水中の有機物を分解する際に必要とする酸素量を示す。
数値が高い程汚染度が高い。[資料:1995年度環境庁]

0.9 石狩川
1.1 十勝川
岩木川 3.0
北上川 1.4
最上川 1.0
九頭竜川 1.8   信濃川 3.2   阿武隈川 2.6
江川 1.6   加古川 3.1   利根川 1.4
遠賀川 3.1   太田川 2.0   多摩川 4.5   鶴見川 2.9
高梁川 2.3   千代川 1.4   木曽川 1.1
筑後川 2.3   淀川 2.3   隅田川 7.6
四万十川 0.7   吉野川 1.3   大和川 13
球磨川 1.8   紀ノ川 2.1   天竜川 0.8   綾瀬川 8.8
大淀川 1.2

0
1
2
3
4
5
6
7
8
9以上[mg/L]

A map showing the rate of criminal arrests in Japan.
日本の犯罪検挙率を表すマップ。

D: Yu Osaki

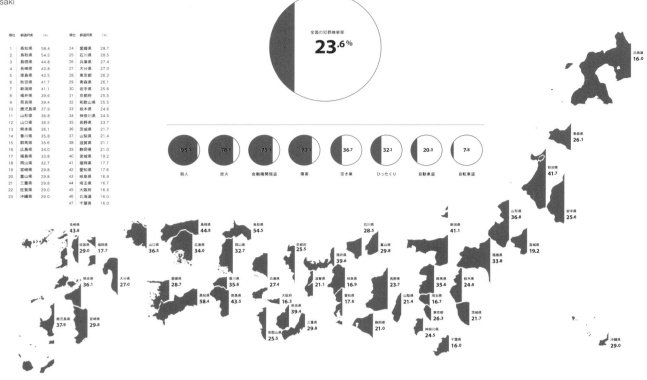

全国の犯罪検挙率
23.6%

順位	都道府県	(%)	順位	都道府県	(%)
1	高知県	58.4	24	愛媛県	28.7
2	鳥取県	54.5	25	石川県	28.5
3	島根県	44.8	26	兵庫県	27.4
4	長崎県	43.8	27	大分県	27.0
5	徳島県	43.5	28	東京都	26.3
6	秋田県	41.7	29	青森県	26.1
7	新潟県	41.1	30	岩手県	25.6
8	福井県	39.6	31	京都府	25.5
9	奈良県	39.4	32	和歌山県	25.5
10	鹿児島県	37.9	33	栃木県	24.6
11	山形県	36.8	34	神奈川県	24.5
12	山口県	36.5	35	長野県	23.7
13	熊本県	36.1	36	茨城県	21.7
14	香川県	35.8	37	山梨県	21.4
15	群馬県	35.6	38	滋賀県	21.1
16	広島県	34.0	39	静岡県	21.0
17	福島県	33.8	40	宮城県	19.2
18	岡山県	32.7	41	福岡県	17.7
19	宮崎県	29.8	42	愛知県	17.6
20	富山県	29.8	43	岐阜県	16.9
21	三重県	29.8	44	埼玉県	16.7
22	佐賀県	29.0	45	大阪府	16.3
23	沖縄県	29.0	46	北海道	16.0
			47	千葉県	16.0

95.0 殺人　78.7 放火　75.0 金融機関強盗　72.0 侵客　36.7 空き巣　32.1 ひったくり　20.3 自動車盗　7.8 自転車盗

A distribution map showing the use of the words "baka" and "aho" (both meaning "fool" or "idiot") throughout Japan.
日本全国の「バカ」と「アホ」ということばの使用分布を示すマップ。

D: Miwa Akabane

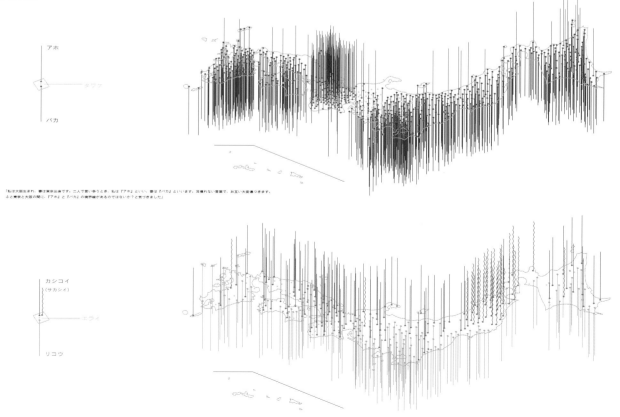

「私は大阪生まれ、妻は東京出身です。二人で言い争うとき、私は「アホ」といい、妻は「バカ」といいます。耳慣れない言葉で、お互い大変傷つきます。
ふと東京と大阪の間に、「アホ」と「バカ」の境界線があるのではないか？と気づきました」

ねじはバカになっても、けっしてアホにはならない。「人をアホにするな」とはいわない。東京では「兄はバカだけど、弟はおリコウさんね」というが、
大阪では「兄はアホやけど、弟はカシコイ」という。

INDEX

CLIENT

The Best Informational
Diagrams 2

ベスト インフォメーショナル ダイアグラム 2

Jacket Design

Hajime Kabutoya
甲谷 一

Designer

Akiko Shiba
柴 亜季子

Editor

Yu Fukushi
福士 祐

Coordinator

Maya Kishida
岸田麻矢

Photographer

Kuniharu Fujimoto
藤本邦治

Translators

Maya Kishida, Pamela Miki
岸田麻矢／パメラ三木

Typesetter

Ayuko Ishibashi
石橋亞由子

Publisher

Shingo Miyoshi
三芳伸吾

2005年1月5日　初版第1刷発行

発行元：ピエ・ブックス

〒170-0005　東京都豊島区南大塚2-32-4
編集　Tel: 03-5395-4820　Fax: 03-5395-4821
E-mail: editor@piebooks.com
営業　Tel: 03-5395-4811　Fax: 03-5395-4812
E-mail: sales@piebooks.com

印刷・製本　株式会社サンニチ印刷

ISBN4-89444-392-9 C3070
Printed in Japan

TRAVEL & LEISURE GRAPHICS 2
トラベル & レジャー グラフィックス 2

Pages: 224 (Full Color)　¥15,000+Tax

ホテル、旅館、観光地、交通機関からアミューズメント施設までのグラフィックス約350点を一挙掲載！！パンフレットを中心にポスター、DM、カードなど…現地へ行かなければ入手困難な作品も含め紹介。資料としてそろえておきたい1冊です！

A richly varied selection of 350 samples of travel and leisure guide graphics. The collection conveniently presents tour information, sightseeing guides, posters, promotional pamphlets from airline, railroad companies, hotels, inns, facilities, and more. Pick up this one-volume reference, and have it all at your fingertrips without having to leave your seat, let alone leave town!

PICTOGRAM AND ICON GRAPHICS
ピクトグラム & アイコン グラフィックス

Pages: 200 (160 in Color)　¥13,000+Tax

ミュージアムや空港の施設案内表示から雑誌やWEBサイトのアイコンまで、業種別に分類し、実用例とともに紹介しています。ピクトグラムの意味や使用用途などもあわせて紹介した、他に類をみないまさに永久保存版の1冊です。

The world's most outstanding pictograms and applications. From pictographs seen in museums, airports and other facility signage to icons used in magazines and on the web, the examples are shown isolated and in application with captions identifying their meanings and uses. Categorized by industry for easy reference, no other book of its kind is as comprehensive—it is indeed a permanent archives in one volume!

NEW COMPANY BROCHURE DESIGN 2
ニュー カンパニー ブローシャー デザイン 2

Pages: 272 (Full Color)　¥15,000+Tax

デザインの優れた案内カタログ約150点とWEB約50点を厳選。WEBサイトはカタログと連動した作品を中心に紹介しています。また各作品の企画・構成内容がわかるように制作コンセプト・コンテンツのキャッチコピーを具体的に掲載しています。

A selection of over 150 superbly designed brochures and 50 corresponding websites. All works are accompanied by descriptions of their design objectives and catch copy, to provide added insight into their planning and compositional structures.

ENVIRONMENT/WELFARE-RELATED GRAPHICS
環境・福祉 グラフィックス

Pages: 240 (Full Color)　¥15,000+Tax

環境保全への配慮が世界的な常識となりつつある今日、企業も積極的に環境・福祉など社会的テーマを中心にした広告キャンペーンを展開しています。国内外の優れた環境・福祉広告を紹介した本書は今後の広告を考えるために必携の1冊となるでしょう。

Environmental conservation is now a worldwide concern, and corporate advertising campaigns based on environmental and social themes are on the rise. This collection of noteworthy local and international environment/welfare-related publicity is an essential reference for anyone involved in the planning and development of future advertising.

PAPER IN DESIGN
ペーパー イン デザイン

Pages: 192 (Full Color) + Special reference material (paper samples)　¥16,000+Tax

DM、カタログをはじめ書籍の装丁、商品パッケージなど、紙素材を利用し個性的な効果を上げている数多くの作品をアイテムにこだわらず紹介。掲載作品で使われている紙見本も添付、紙のテクスチャーを実際に確かめることができる仕様です。

A special collection of graphic applications that exploit the role paper plays in design. This collection presents a wide range of applications—DM, catalogs, books, and product packaging, etc.—in which paper is used to achieve unique visual statements. Actual paper samples accompany each work to demonstrate their texture and tactile qualities.

BUSINESS PUBLICATION STYLE
PR誌企画&デザイン 年間ケーススタディ

Pages: 224 (Full Color)　¥15,000+Tax

PR誌の年間企画スケジュールとビジュアル展開を1年分まとめて紹介します。特集はどういう内容で構成しているのか？エッセイの内容と執筆人は？など、創刊・リニューアル時の企画段階から役立つ待望の1冊です。

Year-long case studies of 40 critically selected PR magazines.What should the content of the feature stories composed ? What should the subject of the essays be and who should write them? This eagerly awaited collection promises to assist in the planning stages for the inauguration or renewal of business periodicals.

SMALL PAMPHLET GRAPHICS
スモール パンフレット グラフィックス

Pages: 224 (Full Color)　¥14,000+Tax

街や店頭で見かける様々な企業、ショップのパンフレットを衣・食・住・遊の業種別に紹介します。気軽に持ち帰ることができる数多くの小型パンフレットの中からデザイン性に優れた作品約300点を厳選しました。

A collection introducing a wide variety of company and shop pamphlets found in stores and around town, grouped under the categories "food, clothes, shelter, and entertainment." 300 small-scale pamphlets selected for their outstanding design qualities from the great many pieces available to customers for the taking.

NEW CALENDAR GRAPHICS
ニュー カレンダー グラフィックス

Pages: 224 (Full Color)　¥13,000+Tax

国内外のクリエイターから集めた個性豊かなカレンダー約200点を、企業プロモーション用、市販用と目的別に収録した、世界の最新カレンダーを特集！！カレンダーの制作現場に、欠かすことの出来ない実用性の高い一冊です。

Over 200 of the newest and most original calendars from designers around the world! Categorized by objective, this collection includes calendars for the retail market as well as those designed as corporate publicity pieces.

NEW ENCYCLOPEDIA OF PAPER-FOLDING DESIGNS
折り方大全集　DM・カタログ編

Page: 240 (160 in Color)　￥7,800+Tax

デザインの表現方法の１つとして使われている『折り』。日頃何げなく目にしているDMやカード、企業のプロモーション用カタログなど身近なデザイン中に表現されている『折り』から、たたむ機能やせり出す、たわめる機能まで、約200点の作品を展開図で示し、『折り』を効果的に生かした実際の作品を掲載しています。

More than 200 examples of direct mail, cards, and other familiar printed materials featuring simple / multiple folds, folding up, and insertion shown as they are effected by folding along with flat diagrams of their prefolded forms.

EVERYDAY DIAGRAM GRAPHICS
エブリデイ ダイアグラム グラフィックス

Page: 224 (Full Color)　￥14,000+Tax

本書はわかりやすいということにポイントを置き、私たちの身の回りや街で見かける身近なダイアグラムを特集しました。マップ・フロアガイド・チャート・グラフ・仕様説明など、わかりやすいだけでなく、見ていて楽しいものを紹介しています。

This collection features diagrams of the sort we constantly meet in our daily lives, selected with their ready 'digestibility' in mind. The maps, charts, graphs, floor guides and specifications introduced here are not just easy to understand, they' re fun to look at, too.

SMALL JAPANESE STYLE GRAPHICS
スモールジャパン スタイル グラフィックス

Page: 224 (Full Color)　￥15,000+Tax

日本伝統の文様・イラスト・色彩等、和のテイストが随所にちりばめられたグラフィック作品を1冊にまとめました。古き良き日本の美意識を取り入れ、現代のクリエイターが仕上げた作品は新しい和の感覚を呼びさまします。

Traditional Japanese motifs, illustrations, colors—collection of graphicworks studded with the essence of "wa" (Japanese-ness) on every page. See how contemporary Japanese designers incorporate time-honored Japanese aesthetics in finished works that redefine the sensibility known as "Japanese style."

SCHOOL & FACILITY PROSPECTUS GRAPHICS
学校・施設案内 グラフィックス

Pages: 224 (Full Color)　￥15,000+Tax

「学校」「施設」という2つの大きなコンテンツを軸に、デザイン、企画、コンセプトに優れたカタログ、リーフレットなどの案内ツールを収録。表紙、中ページのレイアウト、構成からキャッチコピーまで見やすく紹介しています。

A collection presenting examples of well-designed and conceptually outstanding guides (catalogs, pamphlets, leaflets, etc) focusing on two broad categories: schools and service facilities. Documentation includes cover and inside pages, highlighting layout, composition, and catch copy.

LAYOUT STYLE GRAPHICS
レイアウト スタイル グラフィックス

Pages: 224 (Full Color)　￥14,000+Tax

カタログや雑誌などのレイアウトをする上で必要不可欠な、目次や扉ページ・ノンブル・柱などの細かい要素。本書はそれらをパーツごとにコンテンツわけして、優れた作品例を紹介します。美しいレイアウトを表現するための参考資料として、グラフィックデザイナー必携の一冊となるはずです。

Table of contents and title pages, pagination,titles, &c. —these are the essential elements of catalog and magazine layout. This collection presents outstanding examples of editorial design broken down and categorized by their key components. A volume that will prove indispensable to graphic designers as a reference for creating beautiful layouts.

A4 IN-STORE LEAFLET GRAPHICS
店頭 A4リーフレット グラフィックス

Pages: 224 (Full Color)　￥15,000+Tax

様々な業種の店頭に置かれた販促用のA4・B5サイズのペラ物や2つ折り、3つ折りのチラシ・リーフレットに限定し約650点を収録。デザイナーを悩ます、文字や写真などの構成要素の多い実務的なリーフレットの効果的な見せ方がわかる1冊です。

A collection featuring 650 flat, single- and double-fold A4 and B5 sized leaflets found in retail environments, representing a wide range of businesses. This single volume presents effective examples of the practical business tool that because of its many compositional elements always poses a challenge to designers.

IDEAS UNBOUND
自由なアイデア & 表現 グラフィックス

Pages: 224 (Full Color)　￥14,000+Tax

本書はコンセプトに基づきアイデアを生かしグラフィック表現されたもの、紙やその他の素材の特徴をうまく生かし表現したもの、最新または超アナログ印刷技術を駆使した作品などを特集したデザイナーのアイデアの宝庫ともいえる必須の一冊です。

This book focuses on conceptual graphic works that exploit the characteristics of paper and other materials to express those ideas, a collection of latest, "state-of-the-art" analog printing techniques and a treasure trove of designers' ideas-a must for anyone who appreciates creative genius.

BRAND STRATEGY AND DESIGN
ブランド戦略とデザイン

Page: 224 (208 in Color)　￥15,000+Tax

「ブランド戦略」にデザイナーが参加することは規模の大小を問わず求められています。今後デザイナーは総合的に戦略を考える力が必要です。本書はデザイナーが積極的にブランド戦略に関わることで認知度アップに貢献した実例を紹介します。

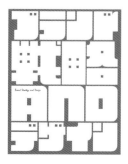

In projects big and small, designers are being called upon to participate in "brand strategy". In coming years, designers will require the ability to consider brand strategy comprehensively. This book presents case studies in which the designer's active role in brand strategy contributed to a higher degree of brand recognition.

ADVERTISING PHOTOGRAPHY IN JAPAN 2004
年鑑 日本の広告写真2004

Pages: 229 (Full Color)　¥14,500+Tax

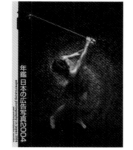

気鋭の広告写真をそろえた（社）日本広告写真家協会（APA）の監修による本年鑑は、日本の広告界における最新のトレンドと、その証言者たる作品を一堂に見られる貴重な資料として、国内外の広告に携わる方にとって欠かせない存在です。

A spirited collection of works compiled under the editorial supervision of the Japan Advertising Photographers' Association (APA) representing the freshest talent in the Japanese advertising world. An indispensable reference for anyone concerned with advertising in or outside Japan.

ADVERTISING GRAPHICS WITH IMPACT
インパクトのある広告グラフィックス

Page: 224 (Full Color)　¥14,000+Tax

ポスターを中心に雑誌広告などから、コミカルで笑いを誘う作品、衝撃的で目を引く作品、意表をつく奇抜な作品、豪快で驚異的な作品などを紹介。五感に訴え、心に強く残り、高い広告効果をあげているインパクトのある作品の特集です。

A collection of select world advertising with IMPACT! Laughter-provoking comical works, attention-getting shocking works, unconventional works that take viewers by surprise. A collection of primarily poster and magazine ad graphics that appeal to the five senses, demonstrating a wide range of ways to have IMPACT.

NEW SEASONAL CAMPAIGN GRAPHICS
季節別 キャンペーンツール グラフィックス

Page: 224 (Full Color)　¥15,000+Tax

企業やショップが展開している様々なキャンペーンの中からクリスマス、お正月、バレンタイン、母の日、父の日、サマー・ウィンターセールなど、特に季節を感じさせるものに対象をしぼり、そこで使用された優れたデザインの販促ツールやノベルティグッズを紹介します。

Christmas, New Year's, Valentine's Day, Mother's and Father's Day, summer and winter sales, &c, this collection presents outstandingly designed corporate and retail campaign materials and novelties with a season-specific focus.

PACKAGE & WRAPPING GRAPHICS
パッケージ & ラッピングツール グラフィックス

Page: 224 (Full Color)　¥14,000+Tax

様々な商品パッケージには、販売対象やブランドイメージに沿ったデザイン戦略がなされており、商品イメージを決定する重要な役割を担っています。本書は世界中からデザイン性の高いパッケージとラッピングツールを多数ピックアップし、食・美容・住にコンテンツわけして紹介しています。

Package is based on carefully developed design strategies to appeal to target customers and to build brand and protect image. This collection presents a wide variety of packages and wrapping materials from around the world reflecting the state of the art. It is grouped loosely under the categories food, beauty and living.

ENVIRONMENTAL COMMUNICATION GRAPHICS
環境コミュニケーションツール グラフィックス

Page: 224 (Full Color)　¥14,000+Tax

環境リポートや、環境をテーマとしたリーフレット、チラシ、ポスターなど、環境コミュニケーション・ツールを一堂に会し、業種別に紹介します。本書は、会社案内や各種パンフレット制作などあらゆるクリエイティブのアイデアソースとしても、利用価値の高い1冊です。

This book provides an overview of environmental communications tools, including leaflets, handbills and posters that focus on the topic of the environment, classifying them by type of business. This book is indeed a valuable source of creative ideas that graphic artists can use in creating company brochures and many other brochures.

DIRECT MAIL COMMUNICATIONS
ダイレクトメール コミュニケーション

Pages: 224 (Full Color)　¥14,000+Tax

本書は、顧客とのダイレクトなコミュニケーション・ツールとして活用する、様々な招待状、案内状をまとめたデザイン書です。伝えたい情報が、美しく、分かりやすくデザインされているものや、顧客の遊び心をくすぐるための、仕掛けのあるものなど、様々なタイプのダイレクトメールを多数収録します。

A design book focusing on invitations and announcements designed to function as communications tools that speak directly to their target customer. This collection presents a wide variety of direct mail pieces that deliver their messages beautifully, loud and clear, with tricks and devices, by tickling the playful spirit, and many other unique and interesting ways.

PUBLIC RELATIONS GRAPHICS
パブリック リレーションズ グラフィックス

Page: 224 (Full Color)　¥15,000+Tax

企業、団体、店舗で発行されている多様な広報誌・PR誌・フリーペーパーを特集しています。人目を引く表紙、見やすいレイアウト、読まれる特集とは？表紙、中ページを見やすく紹介した本書は、デザイン・編集・企画にきっと役立つ1冊となるでしょう。

A special collection focusing on the various public relations magazines, bulletins and free newspapers published by companies, organizations and retailers. What makes eyecatching covers, visually accessible layouts, and features people read? The answers are obvious in the covers and inside pages presented in this single volume —certain to serve as a valuable reference to anyone involved in the design, editing, and planning.

DESIGN IDEAS WITH LIMITED COLOR
限られた色のデザインアイデア

Page: 208 (192 in Color)　¥13,000+Tax

限られた刷り色で効果的にデザインされた作品を、使用された刷り色の色見本・パントーン（DIC含む）ナンバーと併せて紹介。色の掛け合わせと濃度変化がわかるカラーチャートを併載。無限大のアイデアを探し出すときに必要となる1冊。

A collection of the latest graphic works effectively reproduced using limited ink colors. Presented with color swatches and the Pantone/DIC numbers of the ink colors used, gradation and duotone works also feature simple color charts indicating screen and density changes. A reference of limitless ideas for anyone specifying color.

WORLD CORPORATE PROFILE GRAPHICS

ニュー 世界の会社案内 グラフィックス

Page: 256 (Full Color) ¥14,000+Tax

世界から集めた最新の会社案内・学校・施設案内とアニュアルレポートを業種別に紹介。作品を大きく見せながらも形態、デザイン制作コンセプト、コンテンツ内容を簡潔に掲載しています。世界のデザイナーの動向を掴む上でも貴重な1冊です。

The latest exemplary company, school and institution guides and annual reports collected from diversified industries worldwide and grouped by line of business. Shown large scale, the pieces are accompanied by brief descriptions of their content and the concepts behind their design. Valuable for gleaning the latest trends in corporate communications.

GRAND OPENING GRAPHICS

オープン ツール グラフィックス

Pages: 216 (Full Color) ¥14,000+Tax

ショップや施設をオープンする際に制作するグラフィックツールは、新しい「空間」のイメージを消費者へ伝える大切な役割を果たします。本書ではオープン時に制作された案内状やショップツール、店舗写真などを業種ごとに多数収録。

The graphic applications created for the openings of new stores and facilities play a critical role in conveying store image to customers. Categorized by line of business, this book presents the wide range of graphics — from invitations to in-store collateral – that form the first impressions in building strategic store identity.

OUTSTANDING SMALL PAMPHLET GRAPHICS

街で目立つ小型パンフレット

Pages: 240 (Full Color) ¥14,000+Tax

街やショップの店頭で手に入る無料の小型パンフ。50ヶ所以上の街で集めた約1,000点から、販売促進ツールとして効果的に機能している作品を厳選。衣・食・住・遊の業種別に分類し機能的で美しい小型パンフレットを約250点紹介します。

250 small-scale pamphlets selected for their beauty and function as effective sales promotional tools from roughly 1000 pieces available to customers at more than 50 locations. Grouped for valuable reference by type of business type under the categories: Food, Clothing, Shelter, and Entertainment.

WORLD CATALOG EXPO

ワールド カタログ エキスポ

Page: 192 (Full Color) ¥5,800+Tax

一目でわかるように、衣食住のコンテンツは色分けされています。高級感あるスマートな作品、楽しくカラフルな作品、斬新なアイデアの作品など、ページをめくるごとに様々な作品の個性が広がる、国際色豊かな1冊です。

A survey of outstanding catalogs from around the world: simple and refined, colorful and playful, full of novel ideas. Color-coded for easy identification under the categories: Fashion, Food, and Living. Highly original works, international in flavor, spill out with each turn of the page.

FOOD SHOP GRAPHICS

フード ショップ グラフィックス

Page: 224 (Full Color) ¥14,000+Tax

レストラン・カフェ・菓子店など、国内外のオリジナリティ溢れる飲食店のショップアイデンティティ特集です。メニューやリーフレットなどのグラフィックと、内装・外装の店舗写真、コンセプト文を交え、約120店を紹介。

Restaurants, cafes, sweet shops... 120 of the world's most original food-related store identities. Together with graphic applications ranging from menus to matches, each presentation features exterior and interior photos of the shops and brief descriptions of the concepts behind them.

365 DAYS OF NEWSPAPER INSERTS Spring / Summer Edition

365日の折込チラシ大百科 春夏編

Page: 240 (Full Color) ¥13,000+Tax

全国の主要6都市から厳選された春夏の新聞折込チラシを一挙に掲載。優れたデザインや配色、目を引くキャッチコピーの作品が満載。お正月、成人の日、バレンタイン、お雛様、子供の日、母の日、父の日などの作品を含む季節感溢れる1冊です。

Volume 3 of our popular series! Eye-catching newspaper inserts – outstanding in design, color and copywriting – selected from 6 major Japanese cities between January and June. Brimming with the spirit and events of spring: New Year's, Valentine's Day, Girls'/Boys' Days, Mother's/Father's Days, and more.

カタログ・新刊のご案内について

総合カタログ、新刊案内をご希望の方は、はさみ込みのアンケートはがきをご返送いただくか、90円切手同封の上、ピエ・ブックス宛お申し込みください。

CATALOGS and INFORMATION ON NEW PUBLICATIONS

If you would like to receive a free copy of our general catalog or details of our new publications, please fill out the enclosed postcard and return it to us by mail or fax.

CATALOGUES ET INFORMATIONS SUR LES NOUVELLES PUBLICATIONS

Si vous désirez recevoir un exemplaire gratuit de notre catalogue généralou des détails sur nos nouvelles publication. veuillez compléter la carte réponse incluse et nous la retourner par courrierou par fax.

CATALOGE und INFORMATIONEN ÜBER NEUE TITLE

Wenn Sie unseren Gesamtkatalog oder Detailinformationen über unsere neuen Titel wünschen.fullen Sie bitte die beigefügte Postkarte aus und schicken Sie sie uns per Post oder Fax.

ピエ・ブックス

〒170-0005　東京都豊島区南大塚2-32-4
TEL: 03-5395-4811　FAX: 03-5395-4812
www.piebooks.com

PIE BOOKS

2-32-4 Minami-Otsuka Toshima-ku Tokyo 170-0005 JAPAN
TEL：+81-3-5395-4811 FAX：+81-3-5395-4812
www.piebooks.com